Praise for
THAT'S WHAT SHE SAID

"This is the perfect time for this book, and Joanne Lipman is the perfect person to write it, both in terms of her own experiences and her multiple talents. She's a terrific writer, a savvy reporter, and smart thinker, and all of that comes together in a great read."

—Steven Brill, founder of Court TV and *The American Lawyer* and
bestselling author of *America's Bitter Pill: Money, Politics, Backroom
Deals, and the Fight to Fix Our Broken Healthcare System*

"It's great we are talking the talk, but Joanne Lipman's cutting-edge research and razor-sharp advice will help men and women alike start walking the walk (toward a more equitable workplace)."

—Katie Couric

"At last! *That's What She Said* is so timely—and so needed. It's the ultimate guide for women (and men) who are determined to close the gender gap. Lively and readable, it's a game changer in how we understand gender relations—and how we can break down barriers, right now."
—Sallie Krawcheck, CEO, Ellevest

"Joanne Lipman leaves her soapbox at home, rolls up her sleeves, and provides real solutions to complex problems. Her valuable insights are a tool kit for men and women to not only work alongside each other, but also to bring out each other's best."

—Glen Mazzara, executive producer, *The Shield* and *The Walking Dead*

"Insightful and timely. The points Joanne Lipman makes in *That's What She Said* are right on target for today's new workplace. It will resonate whether you're male or female, young or old, manager or managed, a long-term employee or just starting your career."

—Andrew H. Tisch, Cochairman of the Board, and Chairman of the Executive Committee, Loews Corporation

"*That's What She Said* is an instant classic. It's a must-read for two groups of people: men and women."

—Roger McNamee, venture capitalist

"Joanne Lipman has written an urgently needed exploration of how men—alongside women—can close the gender gap at work and in life. Now, more than ever, we need this book and its real, pragmatic solutions. By rooting her insights in real-world examples, extensive academic research, and stories that are a joy to read, she has provided an essential primer on how we can all succeed together."

—Charles Duhigg, bestselling author of *The Power of Habit* and *Smarter Faster Better*

"Lipman, editor-in-chief of *USA Today*, makes a bold statement with this important book examining biases favoring men in business. . . . This book goes a step further than Sheryl Sandberg's bestselling *Lean In* and challenges both men and women to examine their own prejudices and actively reshape work cultures to be more welcoming to women."

—*Publishers Weekly* (starred review)

That's
What
She
Said

What Men and Women Need to Know About Working Together

That's What She Said

Joanne Lipman

WILLIAM MORROW

An Imprint of HarperCollins*Publishers*

Avenue Q lyrics used herein reprinted with permission of co-creator Robert Lopez.

"Woman" by Ingibjörg Haraldsdóttir reprinted with permission from the publisher and the author's estate.

P.S.™ is a trademark of HarperCollins Publishers.

HarperCollins books may be purchased for educational, business, or sales promotional use. For information, please email the Special Markets Department at SPsales@harpercollins.com.

A hardcover edition of this book was published in 2018 by William Morrow, an imprint of HarperCollins Publishers.

FIRST WILLIAM MORROW PAPERBACK EDITION PUBLISHED 2019.

Designed by Bonni Leon-Berman

Library of Congress Cataloging-in-Publication Data has been applied for.

ISBN 978-0-06-243722-8

19 20 21 22 23 LSC 10 9 8 7 6 5 4 3 2 1

For Tom, Rebecca, and Andrew
And for Diane Lipman, matriarch of four generations of strong
women—and men

Contents

Introduction:
Men Aren't the Enemy

This book began with a flight to Des Moines. In most ways, it was uneventful. The businessman sitting next to me couldn't have been friendlier. Over plastic cups of white wine, we chatted about his business, his new house in a New York suburb, and his kids' sports teams.

Then I mentioned I was on my way to speak at a women's conference. Suddenly my neighbor froze.

"Sorry!" he snapped. "Sorry I'm a man."

I looked down awkwardly into the bottom of my wineglass. My seatmate gave me a sideways glance and reached for an explanation.

"I had to go through diversity training a few months ago. It was awful."

The words tumbled out of him. The facilitator had beaten up on him and his male colleagues, he said. It felt like being sent to the principal's office, or being sat in the corner. Hours of his life, wasted. And the message he and his male colleagues took away, he told me, boiled down to one accusation.

It's all your fault.

My seatmate's words struck me. The truth is, I'd heard some version of them dozens of times before. I'd seen the body language, the *Don't yell at me!* flinch, more times than I cared to remember. I'd watched self-assured, confident men curl into that defensive crouch when the subject of women—or God forbid, the phrase "gender equality"—had come up.

My seatmate and I spent the rest of the flight in awkward silence. The next morning, several hundred women gathered in a hotel

ballroom. I had been invited to speak about some of the most common issues women face at work—being overlooked in meetings, being underestimated, watching men getting credit for our ideas. As I spoke, I watched those several hundred female heads nodding in recognition.

I stopped right in the middle of a sentence.

"We already know all of this," I said. "We need men in this room to hear the message instead."

••

FIRST THINGS FIRST: There will be no man shaming in *That's What She Said*. No male bashing. No finger-pointing.

For years, the fastest way to drive men from a room has been to mention women's equality. And who could blame them? The conversation implicitly made men the villain. Long before my epiphany in Des Moines, back in 1859, a *Harper's Weekly* cartoon depicted men cowering in a courtroom while suffragettes berated them. In an 1875 cartoon, a gaggle of women yell at a wincing man, above the caption: "Female Suffrage, Male Suffering."

Men felt demonized. They still do. A recent Harvard study found that corporate "diversity training" has made the gender gap worse, in part because it makes men feel bad about themselves. Which, as it happens, is what it was engineered to do. "We used to do it with a two-by-four," Howard Ross, a veteran diversity trainer, told me. "We beat 'em up until they saw the error of their ways. If somebody cried, that was great."

Women, meanwhile, have pretty much wiped our hands clean of men, cutting them out of the conversation altogether. An entire industry of books, conferences, and networking groups has blossomed to tell us that closing the gender gap is up to us, not them. We're told we need to speak up, to be more confident, to demand to be paid what we're worth. We talk endlessly among ourselves about all of this. What we don't do is talk to men about it.

FEMALE SUFFRAGE, MALE SUFFERING.

John Bull thinks it scarcely necessary that ladies who are already all mouth should have any more voice in public matters.

That disconnect between men and women makes no sense to me. If women only talk among ourselves, we can only solve 50 percent of the problem. We need men to join the conversation, to be our partners. And as for the men, most of them aren't anywhere near villains. They don't need beating up with a two-by-four. They'd like to see an equitable workplace, they just can't figure out what they're supposed to do about it.

And yet men often recoil from the conversation about closing the gap. Some simply aren't interested. Others are sure they have no problem with women themselves; it must be some other guys who do. And some feel victimized, as if the very topic is an implicit

accusation. They're sure the gap doesn't exist at all, that if anything, women are getting an unfair advantage when it comes to jobs and opportunities.

Indeed, by some measures outright hostility toward women has increased, or at least become more visible, over the past decade. It's been fanned both by the Wild West of the Web, where misogyny and racism thrive, and by the same deep frustrations and rejection of "political correctness" that powered Donald Trump into the presidency.

Misogynistic corporate cultures have flourished at companies including Fox News, Uber, venture capital firms, film studios, media companies, and more, though when exposed the result has been the ouster of top executives. The tech industry has been roiled by multiple sexual harassment scandals. In Hollywood, after producer Harvey Weinstein was accused by multiple women of sexual assault, thousands of women in other industries came forward with their own tales of abuse, igniting the #MeToo movement that has since toppled scores of powerful men, from former Senator Al Franken to comedian Louis C.K. to CBS chief Leslie Moonves.

The #MeToo movement has brought into sharp focus how sexism remains a deeply ingrained, systemic problem. And it isn't just an American phenomenon. Almost half of women as well as men surveyed in Russia and India believe women to be inferior. And this was a survey done in 2017.

Those attitudes make it even more difficult for men who *do* want to reach across the gender divide. When Robert Moritz, chief executive officer of consulting firm PricewaterhouseCoopers, wrote a LinkedIn post about why the firm values diversity, commenters—professional men, using real names—called his ideas "repellent," "an affront to every white man," and argued there's "no such thing as a real business run by a non-white man." One suggested that he "surrender [his] job to a diversity hire and stay at home as a house husband."

It's no wonder that men feel stymied, fearful of speaking out on behalf of women. While he was a student at Harvard Business School in 2012, management consultant Kunal Modi published a piece in the *Huffington Post* arguing for gender equality. "Man up," he wrote. "Men, just as equally as women, must take ownership of these family issues, which are core to American economic competitiveness." He offered five pieces of advice, including such commonsense suggestions as "learn the facts," "do your job . . . at home," and "get involved at the ballot box," in which he noted that the U.S. ranks "an appalling 90th in terms of female representation in our national legislature."

Even so, he had to take a hard gulp before pressing the "send" button. "It's hard for guys to do this," he told me later. Men worry: "Do I know enough? Do I have the right to talk about this issue? . . . One of the biggest challenges from a guy's perspective is how do we make these issues discussable."

Indeed, plenty of other men would be happy to join in the conversation. They're just terrified of saying something wrong. When Catalyst, a nonprofit organization focused on working women, asked men what might undermine their support for gender equality, a stunning 74 percent cited fear—fear of loss of status, fear of other men's disapproval, and, most telling of all, fear of making a mistake. Men are walking around on eggshells.

Telle Whitney, president and chief executive officer of the Anita Borg Institute for Women and Technology, has witnessed that phenomenon over and again during her organization's annual Grace Hopper conference for women in technology. The confab attracts not only hundreds of women, but also male executives from the major tech firms, all of which are trying to recruit more female employees.

These men genuinely want to correct the gender imbalance in their industry, Whitney told me. But they are intimidated and uncertain exactly how to act or what to say. When Blake Irving, the chief executive of GoDaddy, a Web domain registry, spoke to the group about how he was trying to change the company's macho culture, in-

cluding eliminating its notoriously sexist ads featuring barely clad women, participants attacked him on social media.

"We have a lot of men come to Grace Hopper, and they feel very confused," Whitney said. "They'd like to help [but] they feel like anything they try, they might get taken to task for."

Those fears have only escalated in the past few years, when the tiniest gaffe can be instantly magnified by the Internet echo chamber. Complicating matters further, the politics and vocabulary of "inclusion"—of not offending any outsider. There are "microaggressions"—hurtful, even if unintentional, slights. There are the controversial "trigger warnings" for potentially offensive material on college campuses. There are "safe spaces," where people can go to avoid upsetting interactions. Plenty of guys—even those with the best of intentions—are spooked.

Their fear isn't irrational. Researchers have found that when a man advocates for women's rights, not only men but women are infuriated and surprised. Wharton psychology professor Adam Grant, who has written about women's issues in collaboration with Facebook executive and *Lean In* author Sheryl Sandberg, says some readers have berated him: "What business do you have writing about women?"

Gender experts Barbara Annis and John Gray note that men in their workshops are terrified that they'll screw up when they speak with women. The men often say they have a history of "saying the wrong thing" to women, a fear that can be paralyzing, they noted in their book *Work with Me: The 8 Blind Spots Between Men and Women in Business.* Even one previous episode of unintentionally offending or upsetting a woman can bring back those horrible feelings from adolescence, when boys are afraid to say the wrong thing to girls.

The problem can be exacerbated when these men become bosses. In one survey, 79 percent of male supervisors reported worrying about giving women candid feedback, and said they felt they had to

provide guidance carefully and indirectly. The irony is that by self-censoring, the men don't give women the feedback necessary for the women to advance.

What's more, that nervousness, that suppression of their natural instincts, makes it all the more likely that the wrong thing *will* pop out of their mouths. The men are baffled, they're uncertain, they feel awkward, and it all rolls up into steering clear of particular topics—or of women altogether.

I've long been puzzled by this phenomenon. I've spent my career as a journalist working primarily with men. All of my mentors were men. Most professional men I've encountered truly believe that they are unbiased. And yet when the subject of women comes up, they are so uncomfortable, or fearful of saying the wrong thing, that they simply shut down.

So where does that leave us? With a conundrum: since neither side is talking openly to the other, lots of men are still clueless about the women they work with every day. Not intentionally. But wow. They unwittingly belittle us, or ignore us, or do something they think is nice that just infuriates us instead. Catalyst's survey found that an astonishing 51 percent of men cited lack of awareness about exactly which issues women are facing.

No wonder almost 30 percent of women say they still endure bias at work, half a century after John F. Kennedy signed the Equal Pay Act. In the male-dominated technology industry, that figure soars to 80 percent, with 60 percent also reporting sexual harassment. The majority of men, meanwhile, report that as far as they're concerned, discrimination doesn't exist. Sexism has already been solved.

It's even worse for women of color, who face a double bind, discounted for both their gender and their race. Strike one for being female: multiple studies have found that when a man and a woman are equally qualified for a job requiring math skills, employers are twice as likely to hire the man. And strike two for race: women of

color are far more likely to experience the "prove it again" syndrome, in which they have to work harder than coworkers and repeatedly prove their competence. A 2014 survey of minority female scientists found that an astonishing 100 percent reported experiencing bias. What's more, while women in the U.S. earn only 80 percent as much as men, the discrepancy for minority women is far steeper: just 63 cents on the dollar for black women and 54 cents for Latinas.

Sociologists have scratched their heads about why this is still the case. Intellectually we know it makes no sense. Women began earning college degrees in equal numbers to men more than three decades ago, and now earn more than half, so there's been plenty of time to fill the "pipeline" that leads to management jobs. When I graduated in the 1980s, my female friends—and our male friends too—assumed it would only be a matter of time, and of mathematical certainty, that women would ultimately hold half of leadership roles. We had competed equally in school. We had applied for and been offered the same entry-level jobs.

A few days before graduation, my roommates and I wrote down our predictions for our lives: Where would we be in ten years? Then we sealed our prophecies in an envelope. At the time, Carol was on her way to law school, Ira was soon to enter medical school, Miranda was headed to graduate school for Russian/Soviet studies, and I had landed a job as a reporter at the *Wall Street Journal*. Peering into our own personal crystal balls, each one of us predicted that we would have satisfying careers—and big families.

It didn't occur to us that this might be an "either/or" proposition. Why would it? After all, we were on equal footing with the guys, and they respected us as equals. As far as we were concerned, the battle for women's rights was over. Women had won.

Some of the most prestigious—and historically male dominated—companies that came to recruit on campus at that time were even hiring more women than men. When Lehman Brothers recruiters

arrived—this was when it was still a king-of-the-world investment bank, long before it almost crashed the economy—my friend Phyllis was one of the lucky ones to snare a coveted spot in its analyst training program. Showing up for her first day of work a few months later, she was surprised—and she laughingly admits, a little disappointed—to find that two-thirds of her entry-level class was female. The dating pool at work was thin.

My friends and I didn't consider ourselves "feminists." That was something of a dirty word among many young women at the time, conjuring images of man-hating women who didn't shave their legs. To us that battle for equality was long over. Men and women would march into the future together, on equal footing. Our professors and administrators kept telling our class that we were the future. We believed them. After all, they didn't add any caveats. They didn't say that only the men would be leaders. They were talking to all of us.

Yet three decades later, the world hasn't turned out at all as we had imagined. We were wrong in our cavalier attitude toward feminists, those women who had sacrificed so much so that we could, unthinkingly, expect we could have it all. Not only were we wrong, but by assuming their fight wasn't our own—and assuming their battles were over—we inadvertently lost some of their hard-earned gains.

Almost all of the women in that Lehman Brothers class ultimately quit the finance business, including Phyllis, who went on to earn an M.B.A. from Stanford and then abandoned her business career to become a screenwriter. As for my suitemates, those little folded scraps of paper with our predictions couldn't have been more wrong. While we did marry and have children, half of us dialed back, quitting jobs or working part-time as we struggled to balance work and family. Those who stayed found that guys whom we'd easily bested in school were suddenly bosses. At our ten-year college reunion, the men swanned around in cashmere sports jackets, sussing out which one of them had made bank managing director first.

The women had already encountered obstacles and difficulties that we'd never imagined.

My college friends and I are in some ways a microcosm of what's happened in the wider world. Even though women earn almost 60 percent of college degrees and more than half of graduate-school degrees, they represent just 5.6 percent of S&P 500 chief executives and 18 percent of board members of Fortune 1000 firms. They are only 19 percent of law partners. A Rockefeller Foundation survey found that 1 in 4 Americans believes we will literally invent time travel before women run half of the Fortune 500 companies.

According to a McKinsey/*WSJ* analysis, at the rate we're going, it will take a hundred years to reach parity in the executive suite. Globally, the situation is worse. The World Economic Forum estimates it will take 170 years to reach economic parity for women and men worldwide.

This is an urgent problem not just for women but for men. If women participated equally with men in the workforce, American gross domestic product—the total value of the country's goods and services, and a key measure of economic health—would increase by 5 percent, boosting the economy for all of us.

Nor is this just an American problem. Europe and Asia are struggling with the same lopsided landscape. They desperately need more women working to jump-start their sluggish economies. At least eight European countries have passed quotas requiring 30 percent of board seats or more to be held by women—including Germany, Norway, Italy, Spain, and France. In the U.K., new legislation requires big companies to publicly report the pay gap between men and women, a chasm that currently tops £300,000 over the course of a woman's working life. Japan rolled out a program called "Womenomics" to encourage more women to work, claiming it will boost the country's economy by 15 percent. Prime Minister Shinzō Abe calls women "Japan's most underutilized resource."

But as long as men are afraid, or don't know how to talk about the issues, or are just in the dark about women, we won't close the gap. Even the most well meaning men have a long way to go. I recently attended an event for the 3o% Club, an organization founded by British finance executive Helena Morrissey that encourages companies to strive for 3o percent female representation on corporate boards. Research has shown that women's views are discounted until they make up almost a third of any given group.

The event, the kickoff festivities for a mentoring program for promising mid-career women, was hosted by Kenneth Jacobs, the chairman and chief executive officer of banking giant Lazard. We filed into the bank's impressive conference space high above Rockefeller Center, with waiters passing delicate sushi rolls and windows offering panoramic views of Midtown Manhattan. Jacobs took the podium and looked slowly around at the hundred or so audience members, an overwhelmingly female crowd in their best business suits. He paused.

"Generally, I'm a pretty good public speaker," he finally began. "But I confess tonight I'm a little nervous. Here I am in front of a room full of women, and that's very unusual . . . I have to say it's a bit intimidating."

The irony wasn't lost on the room, or on me, either. Every woman there knew what it was like to be the lone female in a room full of men. And no woman—certainly not me—would confess to being frightened. Imagine any businesswoman taking a podium and starting her speech by saying, "Wow, here I am in a room full of men, and it's terrifying!" That would be absurd. Only a powerful man could trot out that line as a conversational icebreaker. The fact that he didn't seem to realize the irony was emblematic of how far we have to go in bringing together men and women at work.

It isn't just him. His one-liner is a common trope among men. At an awards luncheon for women in media, host Andy Cohen looked

out at the Waldorf Astoria ballroom filled with more than a thousand women and quipped, "I'm intimidated!" One of the presenters, Michael Roth, chief executive of advertising giant Interpublic, took his place at the microphone and joked, "It's not often I represent diversity." Funny, sure. But also a reminder that these men and so many others don't have to think about what their female colleagues experience all day, every day.

That's why, prompted first by that businessman on a plane ride to Des Moines, I realized how crucial it is for women to let men in on our secrets. And so I went on a quest to understand not just the challenges women face, but to discover what mystifies or perplexes professional men about the women they work with. My goal was to get to the bottom of issues that men face every day: why women often don't speak up at meetings, why they can seem tentative when they do speak up, why there are so few qualified women in the management pipeline despite good-faith efforts to recruit them.

And then I went in search of solutions. I sought out male executives who are trying to get it right. I traveled across the U.S. and beyond in search of new discoveries, research, and real-life experiments. I focused on men, institutions, even countries, that are actively trying to close the gender gap.

What I found exploded everything I thought I knew about gender. Some of the most surprising revelations came from the unlikeliest of sources: from the Enron scandal, from brain research, from transgender scientists, from Iceland's campaign to "feminize" an entire nation. Together these findings offer fresh insights into the way we relate to one another. My hope is that the information in this book will be helpful for men who want to sharpen their competitive edge, and who could use some practical tips to help figure out and engage with women—without judgment or blame.

And for women, my hope is they'll come away with a new set of tools they can use to break down barriers, right now. Women are

accustomed to being passed over and marginalized; we're frustrated because despite lots of talk, there's been precious little action when it comes to gender equity. Yet in some corners there's been remarkable progress, and I've sought to crack the code of how successful initiatives can take root.

So consider this an invitation to join the conversation, to work together to close the gender gap. You may be alternately surprised, relieved, irritated, and delighted. But above all my hope is that *That's What She Said* will become a rallying cry, for both men and women, finally to take real steps toward closing the gender gap at work and in life.

The people you'll meet in these pages don't pretend to have all the answers. Nor do I. But their stories offer reason for optimism. We're on the cusp of a new way of thinking, one that unites men and women rather than divides us—at work and beyond.

1

The Secret Lives of Women
(a Primer for Men)

Let's say you're a guy, and you've done just fine so far. Why should you think about changing your ways to fit in with women? It seems absurd even to consider the possibility.

"Ladies (women? gals? Hell, I don't know!) you need to man up if you want to succeed in a man's world," one *Wall Street Journal* reader wrote after I suggested in an article that men try to better understand women.

As another male reader put it, "Women need to learn the way men interact, and change themselves accordingly."

Actually, women already change themselves plenty. If you're a man, here are a few things you should know. I wear high heels at work because I'm convinced that makes me look more powerful to you. (Research tells me I'm right—taller women earn as much as 8 percent more than shorter ones.) Linda Hudson, former chief executive of defense contractor BAE Systems, hired a drama teacher so she could get rid of her Georgia accent and lower the pitch of her voice, to sound more like you. Dr. Carmen Quatman, a chief orthopedic surgical resident at Ohio State University, sought out coaching to look as confident as you—as if it wasn't enough that she'd already published 20 papers, presented at 17 conferences, and won 6 national awards.

All of us, and countless other women, are attempting to fit into a professional world that was created in the image of men. The way we speak, dress, write emails, present ourselves—we're conscious of how we come across in a culture that's not quite our own. We're always a little bit like a tourist, trying to mimic the habits of the locals so we can blend in. *New York Times* reporter David Streitfeld perfectly captured the impossible balance many women are trying to strike in a piece he wrote about a sex discrimination suit: "Speak up—but don't talk too much. Light up the room—but don't overshadow others. Be confident and critical—but not cocky or negative."

That's one reason why women have been so intrigued by social psychologist Amy Cuddy's work on power posing. She's found that we can improve our confidence and actually increase our testosterone levels—literally appear more like men—by adapting simple "power poses," like standing arms akimbo with hands on hips and legs wide (the "Wonder Woman"), putting our legs up on our desks, or puffing out our chests. The poses not only increase testosterone levels by as much as 20 percent, they also decrease stress levels.

Not surprisingly, these poses come naturally to men, but they are foreign to most women—not to mention difficult to pull off in a pencil skirt and heels. We do them anyway.

We change our appearance to fit in with you too. A woman's looks sometimes count more than her résumé. One study found that women with blond hair earn 7 percent more than brunettes. Women who wear makeup get better jobs and quicker promotions. Thin women outearn heavier women; white women who are overweight pay a financial penalty of a 12 percent drop in their wealth. Multiple studies have found that people of both genders who are more attractive than average earn more money than their less genetically gifted peers. But there too men have the edge: when researchers interviewed fourteen thousand people, they concluded that for women, grooming—hair, makeup, clothes—counts even more than looks when it comes to earnings.

Take it from me, it costs a small—make that more like a large—fortune for all that upkeep. The average woman spends $15,000 on cosmetics alone during her lifetime. And that's just for starters. Women pay more than men for almost all of their necessities, from dry cleaning to razors to shampoo to blue jeans. It's known as the "pink tax," and it's pervasive. The New York City Department of Consumer Affairs found that 42 percent out of eight hundred products it surveyed cost more for women than for men. That can add up to $1,400 a year for women, a California study found. Considering that women earn less than men for the same jobs in the first place, the financial consequences are significant.

Depending on where you work, the costs can be even steeper. The fashion, advertising, and hospitality industries are particularly brutal for women. When I was an editor at Condé Nast, a publisher known for magazines like *Vogue* and *Glamour*, every item of clothing, pocketbook, and pair of shoes I wore was scrutinized, even though I worked at a business publication and didn't share the same elevator bank as the fashion editors. Walking into the company cafeteria, with a sea of eyes staring you up and down, could turn into an exercise of doubt and self-flagellation.

Early on, some colleagues in the photo department kidnapped me, on a "mercy mission," they said only half-jokingly, to save me from myself. Apparently, my amateur makeup application looked "too New Jersey." (Though being born and raised in New Jersey, I didn't consider that an insult.) They brought in a makeup artist who promptly threw out the drugstore mascara and eyeliner I'd been using since I was twelve years old, and loaded me up with expensive designer cosmetics.

All those extra costs don't even include the hours women spend on styling our hair, getting manicures, and putting on makeup. One of my favorite examples of how this plays out comes from the former president of Barnard College, Debora Spar, who in her book *Wonder Women: Sex, Power and the Quest for Perfection* calculated that she

spends 282 hours a year on basic maintenance, versus the 30 hours that her husband spends. "Over the course of a forty-year career, I will spend 10,080 more hours than the average guy sitting next to me—nearly five working years—trying to make myself look presentable," she wrote.

That's a sobering thought, that women need to cram in five extra years over the same time period of our careers just to stay on par with men. And that's before considering the additional time women spend on child care and housework, which despite admirable gains that men have made in these areas over the past generation, still clocks in at about nine hours a week more than men spend.

Women in positions of authority make even more changes, so that they don't appear too threatening to you. One study found that 48 percent of female CEOs and 35 percent of female senators have blond hair, even though only 5 percent of the white population is blond. Hillary Clinton, who in her student days appeared to be a brunette, has long since become blond. Sandra Day O'Connor, first female Supreme Court justice? Blond. Meg Whitman, chief executive of Hewlett Packard? Virginia Rometty, chief executive of IBM, and Kirsten Gillibrand, New York senator? Yep, they're blond too. Researchers theorize that lighter hair color is associated with youth, beauty, and warmth, which helps counteract the harsh trait of aggressiveness that goes against female stereotypes.

Women even change the way they speak to fit in with you. Linguists have documented what most of us have observed in real life: men typically have speech patterns that are more assertive and aggressive, while women tend to be more inclusive and self-effacing. I am reminded of that every time I attend the Matrix Awards luncheon for women in media. Each year, on a Monday in April, a Manhattan hotel ballroom overflows with female television anchors, executives, writers, tech pioneers, and actresses. Onstage, either being honored or presenting awards, are some of the most accomplished

women in the country, from Tina Fey to Toni Morrison to Katie Couric.

The honorees each give a short acceptance speech. And almost every one of them, in some form or another, says the same two words: "I'm lucky." At one awards ceremony, even honoree Lena Dunham, the actress and very model of modern feminism, proclaimed how "lucky" she was—twice.

When men succeed, they attribute it to their own grit and intelligence. Women attribute it to luck. It's hard for us to own our accomplishments. We diminish them, or refuse to talk about them, or give the credit to somebody else. We apologize all the time, even though we aren't sorry. We lard up our work conversations with qualifiers like "This may be a stupid question, but . . ." or "I don't want to bother you, but . . ." We make statements that sound like questions, even when stating facts ("Shouldn't we turn right here, not left?"). We use language that makes us seem hesitant, that downplays our own status, and that implicitly cedes more power to the other person in the conversation—especially if it's a man.

We also are highly aware of this, and are trying desperately to change it. We know that to men, our natural speech patterns can be misconstrued as a sign of weakness or indecision.

Comedian Amy Schumer spoofed the tendency for women to apologize in a hilarious skit in which the women speaking on a "females in innovation" panel, including a Pulitzer Prize winner and a Nobel Prize winner, trip over each other as they apologize for increasingly absurd scenarios, culminating in one of the women being fatally burned by scalding-hot coffee spilled on her by a man ("Sorry, is this coffee? Sorry, this is my fault"). It wasn't that far off from the truth; Hillary Clinton became the first presidential candidate in recorded history to say "I'm sorry" in her concession speech.

So we try to erase our own natural speech patterns, to sound more like you. Some female executives keep a "Sorry Jar" on their desks,

contributing a dollar each time they find themselves uttering the word. Google even offers a gmail plug-in for women called "Just Not Sorry." It highlights those undermining words and phrases with a red underline, as if they are misspelled. It is a reminder to women to stop sabotaging ourselves in your eyes.

All of this is simply to fit in with you, to be as unobtrusive as possible so that we can be recognized for our work, and not penalized for the way we dress or speak or look or act. It takes hours of effort and hundreds of tiny daily conscious and subconscious decisions about what to say, when to speak, what to wear, whether to acknowledge we have a sick kid at home—moves we make to protect ourselves and that are completely invisible to most men.

My point isn't to blame men, who for the most part don't realize any of this is happening. I'm simply stating the facts. This is the reality for the women who work with you.

••

LINGUIST DEBORAH TANNEN, author of *Talking from 9 to 5*, has famously argued that all of these verbal and behavioral tics—the "upspeak" at the end of sentences, the apologies, the hedging, the self-effacing language—date back to childhood. Little girls learn to play with other girls by collaborating, while boys learn to play with other boys by trying to one-up each other. Girls who try to grab power are shunned. Observing children play, Tannen noted that young girls in a group use language and actions that assure others they are all equal. Girls who overtly jockey for status are ostracized by the group. Boys gain status by winning and one-upping others, while girls lose status for precisely the same behavior.

Girls who violate the norm aren't seen as "nice." They're "bossy" or "nasty." And of course who doesn't want to be seen as nice? I certainly do. Girls learn early that we pay a price for acting differently than what is expected of us.

Tannen wrote her seminal book about these miscues between the sexes more than two decades ago. It's troubling to her that its insights remain as fresh now as ever. When the book was first published, "If you asked me, 'Will everything be the same in twenty years?' I would have said, 'I hope not,'" she told me. She sighed. "But no, things haven't changed."

All of this adds up to one exasperating, infuriating fact: despite the decades that men and women have been working together, we still haven't quite figured each other out. Men, even the most enlightened of them, often remain oblivious to the issues facing their female colleagues sitting in the next cubicle. It's no wonder. They've grown up with the concept that "equal" at work has meant "the same"—a notion that has done us all a disservice. It doesn't allow for the many differences that may inadvertently reward men while penalizing women. It smooths over and ultimately negates the challenges that women face every day, which in turn makes their experiences invisible to men.

That's a dangerous situation for men and women alike. If men are blind to the gender gap experienced by women, we can hardly expect them to care about it, or to be partners in helping to close it. Perhaps it shouldn't be surprising that a recent Pew survey found that the majority of men believe obstacles to women's success "are largely gone," while the majority of women believe "significant obstacles" are still in the way.

The same goes for sexist behavior, which men consistently underestimate. While the majority of women in a nationwide poll said they had been touched inappropriately by a man, only a third of men thought their partners had experienced that kind of harassment.

The bid for gender equality still is perceived largely as a female struggle, led by women for the benefit of women. As sociologist Michael Kimmel has said, "Most men do not know they are gendered beings. When we say 'gender' we hear 'women.'" That explains why

one study found that 43 percent of women agreed with the statement "Women have fewer opportunities than men"—while only 12 percent of men agreed. The men simply couldn't quantify what they couldn't see.

Men who can't see the problem end up instead exacerbating it. Being blind to the issue emboldened Kevin Roberts, then-chairman of Saatchi & Saatchi, one of the world's largest advertising firms, to publicly insist that gender diversity is "an issue that isn't really there," that "the f—ing debate is all over," that the lack of female leadership in his industry isn't "a problem," and that he spent no time on "supposed gender issues."

He didn't make those comments fifty years ago, as you might expect. He made them in 2016. This despite the advertising industry's significant gender gap in leadership; while the industry as a whole is evenly split between genders, women make up only 11 percent of creative directors. His comments provoked such fury that he ultimately resigned.

That blind spot also helps explain why the following year John Allan, the chairman of British supermarket giant Tesco PLC, complained that white men are "an endangered species" on U.K. corporate boards, despite the fact that just 29 percent of directors appointed the previous year were female, and his own board of eleven members had only two women. (He later backtracked on his comments after women threatened to boycott his stores.)

What set these men apart wasn't their boneheaded comments. It was that they said them out loud, in public. Decades of research has shown that their perceptions are common: men tend to overestimate not only women's progress, but their presence. The Geena Davis Institute on Gender in Media found that on average, only 17 percent of the people in film crowd scenes are female, but the perception among men is that 50 percent are women.

Men also believe women speak more than they do in reality. While

they perceive that women talk more than men, women actually don't even get equal time in group discussions unless they make up a majority—60 to 80 percent—of the group. That goes for films too: USC's Annenberg School for Communication and Journalism found that in 2015, female characters made up less than a third of speaking roles in movies.

The reality is that even today, being male is the norm. Being female is the outlier. This isn't just the case at work. "Male" is the default mode around the world—at home and in school, at the mall and in the doctor's office, online and in real life. Even the words we speak are primarily male. In European and Asian languages, the default form of any word is male; you need an alternate form—an added *esse* or *ette*, for example—to transform it into the female equivalent. The male variant is taken more seriously. A "movie star" has more gravitas than a "starlet." And who would want to be operated on by a "surgeonette"?

••

ALL OF WHICH is to say that women are already living in a man's world. We're adjusting to you, every day. The more intriguing notion to me, though, is that men are starting to meet us halfway. They're recalibrating their behavior, just as we recalibrate ours. And in doing so, they are transforming a one-sided conversation—women talking to and about women—into something far more powerful. When men and women both reach across the gender divide, we actually will have a shot at closing the gap.

Consider Glen Mazzara, an executive producer of the hit television series *The Shield*, about a Los Angeles police squad. The characters in the show are diverse, yet when he first began working on it, "I looked around the writers' room and a lot of my fellow writers were white, middle-aged guys," he recalled. Even when he asked talent agents specifically for female writers, they kept sending over white guys.

They didn't believe he was sincere; one agent even told him, "I was just trying to cover my ass." Mazzara began to believe that "the system is rigged to accept white males, to train them and keep them in the pipeline." Indeed, less than a third of film and television writers are female, while in 2016, just 7 percent of the 250 top-grossing films were directed by women.

Ultimately the show brought in a two-person female writing team. But then another problem emerged: the women weren't contributing in the writers' room. They didn't have a chance. Every time they tried to present prepared material, some guy would cut them off. Worse, Mazzara realized, this had been going on for quite some time. It took him too long to notice it himself. "I was complicit in this because my male ear was tuned to the interrupting male voice," he said. "So I realized I had behavior that I had to unlearn."

Mazzara's realization that the women were being shut down may have been news to him—but it's familiar to women everywhere. Visit any meeting, at any company, anywhere in the world, on any given day, and you'll find the same scenario. Men dominate. Women often don't speak at all, or self-censor, or tentatively pose statements as questions. Women who do speak up are interrupted or ignored. If they do manage to get an idea out before being shut down, a guy inevitably will grab credit.

If an alien landed in the middle of a quarterly budget report at a typical company, the imbalance would be easy for the alien to spot. Yet to most men, it is invisible. Meetings, quite simply, are the killing fields of a woman's career.

This too dates back to the sandbox. Linguist Tannen has found that little boys don't listen to girls. Even as youngsters, boys "pay less attention to females of their own age than to other males," she says. "And the experience of women at meetings indicates the same is often true for adult men and women."

Indeed, women who do speak up at meetings are often penalized just as little girls are. A Yale study found that male executives who

spoke more than their peers were viewed as more competent. For the female executives, it was the reverse. If they spoke more than their peers, they were judged 14 percent *less* competent. And when researchers observed company meetings for a 2012 study, they found that men speak a whopping 75 percent of the time—and that women as a result have little impact on decisions.

This is as true for world leaders as it is for company trainees. Christine Lagarde, head of the International Monetary Fund, said that in a meeting, when a woman speaks, "many of the male board members start to withdraw physically, they start to look at their papers, to look at the floor . . . and you need to disrupt that." She doesn't hesitate to call them out on it: "When you're the chair, you say 'Somebody's talking. You should be listening.'"

Similarly, Linda Hudson, the former BAE chief executive, has noticed the phenomenon throughout her career. "You can see it. . . . around the conference table," she told me. In a meeting, "the men who speak will pay more attention to other men than to women. It's just a dynamic that has developed over decades and lifetimes, the view that somehow what the man has to say is important. It might matter more than what a woman has to say."

Dozens of studies have concluded that women are interrupted more frequently than men, and that men do so to display their power. Kieran Snyder, a tech executive with a Ph.D. in linguistics, calculated interruptions in meetings at her own company, and found that men were three times more likely to interrupt women than other men. Perhaps even more dispiriting, though, the very few women who did interrupt others overwhelmingly cut in on other women—a stunning 87 percent of the time. They almost never interrupted men.

Not even the Supreme Court is immune. A Northwestern University analysis of Supreme Court arguments over a dozen years found that the three female justices were interrupted three times more frequently than their male counterparts. As powerful as these women are, they "are just like other women," the researchers wrote,

"talked over by their male colleagues." Interestingly, though, the longer the female justices sat on the court, the more they adopted speaking patterns similar to those of the men, using fewer polite qualifiers like "excuse me" or "sorry," and speaking in a more aggressive, declaratory style.

Like the justices, tech executive Snyder concluded that women need to change their behavior, to act like men in order to be heard: "Women don't advance in their careers beyond a certain point without learning to interrupt."

Even then, they face steep odds. I was reminded of that at a recent meeting of the World Economic Forum in Davos. Each year, billionaires, CEOs, and world leaders descend on this tiny Swiss ski resort town for a weeklong orgy of backslapping, schmoozing, partying, and amassing bragging rights for running into George Clooney or Xi Jinping. And, oh yes, solving the problems of the world.

For several years I've been there too, as a journalist covering the proceedings. Each time, I am newly astonished by how few women I see. This is a conference of three thousand people, yet there's never a line for the ladies' room. That tells you pretty much everything you need to know about the "global elite."

The forum has made a concerted effort to invite more women. It even took the somewhat desperate measure of allowing companies to bring an extra attendee beyond the maximum four—as long as the extra is female. It reminds me of the dive bars I went to in college: Ladies' Night! In 2017, the conference organizers announced, proudly and with great fanfare, that 20 percent of attendees were female. The audience applauded, to my consternation. Since when is 20 percent, when women comprise slightly more than half the population, something to celebrate?

"It takes endurance," one of the forum participants, Kim Metcalf-Kupres, the chief marketing officer of Johnson Controls, told me during the 2017 meeting. "I'm naturally an introvert, and as a

woman in these forums, this is a forum of extroverts and a forum of big egos."

Most of the action in Davos takes place not in the large formal sessions, but in small private meetings. There, she says, "the men dominate the conversation. Their body language to me is offensive. I find my personal space becomes smaller and smaller and their arm gestures become bigger and bigger. And nobody wants to ask questions. Everybody want to make statements . . . It becomes about grandstanding . . . It's all thought provoking, but they're all talking at each other, past each other."

It takes guts for women to speak up. And sometimes a thick skin too. I know from painful experience. For years I barely spoke at meetings. I feared that others would think my ideas were stupid . . . or that I was. The first time I pushed myself to do so, I was terrified that my remarks would be ignored, or greeted with derision, or dismissed with the journalist's most dreaded insult: "Everybody knows that." Day after day, I would sit silently as men spoke up, making points I had been thinking beforehand but had been too timid to express. Finally, I tried, tentatively, to interject my own ideas. At first, it was liberating. My boss was attentive, my ideas for news coverage were having an impact. So far, so good.

But then one of my more swaggering male colleagues, who considered himself a rival for our boss's attention, pulled me aside. He led me to a vacant office and closed the door. The vein in his forehead was throbbing. "Stop talking!" he yelled. "Just stop. You're not as smart as you think you are."

I was too startled to respond. I was, literally, shaking. I was mortified. And furious. And also . . . wondering if he was right. Maybe everybody else in the room did know more than I did. Shaken, I confided as much to my husband, Tom, that night. My gallant husband's first reaction was to offer to beat up the guy, which I appreciated. But then he shrugged and said, essentially, get over it:

this was simply posturing by a colleague who was vying for our boss's attention.

The next day, gulping in a deep breath, I forced myself to speak. In the following weeks, every day I did the same. Speaking up didn't come naturally—it still doesn't. But my husband was right. My voice was heard. As for my swaggering colleague, he eventually left the company.

My experience, and my self-doubt about the value of my opinion, would hardly surprise sociologists. Not just men but women themselves have a hard time accepting it when a woman's behavior is at odds with long-held stereotypes. One survey asked more than three thousand professional and college-age women what lessons they were taught growing up. Topping the list: "be nice to others," "be a good student," "be respectful to authorities/elders," and "be helpful." At the bottom? "Be a good leader," "make a difference in society," "master a skill," and "share your point of view."

When women do force ourselves to speak, that's just clearing the first hurdle. The next may be even harder: when women's ideas are accepted, it's often because the credit goes to a man. Olivia makes a smart comment and no one seems to hear it. Then Bill paraphrases it, and suddenly he's a genius: "That Bill! What a sharp thinker he is." The women in the room, meanwhile, are all thinking the same thing: "WTF?? That's what she said!"

Almost any woman you ask is familiar with the experience. It's so common that *Mother Jones* ran a list headlined "Ladies Last: 8 Inventions by Women That Dudes Got Credit For"—including the double helix (Rosalind Franklin), computer programming (Ada Lovelace), and the game Monopoly (Elizabeth Magie). The classic example is Kanye West, who took credit for singer Taylor Swift's success: "I made that bitch famous. God damn, I made that bitch famous."

"It happens to all of us, every day," Metcalf-Kupres of Johnson Controls told me, laughing ruefully. "They don't even know they're doing it."

I once referenced the phenomenon in a speech before a group of lawyers. During the Q & A afterward, one of the men in the audience raised his hand, eyes wide. He was part of a working group in which the majority of an assignment was done by a female lawyer, he said. But when the work was complete, one of the men in the group gave the final presentation to the senior partner and got the credit. As he spoke, he seemed stunned by this new and sudden realization. All around him, a hundred female faces looked bemused, and just a tiny bit annoyed. I could almost hear their collective response: *Duh.*

And yet men who become aware of this dynamic are in the best possible position to help us change it. That's why Glen Mazzara's epiphany, that he needed to "unlearn" some of his own behaviors to make sure women were heard, is so critically important. When he realized that female writers were constantly being interrupted by their male counterparts, he came up with a new rule: No interrupting during prepared presentations. For anyone. The idea wasn't to coddle women; it was to make sure the best ideas got surfaced, and the worst were summarily killed.

Every writer is entitled to present their pitch, to its conclusion, without anyone else jumping in, Mazzara explained. "Then, when they finish, then you can rip it apart and leave them in tears—whether they're male or female." Mazzara has since gone on to become the showrunner for multiple hit series, including *The Walking Dead,* and has brought the practice to each.

••

THOUGH MEN MAY not realize this, women have been coming up with similar kinds of life hacks for years, in order to be heard. Jennifer Allyn, PricewaterhouseCoopers managing director for diversity, advocates the "brag buddies" approach. Women have a difficult time talking about their own achievements, and are viewed unfavorably when they do. It's the "humility trap," she says, the idea that "good girls don't brag." So she recommends that women instead trade

success stories with one another. Then each makes it a priority to talk up the others to colleagues; they support each other by pointing out the others' achievements.

The women working in President Barack Obama's administration invented their own twist on this idea. Obama prided himself on championing women. The first bill he signed into law when he took office in 2009 was the Lilly Ledbetter Fair Pay Act, effectively extending the statute of limitations on equal-pay lawsuits. By the end of his tenure, women made up 44 percent of his top staff.

And yet women in his administration still felt overlooked and bulldozed by the men in meetings. So much so that they created an echo-chamber solution they called "amplification": when one woman spoke up, another would repeat her idea and give her credit for it. The women reinforced one another, allowing them to take ownership of their ideas before a man could steal them.

I'm encouraged to see that more men are embracing these kinds of tactics too. After he became a manager, Paul Gotti, Cardinal Health's vice president of nuclear pharmacy services, noticed that in meetings, a woman "will say something, and it's not acknowledged until a guy says it later." So now he makes sure to credit the woman and then bring her back into the discussion, asking her, "Why don't you elaborate on that?"

The beauty of Gotti's solution is its elegant simplicity. You don't need to be the boss to recognize when a woman has a great idea that's been overlooked or credited to someone else. Any one of us, male or female, can speak up and give her credit on her behalf.

••

THE MYRIAD WAYS in which women are adjusting to you, all day every day, nevertheless remain stubbornly invisible to most men. It's time to put a stop to that. And that's where this book comes in. Whether you're a man or a woman, whether you're just starting out in your

career or are a senior manager, whether you're a father or a mother, it's time to acknowledge the gap and understand how we can work together to close it. I've been on multiple sides of this equation, as an employee and a boss and as a mom to a daughter and a son, both of whom I hope will experience a more equal world—something my husband wishes for as fervently as I do.

Wherever you stand, once you see the gap—women being overlooked, interrupted, their ideas credited to a man—you'll notice it everywhere. The good news is, that's the first step in closing it. As I traversed the country and the world, speaking with scores of executives and academics who are making an effort to reach across the gender divide, they all noted this same essential step. Awareness, like sunlight, isn't just the best disinfectant. It's the cure. The men I met who became attuned to the issues told me they modified their own behavior, and tried to change the culture of their own workplaces too.

These men are already making a difference. Consider my college pal Matt Krentz. We became fast friends freshman year, when he and a group of boys lived directly above my own suite of five girls. They were like brothers, who alternately protected and tortured us. Once, my roommates and I came back from dinner to find all of our furniture—which we had pooled our meager resources to buy from the Salvation Army—was gone. We panicked and called the police. The guys, realizing we were too naive to understand that no self-respecting thief would want our tattered plaid couch, had to admit they had stashed it in their own suite as a practical joke.

After graduation, Matt landed an entry-level job at Boston Consulting Group (BCG). Matt hails from a family of strong women: he has two brilliant sisters, a mother with an advanced degree in English, and he met his wife when they were classmates in business school. So he was perplexed to find that, as the years went by and he rose through the ranks, at each level he had fewer female

colleagues. Ultimately promoted to run the firm's Chicago office, he looked around and realized there were no female partners at all in his group. That's when he began assessing the issue in earnest.

Matt became an anthropologist in his own firm, studying the habits, habitats, and interactions of the men and women around him. Consulting is a difficult career for anyone. The path to partnership, designed decades ago for men with wives at home, typically takes about eight years and requires continuous travel to embed with clients.

But Matt and other firm leaders began noticing other, more subtle issues that were alienating to women in particular. For example, "We are a very critical culture. We often tell people what they need to get better at"—a message that was effective for many men, but was devastating to many of the women. Indeed, researchers have found that some women react to negative feedback far more strongly than men do. When given a mix of positive and negative feedback, men focus on the positive—while women put greater weight on the negative.

At BCG, women took that critical feedback to heart so strongly that it undermined their confidence. Even for high-performing women, the firm's feedback often was "You need to be more edgy, more confrontational," which inadvertently sent the message that they were supposed to act like men.

For men, "that environment doesn't feel foreign," Matt said. But "the women become much more disconnected, and we lose the opportunity to retain them." Not only were women quitting at higher rates than men, those who didn't leave voluntarily were being cut at a disproportionately greater rate than men.

Matt and like-minded colleagues took a hard look at their own behavior, and realized that "we need to change the environment in which we work, how we give feedback, and more proactively engage on how we are mentoring, sponsoring, guiding" women, he told me. Among other steps, he paired women with successful partners so

they could model real-world success. The partners didn't just offer advice and moral support; they were able to advocate for the women they worked with.

"A mentor isn't good enough. You need someone who will stick their neck out and say, 'Yes, I will vouch for this person,'" Matt found. By the time he moved on to his next role, close to 20 percent of the partners in the Chicago office were women.

Today, Matt is one of BCG's most senior leaders, a member of the executive committee and head of the global people team. (And I assume no longer pilfering his friends' furniture!) His work helped lead to a program called Apprenticeship in Action, which, among other things, helps junior employees develop professional relationships.

Performance evaluations have changed too, to focus on strengths, not just weaknesses, and link those strengths to areas for development. Managers check to make sure they don't fall back on the male-dominated tropes like "'You need to be more confrontational in meetings, you need to speak out more,'" Matt said. "Just telling someone to do that and then watching to see if they can do it is poor development, but we default to that because men will respond." From 2011 to 2016, the number of female consultants grew by 70 percent.

The bottom line is, "our male leaders need to be engaged on this," Matt told me. "We have to behave differently."

We have to behave differently. Think about that for a moment. Women spend our whole careers trying to fit in with men. But when men like Matt Krentz and Glen Mazzara change their behavior to adapt to us as well, the landscape suddenly shifts. The old saw about Ginger Rogers—"she did everything Fred Astaire did, but backwards and in high heels"—has been a pretty accurate description of how women feel at work. When more men reach across the gender divide, we can work side by side instead—facing forward together.

2

She'll Make You More Successful

One day in 1945, a failed landscaper stumbled on an idea he was sure would make him rich.

Earl Silas Tupper had already gone bankrupt once, and may well have been on his way there again. He had lost his Massachusetts tree surgery business during the dark days of the Depression. Who cared about pruning your trees when you couldn't feed your kids? He had tried his hand as an inventor too, but nobody wanted to buy his fish-powered boat or his dripless ice-cream cone.

Desperate for work, he had taken a job in a plastics factory. After scraping together enough savings, he bought some molding machines and went into business himself. When World War II erupted, he turned himself into a military contractor and churned out plastic parts for gas masks and jeeps.

But when the war ended, demand for gas masks evaporated. What's worse, so did the raw materials he needed to keep his plants running.

"Sorry, there's just not enough to go around," a Bakelite sales rep told him that day, when Earl went looking for the plastic resin he needed for his molds.

Earl refused to leave. "What else have you got? You must have something kicking around."

The rep shrugged, and handed Earl a rubbery, stinking black substance that left a greasy film on his fingers. It was slag, the waste left over from industrial smelting. The military had used it during

the war to insulate wiring on military devices. But now that the war was over, nobody needed it.

"We have tons of this stuff sitting around and we don't know what to do with it," the rep said. "You can have all of it if you want."

Earl took the greasy hunk home. Thoughtfully, he turned it over and over in his hands. Maybe, he thought, if he could figure out how to liquefy it, he could make something useful out of it. So he threw it in a pot of water and boiled it.

Soon, he was mixing up different concoctions using the slag, technically known as polyethylene. Every night, he would bring home a dozen samples of the stuff, mixed with different chemicals and processed using different pressures. Then he and his teenage son Miles would throw the samples into vats and cook each at different temperatures.

For months, they slaved over the stove, experimenting with different recipes, temperatures, pressures. Finally, they figured out a way to make it malleable—liquefied enough to pour into a mold, supple enough that when it hardened it wouldn't crack, translucent instead of ugly black. Earl even found a way to inject it with pastel colors. He called it "Poly T: Material of the Future."

Then he started making things out of it. Beads. A cigarette case. They were fine, but even he had to admit they were nothing special. It wasn't until he tried making it into a bowl that he realized he was on to something.

Food storage was a problem for the housewives of post-war America. After America's boys came home from battle, they married, had children, moved out to tidy houses in the growing suburbs. As farmland was bulldozed to make way for tract houses, supermarkets sprouted across the country, their shelves groaning with a dizzying array of products, as many as ten thousand in a single store. Ribbon cuttings at huge new A&P and Safeway stores seemed to make the front page every week.

But women couldn't figure out how to keep the food they bought

fresh. Mostly they improvised. One popular method was to cover leftovers with a shower cap. It wasn't much of a solution; air still seeped in, and food spoiled.

That's where Earl saw his opening. He crafted a lid for his bowl, one that would fit so tightly that no air could escape, guaranteeing that your fruit salad or leftover dinner would stay fresh. The only glitch was that to close the seal properly, you had to open a corner just a bit and let out the trapped air.

Earl called it Tupperware.

The reviews for his new invention, which he manufactured in an array of pastel colors, were rapturous. "Fine art for 39 cents," declared *House Beautiful*. New York City's Museum of Modern Art displayed Tupperware bowls in a housewares exhibit.

Orders poured in. One of the biggest department stores in the country, Detroit's J.L. Hudson, put his whole line on display. Earl found himself, at the age of forty, an overnight success. A 1947 *Time* magazine article called him a "one-man boom." He was sure he'd sell a million of his bowls in the first year, according to author Bob Kealing, whose book *Tupperware Unsealed* recounts his history.

A great success story, right?

Not quite.

At stores around the country, the beautiful new bowls sat. And sat.

Women couldn't figure out how to use Tupperware. The few who bought it returned it, saying it was defective, sure that the top didn't fit. It gathered dust in department store displays.

Earl had failed again.

••

THE AMERICAN ECONOMY is fueled, overwhelmingly, by women. Some 75 percent of America's gross domestic product—the value of all goods and services, which is generally used as a measure of economic health—derives from consumer purchases. An astonishing 85 percent of those purchases are driven by women.

Yet just as in Earl Tupper's day, men overwhelmingly control the design, manufacture, and sale of the vast majority of stuff we're buying. This leads to a lot of comically awful product design, marketing catastrophes, and way more "What the hell were they thinking?" moments than strictly necessary.

Even Apple, renowned for its impeccable design sense, infuriated a lot of women when it first introduced the oversize iPhone 6 Plus, sized comfortably for most men's but too big for most women's hands—and pockets. Where were we supposed to keep the thing? "iPhone 6 Plus: Is It Too Big for Women?" asked CBS News. Clothing designers struggled over whether to redesign women's pockets. Adding insult to injury, the phone's camera snared women's hair so often it launched the Twitter meme #hairgate.

Perhaps none of this should have been surprising. Despite concerted efforts to hire women, Apple remains 68 percent male, with particularly bro-heavy design and engineering teams.

Male-dominated design explains so many mysteries of life. Long lines at women's restrooms, for example; the vast majority of architects are men. And, almost every woman I know keeps a sweatshirt, a wool throw, or—like me—a space heater in her office. Sometimes you'll find me wearing gloves while I type. I used to wonder why I was always freezing at work. I asked my doctor about it once. Am I literally thin-skinned?

Apparently not. As the *New York Times* reported, office temperatures have been set since the Mad Men era by using male anatomy as a baseline. Most office buildings use a formula that calculates an ideal room temperature by factoring in the average metabolic rate—the rate at which a body generates heat—of a forty-year-old, 154-pound man. Men typically have a faster metabolic rate than women. So this creaky old formula spits out an office temperature that feels great for a guy in a suit or shirtsleeves, but is frigid for women in dresses and heels.

If goose bumps were the worst problem women had to deal with, we

could shrug it off and buy a sweater. But there are far more serious consequences. A 2011 study found that airbags and seat belts are designed primarily for male bodies—meaning women wearing seat belts are 47 percent more likely to sustain injuries in a crash.

And in 2013, the Food and Drug Administration found that women were routinely being prescribed overdoses of the sleeping pill Ambien. The FDA cut the recommended dosage in *half* after finding that at prescribed levels, women risked dangerous side effects, including impaired driving. How did the dosage go so wrong? Because medical testing of Ambien, as with most testing historically, used men—and men metabolize the drug differently than women.

Indeed, scientists for decades didn't take into account differences in basic biology when figuring out whether drugs work at all. Men were simpler test subjects, since their bodies didn't deal with inconvenient issues like menstruation and hormonal swings. Even today, most medical testing on lab animals uses males.

Now imagine a world where men and women truly work together equally. Where designs and products are created with input from both sexes. What would that look like? For starters, we'd probably have fewer technology startups like Titstare, pitched to potential backers at the TechCrunch Disrupt conference in 2013 as "an app where you take photos of yourself staring at tits." (The crowd of young white guys in hoodies loved it, though it ignited a firestorm of protest on social media.)

It's also a pretty good bet that we'd give the economy a boost. We'd spend more, company profits would rise, employment would follow. "Here's What Would Happen if More Women Designed/Marketed Lady Products" was a headline on the women's blog *Jezebel*. The article suggested products that wouldn't exist (pink razors, pink tools) and those that should (kids' medicine that isn't red, cosmetics that don't explode on airplanes). Buzzfeed weighed in with its own listicle of "21 Pointlessly Gendered Products," including pink earplugs, pens,

and cellophane tape. More practically, rather than complaining about it, a female researcher at MIT Media Lab organized a hackathon to create a better breast pump, a contraption that any woman who has used it can tell you is clunky, awkward, and embarrassingly noisy—clearly designed by people who have never nursed a baby.

Yet it doesn't have to be that way. Remarkable things can happen when men reach across the gender divide. You're probably familiar with the Container Store. It's nirvana for a certain type of neat freaks and neat-freak-wannabes like me. With its perfectly arranged wicker baskets, hangers, shoe racks, closet organization systems, and mul-ticolored containers of every kind, it makes you imagine that you too could have a streamlined, clutter-free life. Its store aisles are arranged to soothe, like a *Real Simple* magazine cover come to life. Every bit of that illusion is intentional.

"Our whole image of that is, it's all about a woman. You're trying to get two kids ready for school, everybody's late, there are tears and stress and it's terrible," company founder Kip Tindell explained to me. "But if you have the organized life, then it's joyful, the little girl's school uniform is perfectly pressed, the husband is a little hunkier. Everything is better."

One of his products in this carefully constructed world, though, wasn't delivering. It was a cosmetics organizer, the kind women stash on a countertop or in a vanity drawer to keep lipsticks and mascara easily at hand. Tindell was perplexed. Women wanted organizers, they came to the store searching for them, so why wasn't this one selling? To get to the bottom of the mystery, he started at the source: Taiwan. That's where the organizers were made. And here's what he found: the designers were all men.

"It was insane," he said. Taiwanese men sat in a room creating "arbitrarily designed" cosmetic organizers that "weren't func-tional . . . no different probably than a fishing tackle box." So he dropped the line and hired American women to redesign a cosmetics organizer. Sales quadrupled.

Tindell since then has not only favored women designers, he favors female executives too. Women, he says, generally have stronger communication skills, empathy, and "emotional intelligence," all of which he finds strengthen company performance. If men champion women at work, he says, "their business will do better. Women make better business leaders."

••

CERTAINLY, THERE'S A strong and wise argument to be made for equality for women as a social good. It's a basic human right. It's simply the right thing to do.

But that isn't Tindell's argument. Instead, he discovered on his own what economists have since concluded as well: if you want to be more successful, about the best thing you can do is hire women.

Multiple studies have found that adding women to all-male teams leads to greater financial success. Companies with female chief financial officers make fewer, better acquisitions than those with male chief financial officers. Female executives make more profitable acquisitions and take on less debt than male executives. Firms with the most female board members outperform those with the least by almost every financial measure. Companies whose top management is at least half female post returns on equity that are 19 percent higher than average. And adding women to work teams tempers risky behavior like the financial gambles that crashed the economy in 2008.

One study concluded that female-led funds outperform those run by men by a large margin. And in a study of thirty-eight thousand households, researchers found that men traded far more frequently—and as a result earned lower returns—than women.

It's perhaps no surprise that Warren Buffett, considered the era's most successful investor, takes a very different approach than other male financiers from his office in Omaha, Nebraska, far from the

testosterone-fueled alleys of Wall Street: investing for the long term, putting money only into companies he understands, and avoiding the frantic trading and panic selling that is the undoing of so many male investors. There's a reason that when author LouAnn Lofton wrote a book analyzing his investment style, she titled it *Warren Buffett Invests Like a Girl*.

The evidence also backs up Tindell's intuition that women make better executives. One survey of 7,280 leaders found that women ranked higher than men in 12 out of 16 competencies, including stereotypically male traits like taking initiative, driving results, and championing change. The researchers found that women were more effective precisely because of the perception that they aren't as good as men; they believed they needed to work harder than men to prove themselves.

"They're afraid to rest on their laurels. Feeling the need (often keenly) to take initiative, they are more highly motivated to take feedback to heart," leadership consultants Jack Zenger and Joseph Folkman concluded. "The irony is that these are fundamental behaviors that drive the success of *every* leader, whether woman or man."

Adding women to all-male groups can be transformative, in sometimes surprising ways. Consider the humble plastic bucket. A few years ago, with its sales slumping, Home Depot decided to try to reinvent the bucket. People buy millions of them every year. You probably have at least one or two that you use for mopping or gardening or washing your car. It's likely in some mildly unappealing color, like jaundice yellow or hospital blue. The plastic bucket hasn't changed in years; you could have bought the same one in 1967, when it was first invented. Not coincidentally, that was the year *The Graduate* was released, along with the memorable advice given to Dustin Hoffman's Benjamin Braddock: "The future can be summed up in one word: plastics."

But by 2010, nobody needed to go to Home Depot to buy a bucket; it was just as easy to stay home in your pajamas and click on Amazon. Home Depot founder Bernie Marcus knew he needed a new reason to bring people into his stores. So the company launched a top-secret program, called Project Whitespace. It had a seemingly quixotic goal: to reinvent ordinary, everyday objects, to improve not just their looks but their function.

Home Depot turned to a California industrial-design firm led by Scot Herbst to puzzle over the bucket. Not many women are industrial designers—by most estimates, just 10 percent or fewer of the industry's employees are female—but Herbst included one on his team. She quickly identified an obvious flaw that fifty years' worth of male designers and retailers had missed: when a bucket is full, it's too heavy for most women to lift. The design team then went into the field, observing real people as they used buckets to wash windows or mop floors. Sure enough, they observed women awkwardly trying to carry full buckets with two hands, or drag them along the floor.

Back in the studio, Herbst and his team designed prototype after prototype to try to solve the problem. Finally, they hit upon a solution: a bucket with a second handhold molded into the bottom, and an ergonomically designed handle to better distribute weight. Women can lift it with two hands, carry it without tipping it over, and pour it more easily. The Big Gripper has since been ordered up by other large retailers like Walmart. It's becoming a new standard.

This wasn't rocket science. Somebody could have figured this out fifty years ago. But nobody had bothered to bring women into the design process. "It wasn't magic," Herbst told me. It was just women.

••

THE PLASTIC BUCKET hadn't yet been invented when Earl Tupper was trying, unsuccessfully, to sell his Tupperware in 1949. While he contemplated failure once again, halfway across the country, in a Detroit

suburb, a divorcée with a young son had discovered she had a gift for selling housewives stuff they didn't know they needed.

Brownie Wise had been scraping by as a secretary when a salesman for Stanley Home Products knocked on her door. She was unimpressed with his sales pitch. I can do better than that, she thought to herself. And so she gave it a try.

Soon she was hosting home parties where she showed housewives the Stanley brooms, brushes, and cleaners they couldn't live without. She was a gifted speaker—a skill honed as a child, when she gave speeches at union rallies organized by her hat-maker mother. She was so successful that she was able to quit her secretarial job.

Her greatest talent, though, turned out to be recruiting other women to host their own parties. She intuitively understood that her neighbors, many of whom had worked in factories during World War II but now were sent back home to the kitchen, longed for the glamour, the respect, and the power that came with a job. They needed the money, for sure. But Brownie's great insight was that they craved the recognition at least as much. Besides, what better job than one that allowed a housewife to stay at home with her children and have dinner on the table for her man every night?

Brownie lavished attention on her growing sales force. She awarded trophies, heralded them in her newsletters, and gave out gifts to her biggest producers. "There is nothing new about the need for personal recognition. It is as old as mankind," she would often say.

By 1949, she was Stanley's star sales manager. She was certain she was in line for a big promotion to a corporate job when she was called to the Massachusetts headquarters. Instead, she got a different message. She wasn't eligible for management, the company founder told her, because the executive suite is "no place for a woman."

Infuriated, she returned to Detroit. She had topped out, her ambitions dashed. "I'll show him!" she vowed to her son.

Perhaps that's why she was so fascinated when a local teenage boy, one of her best salesmen, gave her a gift. It was a curious object he'd found in a local store: a Tupperware bowl. Brownie, like most people, was at first flummoxed by this strange new object. She dropped it and watched it bounce. She puzzled over the lid, trying to figure out how it worked, finally remarking—in what would become a famous marketing refrain—"you had to burp it, just like a baby."

Brownie and her young protégé quickly realized something Earl Tupper didn't: women were never going to buy these odd new bowls on their own. They needed to see how the product worked. Once they saw the magic, she was sure they would flock to it. She soon switched her allegiance—and that of her growing sales force—to Tupperware.

Turns out Brownie was even more successful selling Tupperware bowls than she had been selling mops and brushes. She set her sights on those hordes of housewives who were wrestling with leftovers by covering them with foil and shower caps. She set sales records and recruited dozens more women to join her to host Tupperware parties. "Get rid of your shower caps! Turn your leftovers into makeovers!" was their rallying cry.

None of this had occurred to Earl Tupper himself. He didn't intuitively understand that his overwhelmingly female customers would be baffled by how to use his beautiful bowls. Nor did he realize the frustration of women looking for validation in a world that had sent them back to the kitchen—women who could be mobilized into a powerful sales force.

It wasn't long before Brownie drew the attention of Earl himself—and promptly told him that if he wanted his company to succeed, he must stop selling Tupperware in stores altogether. It should only be sold at home parties. She was insistent that he change his business model. She was certain she knew better than he did.

It's hard to overstate how remarkable a moment this was. Women

didn't tell executives how to run their businesses in the 1950s. This was two full decades before the first woman would be named the chief executive officer of a major company—and that woman, Katharine Graham of the *Washington Post*, inherited the job from her husband. A woman was supposed to stay at home, to keep her husband happy, and to never, ever talk back.

Women weren't believed to have the same capacity for business or the same level of intelligence as men. A Kenmore mixer ad from the era proclaimed, "The Chef does everything but cook—that's what wives are for!" An ad for Lysol disinfectant—which started out its life, astonishingly, as a vaginal douche (and which women used as a primitive, unsuccessful form of birth control)—warned women darkly, "Instead of blaming him if married love begins to cool, she should question herself" and urged women to douche with Lysol to "Keep you desirable!"

In this context, given the overwhelming cultural forces of the era, Earl could easily have ignored Brownie's advice. Instead, almost defiantly rebelling against the conventional wisdom of his time, he took her suggestion. He likely didn't consider the magnitude of this break with tradition. He wasn't trying to advance the cause of women. He was simply trying to save his business. And so he followed Brownie's playbook. He pulled Tupperware out of stores, handing the sales efforts over to this persuasive, insistent woman and her legions of housewives selling Tupperware in their living rooms.

Brownie's insights proved to be precisely right. Earl's once-failing business exploded. Within a few years, Brownie was commanding a Tupperware sales army some nine thousand strong, almost all of them housewives, from headquarters she built in Kissimmee, Florida. Rejected early in her career by Stanley, she now redoubled her efforts to prove that she could be as successful an executive as any man.

Her annual "Tupperware Jubilees" for dealers and managers were

equal parts revival meeting and carnival. At one Florida celebration, she buried mink coats, diamond rings, and television sets, then handed out six hundred shovels for the saleswomen to dig for treasure. She gave out Cadillacs and trips to Europe. She would whip her crowds of acolytes into a frenzy, offering as prizes the dresses off her back and shoes off her feet. Any woman could be a Tupperware star, she promised them. She sometimes ordered a hundred thousand blenders at a time to give out to party hostesses as gifts.

"Brownie had the ability to just talk to your dreams. Things you didn't even know you wanted," as one of her saleswomen put it. "She'd draw these beautiful pictures and you could suddenly see yourself being, you know, something that you hadn't thought about before."

Thanks to Brownie and her team, Earl surpassed even his wildest goals, selling millions of pieces of Tupperware. He became unfathomably rich, a millionaire many times over.

Earl and Brownie, as a team, were able to achieve what neither could alone. He made a great product but didn't understand women. She understood that female employees wanted recognition as much as cash, and that female customers wanted excitement and magic. They were better together than either one could be apart.

The astonishingly successful collaboration between Earl and Brownie predated by half a century research that explained exactly why their partnership was so fruitful. But we know now that they unwittingly had created the precise conditions for men and women to work together with maximum results.

Researchers have found that, just as with the Tupperware duo, when women are added to all-male teams, solutions are more creative than those of single-sex teams of either gender. In one experiment, when male and female students were asked to come up with a new business to fill an empty storefront on campus, the mixed groups consistently came up with more innovative ideas than single-sex

groups of either gender. Researchers found that single-sex groups were quick to agree with one another, which led to limited, unimaginative ideas. The mixed-sex groups approached the problem from multiple viewpoints, resulting in far more inventive solutions.

As with Earl and Brownie, mixed groups are just smarter. An intriguing study that asked groups to solve a murder mystery gives us deep insights into why this is so. Researchers asked homogeneous groups—in this case, a three-person group of male fraternity members and another of female sorority members—to finger the killer in a whodunit mystery. The single-sex groups felt comfortable with one another, and worked easily together. They quickly came up with their solution. They were confident in their answer. They felt good about the process.

Next, researchers sent in an outsider to join the groups—a man into a female group, or a woman into a male group. The group bonhomie evaporated. There was discomfort all around. We naturally gravitate toward those like us, and bringing in an outsider threw off that easy dynamic. Alliances shifted; the "in" group members who agreed with the new outsider's views felt as if their social ties to the rest of the group were strained. The group members as a whole suddenly felt more pressure to justify their answers. These groups had more difficulty solving the murder mystery. They were less confident about the result. The process wasn't pleasant.

And yet, as it turned out, these mixed groups nailed the correct perpetrator far more frequently than single-sex groups. And they did so precisely because of that awkward dynamic. In the mixed group, every individual had to be at the top of his or her game, carefully justifying and explaining his or her beliefs. Researchers concluded that simply by adding in someone of a different gender, the groups became more thoughtful, worked harder to find common ground, and as a result came up with superior solutions.

More than half a century ago, men like Earl Tupper proved it first.

When men reach across gender lines, when men and women work together toward a common goal, great things can happen. All of us are better off for it.

••

EARL TUPPER WAS an outlier in his time, bucking social conventions by bringing in a woman as his business partner. He wasn't trying to promote the cause of women's equality. He was hardly a social activist, as his later life would prove. He was focused, simply, on the bottom line.

In that respect, he was aligned with his modern-day counterparts. While reporting on this book over the course of two years, I interviewed more than a hundred successful executives, physicians, academics, and others who are reaching across gender lines. Virtually all of them shared one distinctive quality with Earl Tupper: like him, most aren't activists agitating for women's rights.

Instead, the common thread among the men with whom I spoke was that, like Earl Tupper before them, most don't view their attempts to close the gender gap primarily as a political statement. These men don't walk around calling themselves feminists. They aren't compelled by grand goals like reversing centuries of male domination, or atoning for their forebears' discrimination, or righting history's wrongs.

They see gender equality simply, instead, as a business imperative. More than one explained the analogy in terms of gym class. When you're the captain of the volleyball team, you want to choose the very best players in the room. If you only get to choose from half of them, but the opposing captain gets to pick from 100 percent of them, you're going to lose. Want to win? You need to pick the best, period, from all the available talent. Cutting out half the population will get you nowhere.

••

YET THERE'S ANOTHER, more alarming quality these men also share with Earl Tupper. Earl faced tremendous social pressures in partnering with a woman. In a perplexing turn of events, the men I spoke with told me they too face hostility. They navigate bitterness and opposition from other men who are suspicious of their motives in championing the cause of women. Their detractors are sure that a woman's success means a man's failure. It's a zero-sum game. If women win, they will necessarily lose.

That zero-sum mind-set has a long and ingrained history. The nineteenth-century British barrister Ernest Belfort Bax warned ominously that women were "working, not for equality, but for female ascendency." His view was a common one in the days when women first began to agitate for the right to vote. A typical early color postcard titled "Suffragists (cq) on the War Path" showed women beating a prostate police officer with umbrellas. The message was clear: these women wanted not equality, but supremacy. Success for women meant failure for men.

Fast-forward to today, and a University of Virginia study of undergraduate couples found that men interpret a girlfriend's success as their own failure. Researchers in that study gave couples a test that they were told measured problem-solving and social intelligence. In reality, the test did neither. Instead, researchers randomly assigned test scores to each individual. Then the couples were told how each of them had fared. In some cases the man "outscored" his girlfriend; in other cases it was the reverse.

Afterward, the researchers measured each participant's self-esteem. Astonishingly, the men who were told their girlfriends scored at the top felt worse about themselves; their self-esteem took a hit. But if their girlfriends scored poorly, it actually *boosted* the men's self-esteem. (Women's self-esteem, meanwhile, didn't change regardless of how their boyfriends scored.)

Similar experiments with students in the Netherlands and with

volunteers recruited in an online survey came up with the same results. When a man so much as thought about a girlfriend's success, his own self-esteem plunged.

There are powerful cultural forces shaping these reactions. From birth, men are conditioned to see the world in terms of winners and losers. Recall from chapter 1 that Deborah Tannen has found that young boys play with one another by competing, while young girls learn how to play by collaborating. For boys, the goal is to one-up each other. When these boys and girls grow up, the dynamics remain much the same.

As adults, men associate being the breadwinner with masculinity—and with winning. Even among young men in their twenties and thirties, a generation that prides itself on sharing equally in marriage and parenting, "one thing that hasn't changed is the role of being a financial provider," says Fordham psychology professor Jay Wade, who has studied the connection between earning power and masculinity. "A man feels that if he's going to get married and have children, he should be able to provide for his wife and children. I think that is as true today as it was when my father in the 1950s was having his family."

The hit to men's self-esteem is made worse because men consistently view themselves as smarter and more competent than they actually are. One study found that men routinely overestimate their IQ by five points, while women underestimate theirs by the same amount. In another experiment, after men and women each took a math test, men overestimated their performance by 30 percent, twice as much as women did.

Let's be absolutely clear on this: The men weren't lying. They truly *believed* that they performed far better than they actually did. They were quite confident that their performance was superior. It can be devastating, then, to be faced with a woman who is more successful—implicitly suggesting the man has failed.

Some men respond by lashing out. Researchers have found that when a woman outearns her husband, her husband is more likely to cheat. Worse, the more the woman earns, the more likely it is her husband will have an affair. Yet the reverse is true for women: when she outearns her husband she is *less* likely to cheat. One study found that instead, she'll take steps to shore up her husband's masculinity. She'll minimize her achievements or increase the amount of housework she does.

That harsh reality makes plenty of men fearful of openly supporting women, even if they want to. Adam Grant, who has cowritten several pieces about women in leadership with Facebook executive and *Lean In* author Sheryl Sandberg, has experienced that kind of backlash firsthand. Readers have attacked him for attempting to take the side of women. "Many men who would like to see more women leaders are afraid to speak up about it," he concluded in *The Atlantic*.

Robert Moritz, the PricewaterhouseCoopers (PwC) CEO, didn't anticipate how harsh the backlash would be when he wrote his LinkedIn post about diversity. He has long been a champion of working women. In 2010, his firm launched a program with the very deliberate name "White Men and Diversity"—an acknowledgment that 79 percent of the firm's partners were, yes, white men. Among other things, the program works with partners to help them acknowledge blind spots about women and minorities, and suggests ways in which they can bridge the gap. For example, it encourages men, before meetings begin, to talk to the woman sitting by herself in a corner rather than joining in with the guys debating the latest NFL draft pick.

Working with women and other underrepresented groups "makes you a better leader, because the world's not getting any whiter and our clients aren't getting any more homogeneous," as PwC's Chris Brassell, director of the U.S. Office of Diversity and Inclusion, puts it.

Moritz, in his LinkedIn essay, was thoughtful and measured,

explaining some simple actions he's taken at his own firm that others can follow, like hosting dinners with female partners to hear their concerns. Men "can be so worried about saying the wrong thing that sometimes we default to saying nothing instead," he wrote. "But that is a mistake."

His suggestions, which also included "make it personal" and "ask questions, listen to someone else's perspective, and show them that you care," were hardly radical. But commenters, more than two hundred of them, immediately attacked, lashing out as if he were out to destroy them:

- Diversity = secret code for "get rid of the men."
- "As a 'white guy' I wonder why it is always my fault? We are in 2015 and I am sick of this 'white men are the root of all evil' nonsense."
- "White men are the most discriminated group on this earth."

Nor did the commenters spare Moritz himself, calling him—among other epithets—a "white coward."

For men like Moritz who are trying to change the culture and to be more equitable toward women, the pressure to back off, and to conform to the status quo, is intense. It takes courage and conviction to push against that tide. The truth is, Moritz's kind of advocacy goes against the very nature of human beings; we are wired to be suspicious and distrustful of those who support groups that they aren't a part of themselves.

Researchers have found that people are actually resentful of men who promote women's rights, because it isn't viewed as their fight. Men who do so anyway, violating cultural norms, are often attacked, as Moritz quickly learned. What's more, championing diversity doesn't benefit male executives in terms of pay or recognition; a *Harvard Business Review* study found that doing so has

no effect on how their own bosses rate them for competency and performance.

Despite the risk of hostility and suspicion, Moritz and his colleagues have been joined by an increasing number of male executives reaching across the gender divide. They're braving abuse and distrust to do so. And they're doing so for a simple reason: it gets results.

Many of the men I spoke with can pinpoint their "aha" moment, that sudden, smack-the-forehead epiphany when they realized that, *yeah, I've got to figure out this woman thing.* For Tom Falk, that moment came during a board meeting. Falk is the chief executive officer of Kimberly-Clark Corporation, the company that makes consumer brands like Huggies, Kleenex, and Kotex.

At one meeting, Falk and the male executive who ran the Kotex business were attempting to explain tampon strategy. A board member quietly approached him afterward and asked a simple question: "Don't you think you can get a female to present the strategy to us?"

Back at his office, Falk took a look at his organizational chart— and noted that 81 percent of top jobs were held by men, even though the company's customers are overwhelmingly female. If you've ever wondered why tampon commercials feature gleeful women twirling around in all-white spandex—something no actual woman having her actual period has ever willingly done—now you know.

Falk already considered himself a champion of diversity. He viewed himself as fair and unbiased, and assumed that his enlightened attitude percolated throughout the company. But the numbers he saw on his spreadsheet told a different story. "My board gave me a kick in the pants," he later told me. "I looked in the mirror and said, it starts with me. I'd been to all the [diversity] events, but I hadn't put it enough on my personal agenda."

So Falk began making changes. He spoke out about diversity at

company meetings. He presided over enhancements in the work environment, including adding lactation rooms and flexible scheduling. In China, where epic traffic jams at rush hour are common, he changed start and end times to allow new mothers to spend more time with their babies, and linked this with an external Huggies campaign urging other companies to do the same.

Then he went beyond those soft measures, the lifestyle issues that can be difficult to quantify. He built a diversity initiative into the company's financial incentives, adding it to the company's compensation equation. Kimberly-Clark's executives earn bonuses based on four different "buckets" of performance. One of those buckets now includes not just hiring, but training, promoting, and retaining people from diverse backgrounds. Some other companies are starting to adopt similar policies, including Intel, which now links bonuses in part to diversity goals.

The transition hasn't always been easy. Overhauling the corporate culture at a giant corporation is a complex, difficult task to navigate in the best of circumstances. And just as Moritz found at PwC, Falk faced a powerful backlash in some quarters. The zero-sum-game mentality is a hard one to shake. Some men at Kimberly-Clark pushed back. They were "threatened by this," said Sue Dodsworth, the company's global diversity officer. Even a man she had worked closely with, someone she assumed would be an advocate, complained to her, "I cannot support this. If you keep pushing this, I'll never get promoted again." He ultimately left the company.

Other male executives dragged their feet. They insisted that they supported the diversity initiative while not taking any actions to push it forward. "We try to pull them in one by one," Sue Sears, vice president of global diversity and inclusion, told me. "You look at who are the champions and you give them the podium. They start getting recognized by the CEO and promoted because they're creating diverse teams and getting better results."

Ultimately, that's exactly what proved to be the key at Kimberly-Clark: better results. It's astonishing what a little bit of female influence can do. Kimberly-Clark employees often make what they call "mom visits" in order to get to know their customers better. A small group will visit with a woman at her home and ask her to show them her cleaning products, or to talk about her menstrual cycle.

At one such visit in Israel a few years back, Falk had joined an all-male group to question a teenage girl about her period. Not surprisingly, it was an uncomfortable and rather fruitless encounter all around. Other times, to gather information on customers, executives will visit drugstores to watch consumers make purchases. "Nothing like five guys in suits watching women shop in front of the fem care section," as Falk notes dryly.

Adding women to those teams made all the difference. During a home visit in India, a female member of an otherwise all-male team noticed that a new mother's in-laws also lived in the home—and she sensed that the grandmother was calling the shots, not the mom. Her team was able to use that intelligence to adjust how it markets baby products in the country. In the U.S., an all-female team was able to push past the embarrassment factor in interviewing women about bladder leakage for the Poise adult diapers line—leading to a comic campaign fronted by Whoopi Goldberg, who on the talk show *The View* admitted to wearing them, and who starred in a series of lighthearted commercials in which she posed as Mona Lisa and Joan of Arc ("When I laugh, I kind of spritz").

Indeed, one of the first Kimberly-Clark departments to get an overhaul was marketing. And one of the first moves it made was to throw out those old Kotex ads. A tongue-in-cheek new commercial mocked its previous campaigns, showing a montage of those ecstatic ladies gamboling in white, as a woman wryly narrates: "How do I feel about my period? I love it. It makes me feel really pure. Sometimes I just want to run on the beach. I like to twirl, maybe in slow motion.

And I do it in my white spandex. And usually by the third day, I really just want to dance."

The campaign was dubbed "Apology."

Falk openly admits he didn't hire and promote more women to be politically correct. "It was about getting the best talent," he told me. So what ultimately happened to the men of Kimberly-Clark? Well, for one thing, they got richer: Kotex sales surged, and the company's stock price more than doubled since Falk embarked on his initiative in 2009—a boon for the men working there as well as the women.

••

PERHAPS EARL TUPPER could have predicted as much more than half a century ago. Then again, maybe not. Despite his forward-thinking partnership with Brownie Wise, he ultimately was a creature of his time, succumbing to the cultural pressures arrayed against him. Even he never quite got his arms around the fact that women and men can succeed, side by side. He never quite understood that life isn't a zero-sum game. He couldn't accept that Brownie Wise's achievements, as significant as they were, didn't detract from his own success. He couldn't quite comprehend the true synergy that comes from men and women working together, that in doing so they create far more value than either can create alone.

The coda to their successful collaboration underscores why, even though the benefits seem so blindingly obvious, we still live in a world that is largely run by white men. For a while, the partnership between Earl and Brownie couldn't have been sweeter. Their strengths seemed ideally aligned. Brownie Wise was in her element, inspiring women to sell Tupperware and housewives to buy it, rocketing Earl Tupper from obscurity to become one of the most successful businessmen in the country, the overlord of the Tupperware empire. If not for her, Tupperware, Earl's greatest and most

enduring invention, would most likely have been consigned to the junk heap of history long ago.

Their personalities seemed aligned as well. Earl shunned publicity, while the vivacious Brownie adored it. He was satisfied to stay in the background and watch his empire grow, while she delighted in serving as its public face. With the help of Tupperware's publicity team, she was transformed into a media darling, fawned over on talk shows and in women's magazines like *McCall's* and *Cosmopolitan*, which dubbed her the "Sunshine Cinderella." The two balanced each other in a way that helped the business soar.

Until, that is, April 17, 1954. That's the date Brownie Wise became the first woman in history to be featured on the cover of *Businessweek*. This was no ladies' magazine or television talkfest. This was the bible of business, read by men, by successful men—the men Earl considered his peers. And Earl barely even got a mention in the piece. How dare Brownie hog the credit!

Brownie Wise had become the most successful businesswoman in the country, perhaps even the world. She was a household name. And after the *Businessweek* cover, even more adoring press followed. Brownie herself published an inspirational book for women called *Best Wishes* ("It's wonderful to be a woman. Women and wishes just seem to go together!") and convinced her idol, inspirational preacher Norman Vincent Peale, to write the foreword.

And so Earl did what he needed to do.

He fired Brownie Wise.

After almost eight years working together, he cut her off. He instructed his staff to bury every copy of her book in a pit in back of Tupperware's headquarters. He had never given her stock in the company, nor did she have a severance agreement. After she sued him, he reluctantly gave her one year's salary, about $30,000. A few months later, he sold the company for $16 million—the equivalent of $132 million today.

••

BROWNIE WISE DIED in obscurity in 1992. The onetime celebrity is long forgotten (though she does now merit a page and an exhortation—"Be like Brownie!"—on Tupperware's website). Earl had died almost a decade earlier. In their post-Tupperware years, neither one alone ever again achieved the pinnacle of success that they had reached together.

And as for Tupperware? In 1992, the year that Brownie passed away quietly at her Florida home, Rick Goings joined the company as an executive. An ebullient man, with an unusual background as a veteran of both the U.S. Navy and Avon cosmetics, he walked into a firm that still reflected Earl's sad legacy. Brownie Wise had been erased from the company's history. Women played almost no role in company leadership. The product lineup was stale. Tupperware was a fading brand. It was something your mom used to buy, in awful pastel colors. Sales were struggling.

Goings immediately set to work to turn things around. Among his first initiatives was to recruit more women. The amiable seventy-one-year-old, who remains just as passionate about Tupperware today as he was on that first day twenty-five years ago ("There's a Tupperware party starting every 1.3 seconds!" he announces when we meet), admits it's been a heavy lift. It's also an effort he has continued since being named chief executive officer in 1997. For the first time in the company's history, a woman is president and chief operating officer; half of the board members are female, as are a third of managers—a ratio Goings hopes to move to 50 percent.

In the process, Goings has overhauled Tupperware's business model. By the time he joined the firm, American women were pouring into the workplace. The bored housewives that Brownie Wise had counted on to be her sales team were a dying breed.

So Goings quickly shifted the company's focus to overseas, where 90 percent of sales now originate. In the small U.S. market, Goings

has more recently pinned his hopes on millennials, those young people who are part of the "gig economy," taking on freelance work rather than permanent jobs. Eternally optimistic, he cites a statistic that 58 percent of millennials "don't want jobs. They care about relationships more. You're seeing this shift. Look at millennials on a date—there are seven of them!"

Overseas, meanwhile, he's found success in China, where water quality is poor and Tupperware water-filtration products are in demand, and in Third World countries, where women have had few economic opportunities. An evangelist for Tupperware, a true believer, Goings is passionate as he tells me about how selling Tupperware lifts impoverished women out of poverty "to feed her family." I know he has given this same spiel to audiences around the world about a million times, and yet he's mesmerizing, all but jumping out of his seat and grabbing me by the lapels. You'd think he was saying this all for the first time.

As idealistic as Goings is, though, he switches his tone, back to pragmatic CEO, when the subject turns to women in the workplace. It occurs to me that while Earl Tupper probably wouldn't recognize the company he created today, there's one crucial quality that he and his successor share. Like Earl Tupper before him—and like Kimberly-Clark's Falk and PwC's Moritz—Rick Goings isn't hiring women to be politically correct. He's more realistic than that.

This is, after all, an executive who has held on to the top spot of his company for more than two decades. He's looking out for what's best for his business. It all goes back to that analogy about gym class, about picking the best there is, not the best from half the population. The bottom line for him is, bringing in women is about winning.

"Stop leading the cause with 'It's not fair!'" he says emphatically.

"I try to get people beyond the point of altruism," he tells me before we part. "Don't start with altruism. Start with 'It makes good sense to empower women.'"

3

We're All a Little Bit Sexist

One of my son's favorite shows is the raunchy puppet musical *Avenue Q.* It's a hilarious send-up of *Sesame Street,* with a show-stopping number between bickering puppets, "Everyone's a Little Bit Racist":

> You're a little bit racist.
> Well, you're a little bit too.
> I guess we're both a little bit racist.
> Admitting it is not an easy thing to do . . .
> But I guess it's true
> Everyone is just about as racist as you!

The song is bitingly funny in part because it's true. Harvard psychologist Mahzarin R. Banaji has pioneered the study of unconscious bias, the prejudices that all of us have buried so deeply inside of us that we don't even realize that they exist. In their 2013 book *Blindspot: Hidden Biases of Good People*, Dr. Banaji and coauthor Anthony G. Greenwald argue that "hidden biases are capable of guiding our behavior without our being aware of their role."

Multiple studies encompassing millions of people have shown that almost 75 percent of us, for example, are biased against blacks—including more than half of blacks themselves. When it comes to women, the phenomenon is even more pronounced. Some 75 percent of men—and 80 percent of women!—unconsciously equate men with work, and women with family.

To paraphrase the puppets, everyone's a little bit sexist.

That goes for even the most enlightened among us. Not long ago, I met Brian Welle, a data scientist at Google. Slight and soft-spoken, in jeans and a blue polo shirt with a backpack slung over one shoulder, he could easily pass for a college grad student. Over coffee in the large, free café at Google's New York City office, surrounded by dozens of young male engineers in shorts and flip-flops, he explained how he has spent his professional life trying to bust biases.

Dr. Welle, armed with a doctorate in organizational industrial psychology, is part of a team of Google data wizards. But they don't work on the company's search algorithms. Instead, they are charged with turning the company's computing prowess inward, on itself, to learn what makes its own employees tick. It's his job to analyze how fair Google is to its employees, right from the start: Who does it hire, and why?

Google is famously reliant on data in all things. Nothing escapes its scrutiny. It analyzes everything from the placement of the M&Ms in its cafeterias to the color of paint on its walls to the composition of its furniture (hello, soy-foam couches) to the comfort of its toilets (yes, that's a seat warmer and built-in washer/dryer). In designing its website, the company tested forty-one separate shades of blue to analyze which one promoted the best click-through rates on the Google toolbar.

Its hiring process is just as exacting. Early on, the company required applicants to provide SAT scores—even for sixty-year-olds with decades of experience. Members of its People Analytics department had laptop stickers reading "I have charts and graphs to back me up. So f—— off." Would-be Googlers endured up to twenty-five separate job interviews (the company has since tried to cap interviews at four). According to Laszlo Bock, who ran Google's People Operations, as many as 3 million applications pour in each year for just a few thousand openings, meaning your chances of getting hired are about 0.25 percent.

The lucky ones who make it through the initial screening face group interviews and epic problem-solving exercises in which they tackle equations on a whiteboard in front of the room. For years, Google was also infamous—as immortalized in the comedy film *The Internship*—for throwing candidates off balance with wacky, brain-twisting questions. "How many piano tuners are there in the entire world?" an interviewer might ask. Or "How many golf balls would fit inside a 747?"

Not that the questions necessarily had a right answer. After all, to know how many piano tuners there are in the world, you'd need to know how many pianos there are, and how many pianos one person can tune in a day, and for that matter, how often pianos need tuning. But the point wasn't really about the question. It was about how the job candidate thinks. The theory was that Google needed people who were creative, and quick, and could match wits with the brilliant programmers and engineers bicycling around the Googleplex campus.

Google's hiring system was meticulously designed not just to pinpoint the right candidates. It was intended to weed out the wrong ones. Many of those who applied were brilliant, of course. But Google needed to exclude those who wouldn't fit in, who didn't mesh with Google's freewheeling culture—who didn't embody what the company calls "Googleyness."

"The interview process was very much designed to not have false positives," as a former senior engineer explained to me. "We tried very hard not to hire the wrong people, and we were willing to not hire some of the right people. The logic is, someone who is wrong for the company can cause so much damage that it's not worth the risk."

But that painstaking hiring protocol had a curious side effect. It shut out women. It didn't matter whether they had great résumés or brilliant grades. It didn't matter whether they had advanced degrees in engineering. Women weren't even making it into the applicant

pool. In a company that was already 70 percent male—and where 83 percent of technical employees were men—this was a significant issue. Why was it that so few women were cutting it at Google?

The question puzzled Dr. Welle. It didn't make sense. Google prides itself on its inclusive culture. That's one of the reasons he joined in the first place. Google is the kind of company where "we put a value on uniqueness and individuality, and if someone wants to attend a meeting in a bear suit—which I've actually seen—you can," he told me. "There's a lot of tolerance. A lot of people were outsiders at some point in their life."

Google all but puts out the welcome mat for social misfits. It happily embraces the tech-geek stereotype. The former Google engineer told me a popular joke inside the company:

Q: How do you identify an extroverted engineer?
A: He looks at your shoes instead of his own shoes.

It's hard to doubt Google's sincerity about tolerance and diversity. It boasts more than twenty affinity groups for its employees, including at least two for women, another for gays and lesbians ("Gayglers"), and even one for those the company calls "of a certain age" ("Greyglers"). Yet for all that inclusiveness, not only was Google not hiring enough women, it wasn't promoting the women it did hire.

Dr. Welle was stumped. Of all the brainteasers Google could have dreamed up, the riddle about why women weren't making it at the company turned out to be the most perplexing of all.

Google's dilemma is playing out, in one way or another, in companies—and countries—around the world. The evidence is clear that if men want to excel at work, about the best thing they can do is include women. Yet in many ways, women's progress has gone backward. The financial services field, for example, is backsliding at such a pronounced rate—hiring and promoting fewer women at every

level—that if unchanged, the proportion of women at senior levels will drop to 12 percent, from 15 percent now, by 2025.

It's mind-boggling. Companies like Google say they want more women to succeed. Countries are passing legislation to help women succeed. Women are trying their damnedest to step up and close the gender gap on their own. And yet none of it has worked. What's going on here? What kind of nefarious force is pushing back against so many attempts, from so many different directions?

At Google, Dr. Welle was about to find out. Glancing through the newspaper one day, he noticed a report about a new study of Yale University scientists—a group of quirky, deep thinkers very similar to Google employees. The researchers asked 127 scientists to evaluate résumés for a lab assistant position. All the résumés were identical—except for the applicant's sex. The scientists, like Google executives, were certain that they were making evidence-based decisions. Yet they judged the "male" applicants to be more competent, and offered them salaries that averaged $4,000 more than the women's. The scientists were biased against women in ways they weren't even aware of.

Boom. That was it! That's what was happening at Google too. The study was an "instigating moment," as Dr. Welle put it. He realized the problem wasn't the women at all. It was the men. They had biases they couldn't even imagine. "That made us take a step back," Dr. Welle told me, "and say, wait, are we still living in that world today?"

••

DR. WELLE HAD tapped into one of the most seismic cultural shifts of our era. Social scientists are turning upside down our understanding of how men and women relate to one another. They've redefined how to view our relationships at work.

Most men who came of age in the 1980s and 1990s were schooled in the idea that they should be gender-blind. It's wrong to treat

women differently than men at work, they were told. In practice, this meant treating women as if they *were* men, since the de facto culture of the workplace was—and still is—male, created decades ago in a post–World War II era that used the military hierarchy as a model. In 1973, organizational psychologist Virginia Schein even coined the phrase "think manager—think male." She made the observation that successful managers tended to have stereotypically male traits.

This wasn't a terribly revolutionary finding. It was, simply, life. And so women pouring into the workforce adapted by, essentially, acting like men. When I joined the *Wall Street Journal* as a reporter in the 1980s, I wore boxy suits and string ties and, like my female colleagues, cursed like a truck driver, out-machoing the guys. That's what fitting in meant. We weren't trying to change the business world. We were thrilled to be a part of it, to be accepted into the boys' club.

Of course no matter how big our shoulder pads grew—and let's face it, the 1980s was a particularly tragic era for fashion—women aren't men, and pretending we were only got us so far. Researchers of the era found that women who tried to act like men didn't gain the same benefits as men, and in fact were punished for acting counter to social norms. In a 1985 paper, sociologists Mary Glenn Wiley and Arlene Eskilson concluded that the only thing women achieved by talking like men was making people hate them. "Acting as men act (or talking as men do), while it may lead to imputations of success and power, will apparently result in negative evaluations," the researchers concluded.

And yet the gender-blind ideal continued to hold a powerful sway. Even acknowledging sex differences was frowned on in some quarters. Studying sex differences is seen as "anti-American, crazy thinking," as Gloria Steinem once told journalist John Stossel.

But the sad truth was that "gender blind" was just plain blind. We couldn't teach ourselves to be gender blind any more than we could teach ourselves to be taller. Perpetuating the fallacy only made things worse.

Enter Harvard's Dr. Banaji, whose work on unconscious bias, beginning in the late 1990s, explained why we went so wrong. The problem, she argued, was that we had fooled ourselves into thinking we were fair. We truly, fervently believed that we were making unbiased decisions, based on merit. And consciously, we were sure we weren't racist or sexist. How could we be?

But the problem, she found, was that our unconscious doesn't always play by the same rules. Unconsciously we have very different perceptions. She delved deep into our collective psyche to probe biases we don't even know we have ourselves.

These biases, as Dr. Banaji often points out, aren't necessarily bad. They're a survival mechanism that dates back millions of years. All of us are bombarded by information, an estimated 11 million bits of it per second. But we can process just forty bits a second. So our brains take shortcuts.

For our early ancestors, this was literally a lifesaver. If a caveman walked out of his cave and saw an animal, he couldn't take the time to consciously process that it had fur, so it wasn't a human; and strong legs, so it must run fast; and sharp teeth, so it must be a carnivore; and . . . oh, wait, it must be a tiger. By the time he consciously assessed all that, he'd be lunch. Unconscious bias allowed him to understand he was in danger and get the hell away.

Most of us aren't encountering tigers any longer. But unconscious bias still kicks in whenever we see someone not like ourselves. And it reinforces the basest stereotypes.

Google's own search algorithms offer a window into our collective prejudices. Not long ago, I was asked to speak about unconscious bias at a meeting of orthopedic surgeons. Searching for visuals to liven up my presentation, I punched "doctor" into Google Images. Here's what I got:

Almost all men, almost all white.

Maybe that's an anomaly, I thought. So I entered the word "nurse." Here's what popped onto my screen:

Almost all women, almost all white.

Now my curiosity was really piqued. Many of the doctors I would be speaking to ran their own departments. And as a longtime journalist, I often meet with business leaders. So I typed in "CEO." Here's what I got:

Google result for: "CEO"

Yep, you're seeing that correctly. According to Google, the only female CEO meriting a photo on the first search page, and apparently the leading female CEO in the world, is CEO Barbie.

A study of Google ads, meanwhile, found that women searching for employment opportunities are shown fewer high-paying-job ads than men. In a 2015 experiment, Carnegie Mellon University researchers generated a thousand user profiles, split between male and female users, then had each visit a hundred recruitment sites. The most lucrative job ad, for a career-coaching position offering $200,000 a year, was shown to men *six times* more often than to women.

It's possible that these disturbing trends—the Google images, the biased ads—result themselves from hidden prejudices among the overwhelmingly male programmers. After all, the results are spit out by algorithms, all of which are created by coders, most of whom are men. "Code is not neutral. It can't be; it's a creation," as writer Anna Wiener noted in a 2016 *New Republic* article, "Hacking Technology's Boys' Club."

Yet even if that's so, we can't let ourselves off the hook. Google's

autofill shows you popular searches when you enter a word into the search box. It's a pretty fair measure of our unvarnished thoughts. And it offers a chilling window into our uncensored psyche. UN Women, a United Nations initiative focused on gender equality, once ran an ad that simply showed real-life Google autofills:

Women shouldn't . . .
> Have rights
> Vote
> Work
> Box

Women need to . . .
> Be put in their place
> Know their place
> Be controlled
> Be disciplined

These unconscious biases are threaded through all walks of life and every profession. Researchers have found that female economists are twice as likely to be denied tenure as their male counterparts—largely because when women and men collaborate on publications, evaluators give the men as much credit as if they'd written the articles alone, while the women get no credit at all.

Similarly, even though women make up more than half of all doctoral students in biological fields, they're severely underrepresented on science faculties, because the most elite male (though not female) biologists train more men. Top male biologists train up to 40 percent fewer women compared to average scientists.

These biases start young. Moms routinely overestimate the crawling ability of their sons, and underestimate that of their daughters. Parents of male two-year-olds ask Google, "Is my child

a genius?" two and a half times more often than do parents of two-year-old girls.

Once children hit school age, teachers—even female teachers—subconsciously believe boys are better at math than girls. In one study, when a group of teachers graded math tests with no names on them, the girls outscored the boys. But when another group of teachers graded the same tests *with* names, the results were reversed: they gave higher grades to the boys than the girls. All of the teachers, by the way, were female.

As these kids move into middle and high school, the biases are compounded. Not only students, but their parents, are often biased against teenage girls as leaders, a survey of almost twenty thousand teenagers found. By the time these children enter college, it's almost impossible to break free of those constraints. Women are 33 percent more likely to earn a college degree than men. Yet professors are more likely to call on men than on women, and female students are more likely than male students to be interrupted, even though they speak less than their male classmates.

In one study of seventeen hundred biology students at the University of Washington, male students were asked to name peers with a "strong" understanding of the material. They overwhelmingly chose other men. The researchers concluded that in the eyes of the men, their female classmates would need to get an *A* in order to be viewed as equal to a male student who got a *B*. It's a scenario that continues once they graduate. New female grads are paid less than their male peers for the same entry-level jobs, in part because young men are eight times more likely than young women to negotiate for their first salary.

The trend intensifies as these now-grown kids work their way up the career ladder. At every level, women are 15 percent less likely than men to be promoted, according to a joint survey of 118 companies and more than 30,000 men and women by McKinsey & Company and

Leanin.org. In part that's because men get promoted on the basis of their potential, but women are promoted only if they've proven themselves with past performance.

The cycle doesn't end there. Women routinely are caught in the "prove it again" paradox, in which they must continually reestablish their competency. Social scientists have calculated that a woman must be two and a half times more competent than a man to be viewed as his equal.

Adding to the burden is the fact that women in business are presumed to be incompetent until they prove themselves, while men are presumed to be competent, researchers have found. Other studies have concluded that when women do succeed, their accomplishments are more often attributed to luck or other outside causes, while men's success is attributed to skill. When women make mistakes, on the other hand, their missteps are noticed more and remembered longer than similar mistakes by men.

And if a woman does manage to sidestep all of those issues, watch out: both men and women prefer male bosses. In one study, respondents who agreed with the statement "I have no preference for a male boss or a female boss" nevertheless were willing to take a salary that was $3,400 *lower* to work for a man rather than a woman. They literally took a voluntary pay cut in order to avoid working for a woman.

You may be thinking, as many of us do, that all of this describes somebody else. Other people may be biased, for sure, but I'm not. Certainly, I believed that about myself. Want to know for certain? If you're really brave, you can test yourself. The Implicit Association Test (at ProjectImplicit.org) measures your own unconscious bias against a variety of groups, including working women, blacks, and the elderly.

For a test measuring how you feel about working women, it flashes words on the computer screen ("Susan," "office," "children") and

measures how fast you can categorize them as male versus female, or career versus family. Then it mixes things up, measuring how fast you can sort words into a category labeled "male or family" or another labeled "female or career." Almost everyone takes longer to match words to the mixed categories, says Brian Nosek, a University of Virginia psychologist who worked with Dr. Banaji to create the program.

I took the test myself. Even I came out as "moderately" biased against working women.

These tiny biases have outsize impact. Scientists at Rice University were able to show how the smallest bias metastasizes, growing at a warp-speed rate over time. They created a computer simulation of a company with an entry-level workforce evenly divided between men and women. Each worker was assigned a random performance score, but one that was programmed with a miniscule, 1 percent bias against women. The result? By the time you reach the top level of the company, it's 65 percent male.

And you can't get rid of your own unconscious bias, no matter how hard you try. Scientists have investigated all sorts of interventions, without success. Professor Nosek has devoted his career to the subject. "I am as educated as you can be on implicit bias, and yet I still have it," he told me.

Biases infect our every action, whether we realize it or not. In one controversial study published in 2014, scientists concluded that more people die in hurricanes named for women then men—because we take "female" hurricanes less seriously. We assume Hurricane Alexander will be mightier than Hurricane Alexandra, and that Hurricane Victor will be deadlier than Hurricane Victoria. Fewer people take measures like evacuating when a hurricane is named for a woman. Researchers estimated that if Hurricane Charley was renamed Eloise, the number of deaths would have almost tripled.

Even at its most benign, this hidden bias can cause great damage.

Until recently, I'd never heard of the phrase "benevolent sexism." But once you know what it is, you'll see it everywhere. Benevolent sexism is a well-meaning comment or attitude that ends up diminishing or undermining women.

Just one example: after I guest-anchored the CNBC business program *Squawk Box* one day, I received a text from a businessman I know. It said, in its entirety, "You looked mighty cute on TV this morning."

This is tricky. When I speak with audiences of women, I often ask how I should have responded. Point out to him that that really wasn't a compliment? Or should I just say thank you and let the comment slide?

Most audiences are evenly split between those two reactions. In reality, I took the more passive route. I simply said thank you and moved on. But after I told this story to a group of women at a bank, the chief executive officer of the company—the only man in the room— taught us all how to think about this. "That's easy," he said. "The correct answer is: 'I assume you mean I sounded smart. Thank you.'"

••

IF ANY COMPANY could have avoided the trap of bias against women, it should have been Google. The company's roots go back two decades, to 1998, when a couple of Stanford grad-school dropouts were noodling with computer code in a Menlo Park, California, garage.

The World Wide Web was still a relatively new and mysterious thing. The world's first web page had been created only nine years earlier. For most people, the Internet was still a bit of a head-scratcher, something we connected to by using a dial-up connection to a portal like AOL, and that we used mostly for email and amusement. But the two young men had a bigger idea. With the right code, they were sure, they could "organize the world's information and make it universally accessible and useful."

The men had become fast friends and sparring partners after they met at Stanford in 1995. In some ways, they were an unlikely pair. Sergey Brin, with intense dark eyes, preternatural self-confidence, and a penchant for adrenaline-fueled sports like skiing and skydiving, had immigrated from Russia as a child. He barely spoke English when he arrived as a six-year-old, yet by the time he got to Stanford, he had developed into a fierce intellectual with a sense of self-possession so strong it could be unnerving. "He was a brash young man. But he was so smart, it just oozed out of him," one of his Stanford advisors recalled. By contrast, Larry Page had grown up in Michigan as a bookish child who played the saxophone, studied music composition, and spent summers at Interlochen music camp.

But the similarities between the two are perhaps more notable. Most strikingly, both grew up with working mothers—and both moms excelled in male-dominated fields. Larry's mom taught computer programming at Michigan State University, where his father was a computer science professor. Sergey's mother was a NASA research scientist with a degree in applied mathematics.

Women and science mixed easily in both homes. Career women were the rule, not the exception. Both boys were accustomed to their mothers working long hours. "Women's work" meant science and math, not housekeeping. Larry recalled his house as perpetually messy, filled with computers and books and gadgets and magazines. He spent hours immersing himself in old copies of *Popular Science*, and amused himself by taking apart everything he could find in the house.

In college, the young men gravitated toward women who were just as smart and ambitious as their mothers. The garage they found themselves in, that fall of 1998, belonged to a female friend, Susan Wojcicki, a Harvard graduate who had studied history and literature. So when, in September of that year, they incorporated their fledgling project as a company called Google, they hired her. Susan,

their sometime landlord, became Google's sixteenth employee. She would go on to run Google's most high-profile acquisition, YouTube, and become one of the most visible examples of successful women in tech. Admiring profiles never fail to mention that she also is the mother of five young children.

Former Google People Operations chief Laszlo Bock, in his book *Work Rules,* wrote that the company's "efforts to draw more women into computer science started before we had thirty employees." If that's the case, the effort didn't last long. As the company's growth exploded, the thousands of people it hired were mostly men. And while it's laudable that it wanted to draw in women early on, it's perhaps more telling that the company's policy to welcome dogs began even earlier, with its first ten employees.

Maybe it didn't seem necessary to focus on women, since Google's founders assumed they were unbiased. And with their backgrounds, and their own mothers as examples, it seemed hard to argue otherwise. In any case, Google was growing so quickly that it didn't have time to catch its breath and stop to figure out why it wasn't hiring women—or even to realize the lack of women in the first place.

"Google spent many years not focusing on this problem," as the former engineer told me. "Then it woke up and had to aggressively push against the curve to correct it."

The first wake-up call came in 2006, when Bock showed up as head of People Operations and began taking a close look at just who Google was hiring. Or, more accurately, just who it *wasn't* hiring. At the time, Google had a small team focused on diversity. Bock, who joined after stints at McKinsey & Company and General Electric, quickly tasked his entire department with that goal—challenging them to bring in not just women, but other diverse candidates as well.

The group noticed immediately that the problem started at the beginning, with the meager number of women and minorities being hired at the entry level. So it focused on filling the hiring pipeline.

It was a reasonable assumption that Google's problem was an

empty pipeline, and that that simple step, of recruiting more women into entry-level jobs, would fix everything. That's the conventional wisdom in a lot of male-dominated fields. The pipeline theory holds that when there aren't enough women in lower-level positions, or if women leave when they have children, it's impossible to fill the management "pipeline" with sufficient numbers of women who will work their way up to leadership. According to the theory, when women enter the workforce in equal numbers, they will eventually work their way to the top and correct the imbalance.

On the face of it, not just Google but all of Silicon Valley does indeed have a major pipeline problem. Only 18 percent of computer science majors are female, a figure that hasn't budged despite best efforts—and that is only about half of what it was three decades ago, when software engineering was a backwater, before it became a ticket to glamour and riches, and the chief domain of men.

Popular culture representations of the tech world haven't helped the cause of recruiting women. From *Revenge of the Nerds* to *The Big Bang Theory* to HBO's *Silicon Valley,* the stereotype of the *Star Trek*–loving, socially awkward geek who has no idea how to relate to girls doesn't leave a lot of room for female role models.

So Google, along with the rest of the tech industry, threw itself into grooming more young women. Tech firms are backing all sorts of female-friendly initiatives. There's Women Who Code and Black Girls Code, both launched in 2011. There's Girls Who Code, founded the following year. There's FabFems (for women in STEM careers), EngineerGirl (to teach girls about engineering), and *Brainy Girls* (an online magazine about young women in STEM fields), and even a best-selling "you go, girl!" book, *Math Doesn't Suck* (written by former *Wonder Years* star turned mathematician Danica McKellar). Every major tech firm sends top executives to the annual Grace Hopper Celebration of Women in Computing, a gathering named for a pioneering World War II computer scientist famous for—perhaps

apocryphally—removing a dead moth that was bollixing up the machinery, thus coining the term "debugging."

Unfortunately, the pipeline theory has a problem: It's wrong. And not just in tech. The theory has failed in every industry. If it held true, half of all corporate chief executives would be female by now, considering that the average CEO is a fifty-five-year-old man, meaning he graduated from college in the early 1980s—just when women became half of all college graduates.

The same goes for law. In the early 1990s, women actually made up the majority of law students, at slightly more than 50 percent. Yet fast-forward to 2013 to what should have been the prime of those students' careers, and women accounted for just 17 percent of equity partners in law firms. Any industry you look at, the figures follow a similar trajectory: women may enter in large numbers, but somewhere along the way the pipeline spits them out.

A bigger hurdle, once we drill down into it, is the basic assumption that underlies the pipeline theory: that we are fair in the first place. The theory doesn't account for the hidden biases we all have inside of us. Google executives truly believed that they hired and promoted employees based on measureable, objective results. They were certain that bias played no part in it.

That certainty itself turns out to be the problem. Psychologists have found that the more fervently you believe yourself to be fair—or generous, or caring—the less likely you are to act that way. You believe you are, so you see no cause for concern. There's nothing for you to fix. Researchers have found that the industries that consider themselves the most meritocratic, like science, are also the most frequently biased.

In one experiment, psychologists at Northwestern University asked people to write about themselves. One group was asked to use words like "generous" and "caring"; the other was assigned more neutral words, like "book" and "house." After the exercise,

the participants were asked to make a charitable donation. Those who described themselves as "generous" were least likely to give. In fact, they gave at a rate two and a half times below that of people who described themselves in neutral terms. The researchers concluded that those who described themselves as generous didn't feel the need to prove it by acting generously. They convinced themselves that they were generous, and that was sufficient. They were satisfied.

The same holds true for those who insist most firmly that they are meritocratic. In three experiments published by Cornell University in 2010, researchers asked 445 managers to evaluate employee profiles and make recommendations for bonus, promotion, or termination. The researchers consistently found that when the managers were told the company was a meritocracy, they rewarded male candidates more richly than equally qualified female candidates. Because the managers believed they were operating in a meritocracy, they felt confident that their decisions must therefore be fair. They didn't feel the need to check themselves, or to take the time to analyze whether bias played a part in their decisions—a condition the researchers refer to as the "paradox of meritocracy."

You can see how this blind belief in meritocracy plays out in real life. Just take a field trip to GitHub, a popular San Francisco site used by programmers to store and share projects. GitHub is such a nonhierarchical organization that until 2014 it didn't have middle managers, and its chief executive described his title as nominal. It once commissioned a custom rug for its headquarters, modeled on the presidential seal, that read, "United Meritocracy of Github."

The company's site is open-source, meaning that software developers can collaborate, or contribute new code, or suggest improvements to any given project. The project's owner can then approve or reject the code. The company's business model is built on the assumption that the best code will win, regardless of sex or race or ethnicity. It's an ideal real-life laboratory: great code wins, subpar code loses.

That's why, when a group of computer scientists studied whose code was accepted and whose was rejected, they were so gobsmacked by what they found. It turns out that if you judge excellence by looking at whose code is accepted, women win. It's no contest. They are better coders, based on the fact that their code is more likely to be accepted than that written by men. It was an extraordinary conclusion: *Women are better at writing computer code than men*.

But there's a catch. Women only win when no one knows they're female. When the gender of the coder is identified, women's code is suddenly rejected at a greater rate than that written by men.

In part that may reflect overt, rather than hidden or subconscious, biases. GitHub itself is among a number of tech firms accused of fostering a sexist culture where frat-boy antics flourish. Its co-founder resigned in 2014 after he bungled a female former employee's complaints about sexism in the office, including an incident in which she said that male colleagues ogled two female employees hula-hooping.

But in a larger sense, this goes far beyond a straightforward case of sexism, or of boys being boys, of bad behavior among men. It's instead the ultimate expression of implicit bias. The plight of female coders—that their code is considered superior when they are anonymous, but inferior when they are identified—reflects the same paradigm in the rest of the world. Remember the experiment that found teachers gave girls better math grades than boys, but only when the papers were anonymous? The same holds true here. In coding, as in school math—as in life—women are marked down simply for being female.

••

AT GOOGLE, IT was increasingly clear to Bock too that the company's diversity problem wasn't as simple as an empty pipeline. Something systemic was holding women back. Despite Googlers' fervent belief

that their company was a meritocracy, they clearly had blind spots about their own prejudices against women and minorities. So in 2012 Bock asked Dr. Welle and some of his colleagues to come up with a way to combat unconscious bias.

In doing so, Bock and Welle joined a new and growing wave of men who have begun aligning with women to try to close the gender gap themselves. What used to be a cause primarily driven by women is now being taken up increasingly by men.

It's something of an exquisite irony that some tech executives are at the forefront of trying to solve this problem. After all, the industry has a notoriously awful track record with women. A 2008 *Harvard Business Review* study reported that an alarming 63 percent of female scientists, engineers, and technologists had experienced sexual harassment at work, and 52 percent ultimately quit their jobs because of a hostile work environment. A survey of more than two hundred senior women at tech firms found almost 90 percent experienced sexist behavior.

Google itself has been singled out as one of the worst offenders. In 2017, a male Google engineer wrote an antidiversity "manifesto" that went viral, and suggested that the company's gender gap was due to biology, not sexism; that women had more "neuroticism" than men; and that Google "lower[ed] the bar" for diversity candidates. The company fired him for "advancing harmful gender stereotypes." Google has also been fighting U.S. Department of Labor accusations that it systematically underpays female employees; a labor department solicitor characterized the discrimination as "quite extreme, even in this industry." Google has denied the allegations.

But it's also an intriguing turn of events that some male leaders in the tech industry are using their considerable power and resources to try to turn the tide. They are turning their analytical firepower on themselves to figure out why they have a woman problem, and what they can do to fix it. Can they turn around a culture where sexism has

not only been tolerated but in many cases celebrated? If they do crack the code of gender parity, they'll help solve a problem that bedevils not just those in the tech world, but the rest of us as well.

First, though, Dr. Welle had to figure out how to force Googlers to confront their deepest, ugliest, most embarrassing thoughts about one another. He would have to lead them to face some uncomfortable, even despicable, truths within themselves.

To do so, he had to figure out a puzzle. He faced two big questions. First, if we all have biases we don't know about, could he construct exact steps, an easy-to-follow road map, that we can take to counteract them? And second, how do we get men to care, to make this fight their own? Two bedeviling questions, with answers that would reverberate far beyond Google's cloistered walls.

4

The Twelve Most Terrifying Words in the English Language

Imagine that you are being asked to hire a police chief. You receive résumés from two candidates. One of them doesn't have much education, but is tough and experienced and has worked in rough neighborhoods—what we might consider "street smart." The other is well educated and has terrific administrative skills, but doesn't have much experience on the streets. This candidate is what we'd think of as "book smart." Which police chief would you choose?

It's an intriguing question. You could conceivably argue for either one. Though if I woke up in the middle of the night to hear a burglar rummaging around in my living room, I know which one I'd want. I'd care much more about whether the police chief is a good shot, and whether he or she can chase down a suspect, than whether he or she got straight *A*s in school. I'd go for street smarts every time.

Yale researchers were fascinated by the question too. They wanted to understand the ways in which people make choices about who to hire, and why. So in a 2005 study, they put the question to a test. They asked participants to choose the best-qualified police chief, based on résumés that emphasized either "street smarts" or "school smarts." Some CVs had the name "Michael" at the top. Others had the name "Michelle." After the participants made their choices, they were asked to explain why.

Take a guess which one won: street smarts or schools smarts? Perhaps by now you won't be surprised by the results. It turns out, neither. The participants didn't prefer streets smarts *or* school smarts. They preferred the male candidate. Nothing else mattered. Whatever quality the man had, participants rationalized, that was the quality most important for the job.

When Dr. Welle read that study, it struck home. What it told him was that no matter how rational we think we are, we are captives to our own hidden biases. They color every move we make. He realized that it would be pointless for him to try to wipe out Googlers' deeply buried biases. Instead, he needed to focus on changing their *actions*. He needed to find a way to subtly subvert employees' deeply held prejudices, and spur them to act fairly *in spite of themselves*.

"We wanted to ensure that every decision we made, from hiring to promotion to pay to performance, didn't have an unintended bias against women, the disabled, African Americans," he explained to me over coffee in the Google café. "What we're looking for is an impeccably fair workplace."

His challenge was all the greater because of the checkered history of corporate efforts to eliminate bias. Decades before the phrase "unconscious bias" was invented, American companies had dreamed up "diversity training," typically a course that lasts anywhere from an hour to a couple of days, with the goal of wiping out biases against women and others from underrepresented groups. For most of its history, diversity training has been pretty much a cudgel—a blunt instrument that pounded white men into submission with a mix of finger-wagging and guilt-mongering.

The first training programs surfaced in the 1950s, after men returned from World War II and were appalled and perplexed to find women in their offices. "You've had your little joke," an employee tells his supervisor after a new female employee shows up, in an unintentionally hilarious 1959 training film called *The Trouble with Women*. The scene continues:

"What's wrong with her?" the boss asks.

"She's a woman, isn't she?"

"We don't have a man with her qualifications," the boss protests.

But women run off and get married, the employee pushes back.

"Okay, Brad, but how many blushing brides do you have?" the boss—the enlightened man in this scenario—responds. "Marriage, absenteeism, personality problems—aren't they really a part of life?" he adds, blithely equating "marriage" with psychiatric disorders.

"I can remember the good old days," the infuriated employee grumbles, "when there were all men in my department, and we didn't have these problems!"

After the passage of the Civil Rights Act of 1964, the training took on more urgency, focusing on teaching men about the new law prohibiting gender and racial discrimination. Within a decade, it had morphed into a knee-jerk response to legal actions, after a series of high-profile sex discrimination suits, including one by the women of *Newsweek* magazine, who were stranded in a pink ghetto, tolerated as researchers but rarely allowed to be reporters. "Women don't write at *Newsweek*. If you want to be a writer, go someplace else," the bosses told them, according to Lynn Povich, one of the forty-six women who sued.

In her lively book about that time, *The Good Girls Revolt*, Povich recalled how the *New York Daily News* reported on the suit. "Newshens Sue *Newsweek* for 'Equal Rights,'" read the headline over an article that began: "Forty-six women on the staff of *Newsweek* magazine, most of them young and most of them pretty, announced today they were suing the magazine." It took two lawsuits and the intervention of Katharine Graham, whose Washington Post Company owned *Newsweek*, but ultimately the magazine agreed that one-third of writers and reporters would be female by the end of 1975.

By the time I entered the workforce almost a decade later, the *Newsweek* suit and others like it, filed by women at *Time*, the Asso-

ciated Press, and the *New York Times,* were mostly forgotten. Diversity training had taken a backseat too. President Ronald Reagan had appointed conservative Clarence Thomas as head of the Equal Employment Opportunity Commission. Thomas wasn't terribly sympathetic to the cause; his former public affairs director told Judiciary Committee investigators that while they were walking to a meeting one day, he casually asked her, "What size are your breasts?"

I don't recall ever hearing the phrase "diversity training" until the 1990s. By then, it had been reconstituted as a feel-good exercise in consciousness-raising. White men were told they should include women and minorities because it's the right thing to do.

But here's the thing about diversity training: it doesn't work.

Harvard organizational sociology professor Frank Dobbin surveyed diversity programs at 829 companies over 30 years starting in 1971 and concluded that "in general, training doesn't do much of anything." The only exception was for white women and black women and men: for those groups, it actually made things *worse.* In other words, companies that introduced diversity training would actually employ more women and blacks today *if they had never had diversity training at all.*

Professor Dobbin and others have since delved into why the programs have failed. Dobbin combed through thousands of reports to look for common themes, and concluded that any training that smells like legal compliance is sure to backfire. He specifically singled out three situations in which training is doomed to fail: when it's mandatory, when it so much as mentions the law, or when it is specific to managers, as opposed to being offered to all employees. Unfortunately, he found, about 75 percent of firms with diversity training programs fall into at least one of those categories.

Perhaps more to the point, though, is that the training infuriates the people it's intended to educate: white men. "Many interpreted

the key learning point as having to walk on egg shells around women and minorities—choosing words carefully so as not to offend. Some surmised that it meant White men were villains, still others assumed that they would lose their jobs to minorities and women, while others concluded that women and minorities were simply too sensitive," executives Rohini Anand and Mary-Frances Winters noted in a 2008 analysis of diversity training in *The Academy of Management Learning & Education*.

Training done badly can even damage perfectly cordial relationships. Women and minorities often leave training sessions thinking that their coworkers must be even *more* biased than they had previously imagined.

Sometimes they're right. In 1996, Texaco settled a discrimination case for $176 million—$35 million of which went to fund diversity efforts—after a tape surfaced of Texaco executives referring to black employees as "black jelly beans." The irony is, the executives had heard that phrase in the firm's diversity training course.

In fact, simply *mentioning* pro-diversity efforts can hurt companies' efforts to close the gender gap. A trio of researchers set up an experiment in which participants, all of them white men, were asked to apply to a fictional tech firm. Each man received a written description of the company. The descriptions were identical, with a single exception: some made a brief reference to the firm's "pro-diversity values," while others didn't. The participants in both groups then went through a job interview, while biofeedback monitors measured their stress response.

The difference between how the two groups of men handled the job interview was striking. The men who read the reference to "pro-diversity" efforts performed worse in the interview, expected unfair treatment, and even had a heightened biological response, with elevated heart rates suggesting higher stress levels than those for the second group of men.

The researchers concluded that the one brief reference to diversity made the men feel that they were being discriminated against. They were certain that "pro-diversity" was code for "anti–white guy." And that, in turn, "interfered with their interview performance and caused their bodies to respond as if they were under threat." The men in the study, in other words, felt just as my seatmate on that flight to Des Moines did: as far as they were concerned, diversity training was an implicit accusation that they were the bad guys, that it was all their fault.

In an even more troubling development, it turns out that telling people about others' biases can actually make their own biases worse. Researchers have found that when people believe everybody else is biased, they feel free to be prejudiced themselves. In one study, a group of managers was told that stereotypes are rare, while another group was told stereotypes are common. Then both groups were asked to evaluate male and female job candidates. The managers who were told that stereotypes are common were *more* biased against the women; they didn't want to work with them and found them unlikeable.

The researchers concluded that because the participants believed everyone else held stereotypes, it made it a lot easier to let their own prejudices roam free. "If we tell people everybody is biased, they allow themselves to stay biased. As individuals, we tend to do what other people are doing," as one of the researchers, University of Virginia professor Melissa Thomas-Hunt, put it.

The evidence is damning. Yet companies continue to invest heavily in diversity training, spending, by one estimate, almost $8 billion a year. It's all led to what *The Economist* has dubbed "Diversity Fatigue." In a recent article, the magazine suggested that twelve of the most terrifying words in the English language are "I'm from human resources and I'm here to organize a diversity workshop."

••

THAT UNFORTUNATE HISTORY made the challenge for Dr. Welle and his team that much more difficult as they sat down to tackle unconscious bias at Google. They were determined to create an implicit-bias training workshop, but knew they had to sidestep the failures of the past.

His team was walking a bit of a tightrope; they had to explain biases without reinforcing them. They had to help people face the ugliest sides of themselves without alienating them. Mostly, though, they had to try to change the way people *act,* even though they couldn't change the way people truly *think*. They had to make people recognize their deepest, darkest prejudices, and then force themselves to do something about it.

As he worked through the obstacles, Dr. Welle seized on an insight that has proven to be a key not just for Google, but for anyone who is trying to wipe out hidden biases. Thomas-Hunt's research had shown that if we believe everybody is biased, we will be too. But the research also demonstrated the reverse: if we believe that everyone around us is trying hard to fight against those stereotypes and prejudices, we'll do the same. Call it peer pressure, or call it a pack mentality. Whatever it is, it works. Our own biases disappear.

Dr. Welle and his team ultimately developed a workshop that strives to mimic those conditions. In a typical session, he explains the science, so that employees can understand that yes, we're all biased and yes, we're all trying to fight it, and don't worry, it isn't your fault. He focuses on four ways to "interrupt" bias, all of which boil down to one word: "awareness."

He encourages employees to use consistent criteria to measure success, and to rely on data rather than on gut reactions when evaluating others. He urges them to notice how they react to subtle cues. In one study he cites, students posing as job applicants at a Texas mall were rejected at higher rates when they wore baseball caps that

said "Gay and Proud" than when they wore caps that said "Texan and Proud." Finally, he encourages employees to call out bias when they see it, even if the culprit is their own boss.

Google's seminar is a model that other companies have adopted too. In just the past few years, this kind of training has exploded at companies across the country. At Google, about 75 percent of its 75,000 employees have taken the workshop, and in 2014 the company spent $114 million on its various diversity programs.

At least 20 percent of companies in the U.S. now offer unconscious-bias training, from Roche Diagnostics to Royal Bank of Canada to consultants McKinsey & Company ("We do that big time," says its CEO, Dominic Barton) to defense contractor BAE Systems. Almost all of the big tech firms already offer it, including Facebook, Salesforce, VMware, and GoDaddy, with more joining by the day. By some estimates 50 percent of all American corporations will offer unconscious-bias training in the not-too-distant future.

Undoubtedly, the popularity of these programs has soared in part because they intentionally don't cast blame. They do away with the cudgel and the finger-wagging. The beauty of the training is that, unlike old-fashioned diversity training, it's guilt-free. Everybody has biases, right? And we're all trying to overcome them, yes? So we're all in this together. Nobody is being singled out. No more white-guy guilt. Bias is a lot easier to swallow when it isn't your fault.

••

BEFORE EMPLOYEES STEP into the classroom for unconscious-bias workshops, they get a warning: They'll be confronting uncomfortable truths. They'll be facing their deepest demons. The warning intrigued me. It made me wonder about my own darkest thoughts. I knew from taking the Implicit Association test that I had biases even against working women. It was terrifying to think of what other

prejudices might lurk within me. But shouldn't I know, so that I had a chance of combating whatever those demons turned out to be?

Not long before Christmas, I drove the short distance from Google's offices to Facebook headquarters in Menlo Park, California. I was nervous, afraid of what was about to unfold. Facebook had invited me to take its unconscious-bias workshop along with its employees.

When I arrived on that overcast December morning, the place was already a hyper-caffeinated hive of activity. In the reception area, hipsters in jeans mingled with suit-and-tie-clad visitors signing in on iPads. Posters plastered the walls with inspirational sayings: "Pride Connects Us," "Stay Humble," "Fortune Favors the Bold."

Outside, the campus was crowded with young employees in hoodies strolling the oval path that connects a series of buildings. The campus itself is a tech fairy tale, a geeky version of Disneyland's Main Street, lined with ice cream shops, dry cleaners, and cafés.

I ducked into one doorway and plunged into blackness. When my eyes adjusted to the dark, I found myself in a fully outfitted game room, just as dim and noisy as the shopping mall arcades of my childhood, already buzzing with young guys playing pinball. Near the entryway stood a vending machine filled with tech gear—phone chargers, earbuds, keyboards. All of it free.

I headed back outside, threading my way through a series of buildings in search of my workshop classroom. Everywhere I looked, there were more inspirational posters. Tech companies are often parodied for their do-gooder earnestness, and it's easy to see why. In the HBO comedy *Silicon Valley*, a running joke among the characters—almost all of them nerdy guys in hoodies—is their repeated declaration that they are making the world better. "I don't want to live in a world where someone else makes the world a better place better than we do," one character laments. More than one person I met in the actual Silicon Valley told me that the program is less parody than reality show. Looking around, you half expected to see the TV cameras taking it all in.

After grabbing a free yogurt and some fruit, I find the workshop conference room just as the session is about to begin. Facebook's unconscious-bias training is voluntary, open to everyone—just as the experts recommend as the right approach. The company says that all of its managers and more than 70 percent of its employees have taken it, though in my session there were just eight of us, including me, the moderator, and my public relations minder. Only one is male. Most aren't white. None are the engineers who make up the bulk of the company's employees. Their absence was notable given an analysis by a longtime Facebook engineer that found female Facebook engineers' code is rejected 35 percent more frequently than that written by men—a calculation Facebook disputes.

The training kicks off with a passionate and fact-filled appeal, on video, from Facebook executive and women's advocate Sheryl Sandberg. Then, for two hours, we learn about the research, about our deeply buried prejudices against not just women but blacks and other underrepresented groups.

In one exercise, we watch short videos of "job applicants" simply introducing themselves. Then we make snap judgments about their skills and competency—our own test of Malcolm Gladwell's hypothesis in *Blink*, his book suggesting that we form opinions of others in under two seconds. I find, to my dismay, that I am as biased as the next person. I jump to the conclusion that the guy in the T-shirt and Cal Tech hat is an engineer, while the blond woman in the conservative suit is a business executive.

Next, we pair off in role-playing exercises to figure out how we would react if, say, we were in a work group in which Agnes did all the work but Eduardo took all the credit. This one I feel a bit more confident about—I know that any member of the group should be empowered to speak up about Agnes's contribution. On the other hand, I'd been researching this book for almost a year, so perhaps I was more attuned than the average Facebooker.

We learn about potential "bias busters" too. As at Google, Face-

book suggests empowering every employee to call out bias if they see it. On a more tactical level, we got a primer on specific phrases that subtly discriminate against women, phrases that most women (myself included) have heard throughout our careers: "aggressive, assertive, pushy, abrasive," plus "self-promotional, political, not a team player." The moderator warns us to look out for such coded language deployed against women, as well as subtle phrases such as "her style doesn't work," or "she is not a good fit with the team."

The session is engaging and immersive. In the following days, I noticed some key changes in my own behavior. When I checked in at a nearby hotel, I stopped myself as I automatically gravitated toward the Asian guy at the front desk. I realized, to my embarrassment, that I had made the unfounded assumption that he would be smarter and faster than the women on either side of him.

But will that two hours of training stay with me for long? Will it change how I conduct myself in my career? I'd like to think so, of course. But I got a perhaps more realistic answer as the Facebook session was winding down, before we were sent scattering back into the crowds milling about outside. As she prepared to dismiss us, the moderator mentioned that this was just a refresher course, since employees had gotten an unconscious-bias-training overview when they joined the company.

That's when my seatmate leaned over to me.

"I don't remember going through unconscious-bias training," she murmured.

The moderator didn't hear her.

"We are a company that gives people voice to their authentic identity," the moderator sang as she dismissed us. "Make this cause your own."

••

AND THAT'S THE trick with unconscious-bias training. How to make it last? Will employees even remember taking it? Can it help to trans-

form a corporate culture? After all, no matter how good it is, the training is only one tool that, on its own, can't reinvent an organization. Facebook's executives have made it clear that diversity is a priority, and since my visit the company has added several more programs to continually reinforce the message, including one on how to be an "ally" to colleagues from marginalized groups. Sandberg herself is the nation's most prominent advocate for women.

Even so, Kayla Smith, a Facebook engineer, said she left after a year because she felt isolated. "I didn't get invited to meetings. I didn't get put on projects. I withered and felt irrelevant," she told *USA Today's* Jessica Guynn. "There is a lot of effort and thought put into diversity at a company level but at individual levels, there are a lot of micro cultures. Diversity did not trickle down to the team I was on."

••

AT GOOGLE, DR. Welle too realized that training alone isn't enough. So in 2013, Google went further, developing a "bias cheat sheet." It's a checklist that managers use when they evaluate employees for promotion. It reminds them of common biases. Among others, it notes the "Horns & Halo Effects," in which a manager's judgment about actual performance is clouded because he has made a snap decision that the employee is either awful or amazing.

Other firms have adopted bias cheat sheets as well, including Royal Bank of Canada, which distributes its guide to managers. "Do I typically hire the same type of person, or personality type?" asks one prompt. "Who do I encourage to lead or speak at meetings?" asks another. Alongside those questions, the cheat sheet lists tips for identifying implicit bias, including "speak out if you suspect a colleague's contribution may be ignored or misappropriated unfairly."

Google began tweaking its hiring practices in other ways too. It trimmed its interview process from as many as twenty-five interviews for one position to just four. And Laszlo Bock put an end to—or at least

tried to put an end to—the brainteasers as well. He found they have no predictive value about how a candidate might perform on the job. The only value they had at all was to make the interviewer feel smart. As a diagnostic tool, they are "a total waste of time," he told me.

But Google does still put a value on that ineffable "Googleyness," which one senior executive defined as "people who are comfortable with chaos, who are self-motivated, and who do the right thing even when no one is looking." In other words, applicants need to be the right cultural fit.

That's an important quality not just for Google, but for other workplaces too. People who fit in are happier, more productive, and tend to stay in their jobs longer. A global survey found that more than 80 percent of employers consider cultural fit a top priority.

Except, as I learned in unconscious-bias training, researchers have also found that those who don't culturally "fit" are disproportionately female. A "good fit in most American corporations still tends to be stereotypically masculine. Consequently, fit can exclude high-performing candidates—female or male—who are stereotypically feminine," noted Lauren A. Rivera, a management professor at Northwestern University's Kellogg School of Management, in the *New York Times*. Other researchers have found that one reason there are so few women who major in computer science in the first place is they fear they won't fit in.

"It's tricky," Dr. Welle acknowledged when we met for coffee at the Google café, surrounded by young male engineers in flip-flops. "You want people you have a connection with. You want to like them, to have conversations that are fulfilling. But a connection is almost always based on similarity, and that is what's operating against diversity."

As Google introduced its new policies, Dr. Welle and his colleagues continued to analyze the results. What they found wasn't always encouraging. Beginning in 2014, under pressure for their

poor records hiring women and other underrepresented groups, the major technology firms began publicly revealing their diversity statistics. The results can be described in one word: dismal. Almost all were overwhelmingly male and white or Asian.

More perplexing, the massive efforts since then to diversify hiring, and to teach employees about unconscious bias, have barely moved the needle. By 2016, women represented less than a third of total Google employees, and far less than that in key tech positions. Apple, Microsoft, Cisco, and Intel had similarly poor showings. In 2017, even Facebook reported that just 19 percent of its technical jobs were held by women, and that women held 28 percent of senior jobs, despite massive efforts at recruitment and training. At the bottom of the heap among tech companies was Twitter, where only 15 percent of technical employees were female.

Part of the issue is that even if firms hire as aggressively as they can, their efforts can only go so far. The math works against them. In 2014, 21 percent of Google's tech hires were female—but that translated into just a 1 percentage point increase in total female tech workers, to a paltry 18 percent.

More significantly, though, is that unconscious-bias training sometimes prompts the same type of backlash as old-fashioned diversity training, the kind that beat up white guys with a two-by-four. Nancy Lee, a former Google head of diversity, estimates that while a third of employees embrace diversity efforts, an equal amount are "resistors"—those like the author of the Google "manifesto," who later described the company's bias training as "lots of just shaming." As James Altizer, an engineer at chip maker Nvidia, told the *New York Times*, "It's a witch hunt . . . When you're discussing gender issues, it's almost religious, the response. It's almost zealotry."

Even the women already working at Google seemed curiously resistant to the company's efforts. Google allows its engineers to nominate themselves for a promotion. But women simply weren't

doing it. The few who did almost always got promoted—usually because they waited so long that they "were probably ready a year ago," Bock told the *Wall Street Journal*.

Women's lack of self-promotion was frustrating, but not surprising. Studies have found that girls don't raise their hands as often as boys in math class, even though the girls more often have the right answers. And in a pattern that repeats itself, grown-up women don't offer their ideas as often as men in business meetings, yet in studies, the women's ideas are judged more valuable than those of the men.

Flummoxed by women's hesitation to raise their hands for promotion, one senior Google engineer jury-rigged his own solution. He began sending out regular "nudge" notes—an email to all technical employees explaining the research and urging women to nominate themselves. We "tell them for God's sake, nominate yourself for a promotion, because you're holding yourself back!" as Bock put it.

The nudge notes have proven to be remarkably effective. When they go out every six months, the number of women nominating themselves for promotions soars. Once, when the engineer forgot to send the note before a promotion cycle, the numbers plummeted into the basement again.

Google executives continue to try to even the playing field. The firm has introduced a "bias busting" workshop, in which employees practice ways to call out bad behavior, by, for example, giving credit to someone (typically a woman) whose idea had been mistakenly attributed to someone else (typically a man). The company even modified its iconic search home page. In 2014, a blog counted up Google's "Doodles"—the cartoons it creates on its home page each day, usually to commemorate a historical event, a famous scientist's birthday, or a holiday. From 2010 through 2014, it calculated, 83 percent of the Doodles were of men. Google took note: it now is trying to keep the ratio even.

And when it opened a new office in 2013, employees noticed that the vast majority of its sixty-five conference rooms—all named for scientists—honored men. Top executives quickly rechristened the rooms, half of which are now named for women. Not that the transition was easy. The succinctly monikered Peter K. Homer Room—named for the winner of a NASA contest to design an improved astronaut glove—has been transformed into the Praskovya Uvarova Room, named for a nineteenth-century amateur Russian archaeologist who took over for her dead husband as chairperson of the Archaeological Society of Moscow.

Despite all of Google's efforts, the one that made the most noticeable difference had nothing to do with bias training, or names of conference rooms, or Google Doodles of women. Instead, it came about as a result of a change in the company's incentive system. And that points up the dilemma that confounds every corporate attempt at social engineering. It doesn't matter how much companies talk about equality and inclusiveness. What matters are the incentives it creates for employees. Those incentives speak louder than any speeches by the CEO, or bias training workshops, or posters on a wall.

For Google, as for others, the key incentive came in the form of family leave. In 2011, Google sweetened its leave policy, extending paid parental leave to five months from three. The result was immediate. Attrition rates for women who had babies plunged by 50 percent.

That set off an arms race of sorts, with a growing number of tech firms offering gender-neutral paid parental leaves to men as well as women, including Twitter (20 weeks), Etsy (26 weeks), Facebook (4 months), and Change.org (18 weeks). Netflix and Virgin Management increased paid parental leave to a full year. The practice is now spreading beyond the tech industry, to other industries as well.

The results of these changes are still unfolding. But they point to

a hard truth. For men as well as women, it doesn't matter how sincere companies are in embracing diversity, if their own policies work against it—and in particular if they make it impossible to balance work with family. America lags far behind most industrial countries in this respect. It is the only industrialized country in the world that doesn't offer paid parental leave. At least ninety-six other countries offer not only guaranteed maternity leave but paternity leave as well, including Gambia, Armenia, Belarus, Azerbaijan, Togo, and Mauritius. Without broad policy changes that allow parents in every industry and at every level to have access to affordable health care and child care, the rest doesn't matter.

What's more, at tech firms, the newly generous parental leave policies are still often undercut by other opposing incentives that are at least as powerful. Apple's sprawling new 175-acre headquarters boasts a 100,000-square-foot fitness and health center—but no day care facilities. At Google, the expanded maternity leave is juxtaposed with a work culture that is still round-the-clock, encouraged by campuses which offer so many life perks—free food, dry cleaning, game rooms—that they incentivize employees not to go home. And when they do go home, workers are expected to be tethered to the office.

Eric Schmidt, Google's executive chairman, proudly acknowledged as much in an interview with *MIT Technology Review.* "A successful life is not completely balanced," he declared. His vision of a great leader, he went on, is one who will "go quiet for a few hours while they're busy taking care of the family or whatever it is they're doing, and then they emerge at 11 o'clock at night, working hard to make sure that their responsibilities are taken care of."

I wondered how those mixed messages land, and whether the efforts of Dr. Welle and other men at Google are making a difference. So I decided to go to the source: I asked some female Google employees.

A friend introduced me to a few women at Google's Chelsea office

in New York City. We gathered in the same café where I'd met Dr. Welle, where you could grab a free organic coffee with soy milk near the salad bar. Classic rock played in the background. To get here, we had strolled through the Lego area, where primary-colored blocks were stacked to the ceiling. Lego creations were displayed on shelves along the walls, as were several giant Lego portraits of tech heroes— all men. We headed past the game room, lined with video games, where a few young men were in a fierce match at one of the Ping-Pong tables in the center of the floor.

The decor was oddly familiar. I felt a curious sort of déjà vu, something that tickled the back of my brain. It took me a moment to figure out why I had this strange sensation. Then it struck me: I used to have this decor in my house, when my son was younger. The vibe of Google's New York City flagship was a ten-year-old boy's bedroom.

"Do you ever go in there?" I asked the women as we passed the Ping-Pongers, who were now grunting and yelling.

They laughed.

"You'll see guys who play Ping-Pong every day. Women have a harder time doing that kind of thing," one of my new friends said.

"But why is it harder for women?"

"I think it's because women are very conscientious and concerned about really doing a good job," she said.

"Wait a minute. Isn't everybody here concerned about doing a good job? Isn't that why you all had to go through the punishing interview process? Isn't that why you're among the gifted point-two-five percent of applicants who made it through the door here?"

My friend tried not to sound as exasperated as she clearly was.

"Women want to be seen as 'being present' and not 'goofing off,'" she said, jabbing at the air with exaggerated air quotes for emphasis. "It's a perception thing."

I tried to imagine how the guys playing Ping-Pong or constructing

Lego creations would feel if Google's office were decorated in equally stereotypical little-girl's-room fashion—let's say, with pink walls and mirrors and Barbie playhouses and glitter guns. How would they react? Would they shrug it off and go about their business as usual, as the women here did?

The very fact that the women I met were comfortable in this environment may be why they're among the few women to make it at Google. Research has shown that all-male environments raise stress levels in most women, and can even turn off women's interest in computer science. When researchers asked undergraduates who hadn't yet declared their majors about their interest in computer science, women's answers actually depended on the decor of the room in which they were questioned. When the room was decorated in a neutral way—with nature posters and coffee mugs—the women were enthusiastic. When it was decked out with *Star Trek* posters and video games, their interest plunged. Notably, the decor—whether neutral or geeky—made no difference in men's interest in computer science.

Google's own corporate website references the study, describing it in a section on "unbiasing the workspace." It cautions about "micro-inequities" that might add to the stress of women. "It's important to consider how workplaces might alienate certain groups," the website says. Yet it adds reassuringly, "This didn't mean Google threw out the Legos, Star Wars posters, or Nerf guns."

As we settled into a booth with our coffee, I changed the subject, asking about the company's impressive unconscious-bias training.

"What?" asked one of the women, an engineer. She was genuinely puzzled.

"Oh yeah, we have it," said another. But she added, "I know we have it, but I didn't take it. There's posters up, and articles, and it comes up at company meetings. Why do I need to take it? They try really hard. I definitely feel like it's overcompensation."

Her engineer friend shrugged. She still couldn't recall any mention of unconscious-bias workshops. "They make us take so many of these things they blend together," she finally said. "On compliance, on ethics . . . most of the time I've got other stuff to do. You just want to get through it and get it done.

"For me, I've always been in heavily male cultures," she added. "I'm much more comfortable in my engineering meetings than in my local mommy meet-ups."

And in the end, that may be the key to women who do succeed at Google. These women reminded me of my early days at the *Wall Street Journal* in the 1980s, back when we female reporters in our linebacker shoulder pads were just as tough as any of the guys—or more so. In tech, there's even a name for this syndrome: "the cool girl trap." The phrase was coined by illustrator Kennedy Cooke-Garza, with a definition that comes straight from Gillian Flynn's bestseller *Gone Girl*:

Being the Cool Girl means I am a hot, brilliant, funny woman who adores football, poker, dirty jokes, and burping, who plays video games, drinks cheap beer, loves threesomes and anal sex, and jams hot dogs and hamburgers into her mouth like she's hosting the world's biggest culinary gang bang while somehow maintaining a size 2 . . . Cool Girls never get angry; they only smile in a chagrined, loving manner and let their men do whatever they want.

The problem with being the cool girl, as Cooke-Garza described it, is that it means she has to do everything she can to make the guys feel comfortable—including putting up with abuse. "She laughs along with their shitty jokes, maybe joins in on them, and certainly never challenges a guy to maybe think more critically about what's falling out of his mouth," she wrote.

In her own experience at a games studio, Cooke-Garza endured a steady slide from juvenile comments into increasingly toxic "jokes" from her male colleagues, as they speculated on how fat she'd get, how many kids she'd pop out, and how much she'd earn as a prostitute. In her case, after she finally discussed the issue with her boss—who assured her he would never put up with sexism in the office—her colleagues froze her out. She ultimately was laid off.

The "cool girl trap," Cooke-Garza found, "is one of the reasons that sexism, racism and other 'isms' are so pervasive in such a homogenized industry."

Still, there are some signs that old attitudes are starting to change, that the work that men like Brian Welle and his colleagues are doing is paying off. Onstage at a panel at the SXSW conference in Austin, three prominent voices engaged in a lively conversation about the importance of diversity—and the two men, Google chairman Eric Schmidt and Steve Jobs biographer Walter Isaacson, both repeatedly interrupted the lone woman on their panel, then–Chief Technology Officer of the United States Megan Smith. During the Q&A session afterward, a Google diversity manager who happened to be in the audience raised her hand.

"Given that unconscious-bias research tells us that women are interrupted a lot more than men, I'm wondering if you are aware that you have interrupted Megan many more times?" she said.

The audience cheered.

Dr. Welle is proud of that progress, but fully aware that there's more to be done. Among his concerns is how long his unconscious-bias training effort will stick with employees.

"Will it last? That is my big fear," he said as we collected our coffee cups and headed back out, past the Lego station and conference rooms named for subway stops. "What worries me now is, how do we make it stick in the culture?"

5

She's Pretty Sure You Don't Respect Her

The elderly man had been in the hospital for a month, recovering from a procedure for esophageal cancer, when surgical resident Andrea Merrill came to say goodbye. She had been caring for him since his surgery, attending to him on her rounds twice daily, checking on his lungs, overseeing his daily care.

As she bid him farewell, he looked up at her from his hospital bed. She had spent countless hours with him, bringing all of her medical training to bear to help heal him.

Now he had a question for her.

"Are you training to be a nurse?" he asked.

Dr. Merrill took a deep breath. She had learned to hide her frustration well. Almost every day, at least one patient would mistake the doctor for a nurse. And while she has great respect for the work that nurses do, she knew the reason her patients made the mistake: it didn't occur to them that this young woman could be a surgeon.

When I first heard about her experience, I was reminded of an old brainteaser, one that I couldn't figure out the first time I heard it decades ago: A man and his son get into a car accident. The man dies, and his son is badly injured. The son is taken to the hospital for emergency surgery. The distinguished surgeon takes one look at the boy and says, "I can't operate on him! He's my son!"

How, the riddle asks, can that be?

Even today, 40 to 75 percent of people can't figure out the answer: the surgeon is the boy's mother.

The old joke isn't funny to Dr. Merrill. It rings too true. "I have had patients literally laugh in my face when I introduce myself as 'doctor,'" as she wrote on *HuffPost*. "I cannot tell you how many times I have walked into a patient's room to find him/her on the phone and hear 'Hold on, honey, I have to go, the nurse is here.'"

I first spoke with Dr. Merrill, now a surgery resident in Boston, after reading that post. She told me she was inspired to write about the issue because, while it is drilled into med students that they should never complain or make excuses, the lack of respect toward female physicians can no longer be ignored. It needs to be brought out into the open. She had had one too many experiences like the time when she and a senior female surgeon went to check on a patient, but the patient only wanted to speak to the "real" doctor in the room—the male medical student who had been observing them.

The assumption that women are underlings is often an innocent, unintentional slight. But for Dr. Merrill and other female physicians, it makes an already demanding job that much more draining. "You have to work harder to get them to trust you and see you as a doctor," she says. It is an extra burden that male doctors rarely experience. When Dr. Merrill raised the issue with some other young surgeons, they were surprised: "My male friends had no idea that happens."

"It kind of grates on you," she adds. "I did all this training," and yet she finds herself constantly working to prove that she is worthy of the same respect her male colleagues receive automatically.

It's an undercurrent that runs through every day, all day. Researchers have found, for example, that female physicians are more frequently introduced by their first names (Sally, Juanita), while male physicians are introduced with the honorific "Doctor." "I

always feel like it undermines me when I'm introduced as 'Andrea,'" Dr. Merrill says.

••

IN MEDICINE AS in business, for most men in a room, respect is a given. Women, though, often feel the opposite: that they're treated as if they don't know what they're talking about until they prove otherwise. In my conversations with professional women around the country, the issue of respect is one of the biggest and most frequent frustrations that they cite.

In their 2014 book *The Confidence Code*, journalists Katty Kay and Claire Shipman spoke to female leaders, including Linda Hudson, then CEO of BAE Systems. She told them that "even in the position I am [in] now, everyone's first impression is that I'm not qualified to do the job . . . When a man walks into a room, they're assumed to be competent until they prove otherwise." For women, it is often the reverse.

It isn't just men who make these assumptions; women are just as likely to show less respect toward other women. A survey of more than 3,500 Norwegian physicians, for example, found that female nurses are less respectful toward female doctors than male doctors, and offer them less help. The nurses frequently ignore orders. Or they'll tell the female physicians to do it themselves. The nurses are eager to "cut them down to size," researchers found. The authors concluded, "Female doctors often find that they are met with less respect and confidence and are given less help than their male colleagues."

Other research has found the same phenomenon across professions. Purdue University researcher Xiaowei Shi noticed that she and her classmates seemed to speak more deferentially to male professors than female professors. To test her assertion, she recruited 212 young professionals, from accountants to software engineers, and described various work scenarios—for example, you have an

idea to improve product testing—and asked each how they would influence their boss. For half the participants, the boss was "Bob," while the other half got boss "Barb." In every case, the employees were more polite and deferential to the mythical Bob. They were far more likely to be dismissive of Barb.

When the participants thought they were talking to Bob, for example, they were obsequious, humble, and quick to recognize his superior standing in the pecking order. "If you cannot do it, I will understand," said one. "I was wondering . . . ," began another. But when Barb was in charge, the participants not only showed less deference; they were more likely to give *her* instructions. "Here are some thoughts I have that may interest you . . . ," as one participant began a memo dictating ideas.

Lack of respect is an undercurrent that runs through work and life, mostly in relatively subtle ways. Since I began researching this book, I've noticed it in my own behavior. At a business meeting not long ago, I was introduced to two executives I'd never met, a man and a woman. I didn't know which one was the boss and which the staffer, yet I instinctively went to shake hands with the man first—catching myself only at the last moment as I realized I had made the completely unfounded assumption that he must be in charge. I was reflexively more deferential to him, with no facts available to me other than that he was a guy.

My own unwitting reaction apparently is common. A 2015 Pew study found that, like me, most Americans believe women are as capable as men when it comes to being political and business leaders. In fact, the Pew survey found women were viewed as superior to men when it came to leadership qualities like honesty, fairness, and compassion.

Yet the same survey found that we still assume that men are more qualified; we subconsciously grant them greater respect. About 40 percent of those surveyed believed that "for women seeking to climb

to the highest levels of either politics or business . . . they have to do more than their male counterparts to prove themselves."

The respect gap even colors the way we view a job title. Imagine a prestigious position—say, a school principal. And then imagine a woman in the post. For most of us, the mere notion that the principal is female lowers our respect for the office itself. Indeed, several studies have shown that a male executive has more power than a female executive with the exact same title—and that dynamic is the case regardless of occupation.

Women may be seen as "illegitimate authorities" who aren't deserving of respect, and thus whose judgement is questioned, Yale researcher Andrea Vial has found. One study, drawing on a large survey of Canadian workers, found that men benefit substantially more than women by being a boss, in terms of autonomy as well as influence. Less respect for women in the same job as men also translates directly into lower pay.

The studies are persuasive. But in truth, we don't need academic research to prove what we see every day in real life. The fact that women get less respect than men is so routine that there's really no debate about the issue. There's a reason that "manterrupting," "bropropriating," and "mansplaining" have all entered the lingo, with the last even being formally inducted into the Oxford Dictionaries in 2014. The official definition: a man explaining something "to someone, typically a woman, in a manner regarded as condescending or patronizing."

••

DR. MERRILL, THE Boston surgical resident, never thought that respect would be an issue for her. She first became interested in surgery as a child in western Massachusetts. An enthusiastic athlete, she grew up playing sports: soccer, gymnastics, lacrosse, basketball—you name it, she played it. She ran track in both high school and college at

Tufts University. She was comfortable with boys; after all, she could outrun most of them. When her brother's soccer team was short on players, she'd jump in and join them. Her athleticism put her literally on an even playing field.

Like lots of dedicated athletes, she also suffered her fair share of injuries. After one of them, she stumbled across a textbook about sports injuries that her father, who had a graduate degree in physical education, had left around the house. She was hooked. She became endlessly fascinated by the anatomy of injuries and the process of healing them. She turned to the Internet, spending hours online looking up orthopedic procedures. She decided to become a doctor—an orthopedic surgeon—so she could heal those injuries herself.

Orthopedic surgery is one of the most male-centric professions in the world (just 5 percent of orthopedic surgeons are female). It's a boys' club still, populated largely by former athletes. The conventional wisdom holds that a surgeon needs to be powerfully strong to manipulate bones, saw through them, and pound in pins. Orthopedic surgery is often, somewhat derisively, compared to carpentry—a job requiring brute force rather than intellectual firepower. It is the most macho of all medical practices.

But Dr. Merrill didn't think that the conventional wisdom applied to her; she had grown up around athletes, and dominated in competitions her entire life.

Then one day, early in her medical training, an older female surgeon took her aside. You can't pursue orthopedics, the woman firmly announced. She launched into a lecture about "boy surgeries"—the prestigious and highly paid specialties, including orthopedic as well as heart surgery, dominated by men—and "girl surgeries," primarily breast-related surgeries. "Bigger surgeries are boy surgeries," the older woman explained.

Dr. Merrill was floored. Whoever heard of "boy" and "girl" pro-

fessions of any sort in this day and age? Yes, at a petite five-foot-four, she had encountered some eye-rolling about her chosen field. "You aren't strong enough to do orthopedic surgery," she heard the skeptics say. But she had shrugged off the naysayers, shooting back that "it isn't so much the strength, it's the physics." As she and other female surgeons explain, the key to doing orthopedics isn't so much unadulterated muscle power as it is understanding the use of leverage in manipulating bones.

Dr. Merrill had no qualms about the physical labor of orthopedics. So why was another woman, a mentor, telling her to back off? Why shouldn't she pursue orthopedic surgery? So what if the profession was mostly male?

The female surgeon sat her down and looked her in the eye.

"You're never going to get business," she explained. "No one will ever refer [patients] to you. They won't send patients to a girl surgeon."

Dr. Merrill is still angry when she recalls that exchange. "I was really put off by that," she told me. "I was taken aback that this woman who I looked up to and respected would say that."

But it turns out the older female surgeon, in many ways, was right.

<p style="text-align:center">••</p>

PERHAPS THE BEST way to understand the respect gap is to listen to those who have experienced both sides of it. One of the most outspoken has been Stanford University biologist Ben Barres. As former chairman of neurobiology at the prestigious university, he is one of the top scientists in his field. He has degrees from MIT, Dartmouth, and Harvard. He is a leading expert on nerve cells called glia.

He also is transgender. Dr. Barres was born as Barbara, and transitioned at the age of forty-two, in the midst of his professional career.

One of the most striking aspects of his transition turned out to be the level of respect accorded to him by others. As a high school

student, Barbara Barres had excelled in math, but her guidance counselor steered her toward a local college rather than her own choice, Massachusetts Institute of Technology. She went to MIT anyway.

But in college, when she was the only student out of hundreds to solve a difficult problem, a professor accused her of cheating: he "told me my boyfriend must have solved it for me." Later, as a Harvard doctoral student, she lost out on a prestigious fellowship despite having published six papers—five more than the male student who received the post instead of her.

After Dr. Barres transitioned, though, all of that changed. Not long afterward, he presented a paper to a group of renowned scientists at the Whitehead Institute for Biomedical Research in Cambridge, Massachusetts. As his presentation came to a close, a fellow scientist in the audience, unaware of his transition, confided to a colleague, "Ben Barres's work is much better than his sister Barbara's."

Dr. Barres later wrote about his experience for *Nature* magazine. "By far, the main difference that I have noticed is that people who don't know I'm transgendered treat me with much more respect," he wrote. His authority isn't questioned as frequently, and he's no longer overlooked in conversations. "I can even complete a whole sentence without being interrupted by a man."

"This is why women are not breaking into academic jobs at any appreciable rate," Dr. Barres has said. "Not childcare. Not family responsibilities. I have had the thought a million times: I am taken more seriously."

His case is hardly unique. *Quartz* editor and author Thomas Page McBee, a transgender male who transitioned at age thirty, noted that now when he speaks, "people don't just listen: they lean in . . . My sense since my transition is people *want* to believe the best of me." When he felt he deserved a raise, he marshalled the advice he had heard before his transition: be unemotional, stick to facts and

accomplishments, don't feel guilty about asking. He took a deep breath, and steeled himself for that inevitably difficult conversation. "After all that," he recalled, "I walked into the meeting, ready to hardball, and my boss *offered* me a raise."

Transgender women, meanwhile, have noticed the reverse. Biologist Jonathan Roughgarden didn't have to worry about the issue of respect for the first thirty years of his career. He commanded plenty of it. He was a renowned ecological theorist who created mathematical models to explain how ecosystems work. He authored textbooks on population genetics and evolutionary ecology. He was at the top of his field.

But in his fifties, Jonathan transitioned to Joan. And Joan immediately noticed that the world treated her differently. She found that now, if she questioned a mathematical concept, new colleagues figured it was because she didn't understand the math. She was astonished at the change. "Men are assumed to be competent until proven otherwise," she told the author Kristen Schilt, author of *Just One of the Guys?: Transgender Men and the Persistence of Gender Inequality*, "whereas a woman is assumed to be incompetent until she proves otherwise."

In a much more public way, the conversation changed about Caitlyn Jenner, after her transition from Bruce Jenner. Bruce was the Olympic champion, patriarch of the Kardashian clan, sharp businessman. Caitlyn, suddenly, was the lovely lady with "ample cleavage," luxurious hair, and, as one headline noted, a size 8 figure—thinner than her ex-wife Kris!

"It's really heartening to see that everyone is willing to not only accept Caitlyn Jenner as a woman, but to waste no time in treating her like a woman," comedian Jon Stewart deadpanned. Or, as *Mother Jones* magazine put it in a headline: "The American Media Is a Sexist Shitshow. Welcome, Caitlyn Jenner."

Perhaps it shouldn't come as a surprise that the highest-paid

female executive in 2013, earning $38 million, was Martine Roth-blatt, a founder of the company that became Sirius XM as well as founder of a biotech firm, United Therapeutics. She transitioned in 1994, when she was already known as a successful male executive. As she told *Fortune* magazine, "I've only been a woman for half of my life, and there's no doubt that I've benefited hugely from being a guy."

"One of the unique insights I have is a huge appreciation for all of the privileges I received as a man," Rothblatt has said. "As the oldest son I was expected to do great things . . . but so many times it's the oldest son that gets that encouragement and not the oldest daughter." Her view is that closing the gender gap, and the wage gap, begins at home: "We need to start by educating our kids and society as a whole that a person's productivity and what they accomplish should not be judged differently because they are female or male."

There are an estimated 1.4 million people who identify as trans-gender in the U.S. alone. As their numbers grow, some in the community—a group uniquely qualified to understand the respect gap—are taking steps to close it. Transgender professionals have suggested a number of ways forward, including increasing diver-sity of all sorts—gender, race, ethnicity—in leadership, and, in particular, in search committees for new positions.

As a case in point of the perils of homogeneity, Dr. Barres noted that in 2014, when the National Institutes of Health (NIH) inaugu-rated its prestigious Pioneer Award, 60 of the 64 judges and every one of the 9 winners were men. The NIH has since revamped the process.

That advice carries to other areas of life as well. Dr. Barres calls for "less silence in the face of discrimination." Anyone—man or woman—can call it as they see it. In Dr. Barres's case, he is still grate-ful to a male medical school classmate who, decades ago, complained to a professor who jokingly included a slide of a nude pinup during an anatomy lecture.

••

OTHER MEN ARE starting to champion the cause too. Sam Polk, a former hedge fund trader, has taken Dr. Barres's advice—"less silence"—to heart. For most of his life, he "listened to men dissect women into body parts. When I was younger, I did it, too," he recalled. But "that was nothing compared with what I witnessed on Wall Street." In 2016, he decided to break Wall Street's unwritten code of silence, writing in the *New York Times* about the debilitating lack of respect for women who try to make their way in the world of finance.

Wall Street, like tech, has long been a stubbornly male dominated terrain. Women run fewer than 3 percent of mutual funds, and make up less than 2 percent of hedge-fund managers. As a World Economic Forum report noted, "There are 11 male hedge fund managers named John, James, William or Robert for every one female hedge fund manager of any name."

No major investment bank has ever had a female top executive. Despite efforts to recruit women into entry-level jobs, the top ranks are almost exclusively male. At Goldman Sachs, which frequently touts its "10,000 Women" initiative to help fund female business owners, almost 80 percent of senior leadership is male.

Yet the evidence is overwhelming that women achieve better financial results. Female-led funds outperform those run by men by a large margin. The same is true for banks with female CEOs or board chairs; one study found that male-led banks were six to seven times more likely to fail during the financial crisis than those led by women.

What's more, male investors tend to suffer from overconfidence, prompting them to trade more frequently and achieve lower results than women. A prominent hedge fund even required one of its traders to take estrogen to reduce risky behavior, a lawsuit alleged. The firm denied it.

Polk got his first, surprising taste of Wall Street's throwback

culture when he was a young intern at Credit Suisse First Boston. While Polk was talking with a managing director in Midtown Manhattan, the man ran ahead to ogle a woman. "I had to get a look at those tits," the senior executive announced.

Later, Polk became a bond trader at Bank of America, where part of his job entailed entertaining clients. One night at dinner, a client declared of a waitress, "I'd like to bend her over the table, give *her* some meat." Polk was disgusted, he recalled, but said nothing.

Polk had heard horror stories from some of his female friends on Wall Street, like the female bond trader who received a smaller bonus after refusing to sleep with her boss. But he came to suspect that Wall Street's problem wasn't simply the revolting acts by a few bad actors. It was the casual disdain, the conversations about women when they weren't in the room. In Polk's view, the problem boiled down to one key factor: a lack of respect for women.

"'Bro talk' produces a force field of disrespect and exclusion that makes it incredibly difficult for women to ascend the Wall Street ladder," he wrote in the *Times* piece, headlined, "How Wall Street Bro Talk Keeps Women Down."

That lack of respect—the demeaning undercurrent, the insouciant assumption that women don't deserve the same respect as the man in the same job sitting next to them—seeps into the broader culture in an insidious way. You see it in the offhand comment, in the casual denigration of a woman's achievements, as when JPMorgan Chase CEO Jamie Dimon dismissed Senator Elizabeth Warren, a former Harvard Law School professor and banking critic, by saying, "I don't know if she fully understands the global banking system." Or when former CIA director Michael Hayden shrugged off a 6,300-page Senate Intelligence Committee report on the CIA's use of torture, saying committee chair Senator Dianne Feinstein was too "emotional" to be fair. Similarly, when Supreme Court Justice Sonia Sotomayor dissented from a 2014 decision to uphold Michigan's

affirmative action ban, critics dismissed her argument as "fueled by emotion."

Almost every woman I know can relate to that casual derision, that flip remark that reminds her she is not being taken seriously. In my own media industry, there's a tumblr, #saidtoladyjournos, where female reporters share such gems as "We only returned your phone call because you were cute," "I'm only talking to you because you have a nice ass," and, to a Washington political reporter, "So, which congressman are you sleeping with?"

Female entrepreneurs have their own version, as reported in "Shit Men Say to Women Founders," including "What's your real job?" and "Good luck with your project," when referring to a growing corporation. Black professional women trade stories about having their credentials dismissed, or even being mistaken for the cleaning crew, using the hashtag #BlackWomenAtWork.

That lack of respect threads its away across industries and across oceans. So intractable has been the problem in the U.K. among financial firms, in fact, that one proposal would peg bankers' pay to the number of women they hire into senior roles. The proposal was specifically geared to wipe out the "laddish" finance culture.

In the U.S., major financial firms have paid out hundreds of millions of dollars in high-profile discrimination suits, yet there's little evidence that's had any impact on a culture where lack of respect for women is rampant. Merrill Lynch alone has paid almost half a billion dollars in multiple settlements over the past fifteen years. Nor has the financial industry as a whole become more welcoming to women. The proportion of white women in managerial jobs in commercial banking actually fell between 2003 and 2014. The proportion of women in investment banking management is even lower, and has been stagnant for almost twenty years.

The situation is if anything even worse in the venture capital industry, which funds technology startups. Ninety-four percent of

investing partners in venture firms are male, and 98 percent of the investments they make are in companies run by other men, even though the startup businesses run by women perform as well or better. The industry's frat-house "bro culture" rewards like-minded personalities, from Uber's Travis Kalanick (who resigned amid allegations of sexual harassment and discrimination), to Ben Kaufman, founder of the tech platform Quirky, who on his own LinkedIn page was described as "He's a dick . . . but hilarious."

Ask any woman who has tried to break into the venture-capital boys' club, and she'll likely have horror stories. One female entrepreneur, Susan Wu, recounted "the countless times I've had to move a man's hand from my thigh (or back or shoulder or hair or arm)," and noted that learning how to reject advances without injuring a man's fragile ego is "a pretty important skill that I would bet most successful women in our industry have."

The "real problem with tech bros is not just that they're boorish jerks. It's that they're boorish jerks who don't know how to run companies," as author Dan Lyons put it. "Toxic workplace culture and rotten financial performance go hand-in-hand."

As for Sam Polk, he ultimately left his Wall Street job. But several years later, he is still ashamed that he kept quiet. "Men rarely do or say anything. Why not? Because it feels really good to be in the in-crowd," he wrote. He acknowledged that he'd never spoken up himself because "it would have been embarrassing and emasculating. And it would have been bad for my career."

Now an author, co-founder and CEO of Everytable, and the father of two young children, he has appealed to men to speak out. Rather than diversity training and women's conferences, "(w)hat we need is something simpler: individuals speaking up," he wrote. He calls for "men of status in our wider culture—managers, coaches, politicians, celebrities" to insist "that women were spoken not just to, but about, with respect."

••

POLK IS MORE right than perhaps he even knows. Men are essential to closing the respect gap. Not just because it's a business imperative, but because women can't do it on their own. When women try to do so themselves, it more often than not backfires.

Women who assert their authority themselves almost inevitably are punished for it. Multiple studies have found that women are penalized for behaviors that are considered stereotypically "male"— including being assertive (for women, that's called "bossy") or self-promotional. An analysis of seventy-one studies of assertive behavior found that women, but not men, are disparaged for such basic maneuvers as negotiating for a raise or simply asking a neighbor to turn down music. (It bears noting that men lose respect if they engage in stereotypical "female" behavior.)

A Rutgers University researcher found, meanwhile, that simply mentioning successes—"pointing with pride to one's accomplishments, speaking directly about one's strengths and talents"—hurts women, even as it helps men. It "can backfire on women," social psychologist Laurie Rudman found, because it goes against gender expectations.

Women who self-promote are considered more competent than those who don't, but commanding that respect comes at a steep price: people don't like them. That's a handicap that doesn't apply to men who self-promote.

What's more, as these women rack up successes and rise through the ranks, resentment toward them grows, isolating them from others. A BCG study of 345,000 people found that senior female managers feel less appreciated than their male counterparts, and their opinions less heard. Senior men, on the other hand, feel more support from colleagues. "When companies don't get engagement right, senior-level women feel the pain disproportionately," BCG reported.

If you're a man, you probably haven't noticed any of this. It isn't part of your everyday life. But any woman who's been a boss knows the delicate dance needed to navigate these traps.

"You're sitting in a business meeting and you censor yourself because you don't want the men sitting all around you to think that you are upstaging them," said former Sony Pictures Entertainment chief Amy Pascal. "You talk around your point. You find ways to make the men feel good even when they're wrong."

Men who do become aware of this dynamic are in the best position to change it. Television producer Glen Mazzara has seen junior men ignore a senior woman, doing an end run around her by coming directly to him to privately complain that "she doesn't know what she's doing." His response: "She's doing a great job. Listen to her. If I disagree with something, I'll address it with her, but right now you're reporting to her." As Mazzara told me, "I did not let them circumvent the chain of command."

And woe to the woman who gets angry at work. Three separate studies found that when professional men get angry in a work context, they are accorded greater respect by others. But when women get angry, they receive *less* respect.

The studies found that it didn't matter whether the woman was a trainee or a CEO; if she got mad, her status among coworkers declined. The reason, researchers discovered, was that men's anger was attributed to external circumstances; the assumption was that he had a reason to become angry. For women, though, anger was attributed to a personality defect, that "she is an angry person," or "she is out of control."

This became a key issue during the 2016 presidential campaign. Then-candidate Donald Trump owned his anger, and was amply rewarded for it. "Yes, I'm angry," as he said at his rallies. "I'm angry because our country is a mess," as he repeated in a primary debate. A CNN poll during the Republican primaries found that voters who

described themselves as "angry" at the federal government favored him by a wide margin over his opponents.

Trump's anger was his calling card, and it worked. Supporters equated his anger with respect—after all, many of them were angry too. His slogan, "Make America Great Again," made "his supporters feel great by feeling respected," as University of Massachusetts sociologist Paul Hollander put it. "The craving for respect is the common denominator of his followers." For Trump, anger and respect were closely, and positively, linked.

Democratic nominee Hillary Clinton, meanwhile, had to carefully modulate every utterance to avoid being seen as an "angry woman." For her, anger diminished the respect she garnered, undercut her authority, and made her seem a less legitimate leader. When she was confronted by an activist during her campaign, one blog reported, "She yelled at a Greenpeace protester, waggling that crooked finger like a lecturing nanny . . . and is getting *shriller than ever.*" A *Politico* piece criticized one of her debate performances by noting that "she wore her anger outwardly and seemed to deliver her lines in an aggrieved husky voice."

Just as the academic studies showed, her anger diminished her. Among those who most energetically demeaned her for sounding angry was, ironically, Trump himself, who dubbed her a "nasty woman" and derided her for speaking too loudly. "I haven't quite recovered" from her "shouting," he said at one point. At another he said, "All you have to do is watch her speak. This is not a president."

The connection between anger and diminished respect for women can impact not just elections, but all kinds of group decisions, including jury verdicts. In a 2015 study, undergraduates were asked to participate in mock jury deliberations, moderated via computer. Participants believed they were interacting with five other people to decide the verdict in a real-life murder case. What they didn't know was that the other "jurors" were fictional computer creations. Four of

those jurors were programmed to agree with the participant, while one was programmed to be an angry holdout, and identified as either a man or a woman.

The results couldn't have been clearer: angry men got more respect, simply for being male, while angry women got less. When the angry dissenter was a man, study participants of both genders became less confident of their own judgment and more likely to be swayed by his opinion.

When the angry dissenter was a woman, though, the result was the opposite: participants dug in, doubling down on their own opinions and discounting hers. She was angry and emotional, so she clearly didn't deserve their respect. The researchers concluded, "expressing anger might lead men to gain influence, but women to lose influence."

••

WOMEN MAY NOT get as much respect as men, but there's something that they do get more of: blame, if things go south. A female leader is more likely to take the fall and get fired if her company doesn't perform, and less likely to be able to get another job of similar stature after she leaves.

A Federal Reserve Bank of New York study found that a company's poor performance is attributed more to female leaders than male leaders, while its success is attributed more to the men. The study found that for every 1 percent decline in a company's value, female top executives' pay is reduced by 63 percent, almost twice the percentage decline for that of male top executives. Yet if a company's value increases by 1 percent, male executives get more credit—triple the percentage pay boost versus that for women leaders.

The media plays into those stereotypes too. According to a study commissioned by the Rockefeller Foundation, 80 percent of news reports blame female CEOs when companies are in crisis, but less than a third fault male CEOs.

What's more, when *Fortune* magazine tracked down female executives who had lost their positions and fallen off its annual Most Powerful Women list, it found that only 13 percent of them had found top jobs at other companies, despite stellar careers and track records, and a determination to get back in the game. As the publication noted, "there is something wrong if so many all-star women at the peak of their careers, with decades of top-level management experience, can't land the ultimate job."

Part of the issue is that women are more likely to get the top job if the enterprise is failing in the first place. A Utah State University study of 50 female CEOs found that 42 percent of them had been named to the position when the company was in crisis, compared with 22 percent of men. Women are marched right off the dreaded "glass cliff," a phrase coined by University of Exeter researchers Michelle K. Ryan and S. Alexander Haslam, who found that women are overrepresented in leadership when companies are in "precarious" shape and thus more likely to implode.

Men also appear to be more likely to try to topple female leaders. In 2015, the *New York Times* found that almost a quarter of the then-twenty-three female CEOs of large companies had been targeted by male activist investors. One aggressor, Nelson Peltz, had attacked the female heads of three companies, Pepsi, DuPont, and Mondelez, leading *Fortune* magazine's Patricia Sellers to ask, "Does Nelson Peltz have a problem with women?" Research suggests that the answer not just for him, but for others, is a resounding yes. Women leaders are disproportionately more likely to be forced out of their jobs than male leaders, a 2013 survey found.

A revealing study by the University of Utah and Washington University suggests one reason why that's the case. Two groups of business school students were shown identical prospectuses for an initial public offering. The only difference was that one group's prospectus listed a female CEO and the other a male CEO. Yet the

students were certain there was a big difference between the companies' leadership and prospects. The female CEO was "perceived as less capable" than the male, and the offerings led by her were considered "less attractive investments" than those led by him.

Indeed, even when men and women read from an identical script, the men get more respect. In one study, groups of students were asked to rank the items an astronaut would need in a moon crash landing, such as a first aid kit or map. Each group included either a man or a woman who, unknown to the participants, had been trained to play the leader.

Afterward, the students were asked to evaluate him or her. Men who played that role were viewed as great guys, with ability, intelligence, and skill. The women who played the same role, in contrast, were described as "emotional, bossy and domineering."

That jives with a *Fortune* magazine analysis of performance reviews for 180 people, 105 of whom were men. It found that women were far more likely to be personally disparaged as "strident," "abrasive," "judgmental," and "irrational." Indeed, the magazine found that those types of personality criticisms were leveled at only two of the men—but at seventy-one of the women. The word "abrasive" was used to describe no fewer than thirteen different women.

Men don't even have to be right to garner greater respect than women. One unintentionally hilarious study found that pundits on television—the people who pound the table and shout their views—are worse at making economic and political predictions than random chance. Literally, you could write out three predictions on scraps of paper and let your cat pick one, and Fluffy would have a better chance of being right than the "expert" on TV.

While that study didn't differentiate between male and female pundits, statistically speaking, prognosticators and other "experts" featured on television and quoted in news accounts are overwhelmingly male. One analysis calculated that 74 percent of the guests on network Sunday morning news shows were men.

••

THE DIGITAL WORLD, where everyone can have an equal say regardless of gender or race, was supposed to wipe away these differences. Men, women, minorities—all were afforded the same platform and, theoretically at least, equal opportunity to express their views. Early on, my fellow journalists and I cheered this turn of events, envisioning a future in which more voices would be heard, leading to more diversity of voices and an equal playing field for all.

Of course, that didn't happen. Instead, all of us were able to create and live inside our own filter bubbles, listening only to people who agree with us, a development that was magnified by social media.

The anonymity of the digital world, meanwhile, enabled hatred to flourish, with virtual crowds gathering to attack religious, ethnic, and racial groups—and women. The result: the respect gap has only widened in recent years. If you were to measure the curve of respect toward women in America, it would have shown a steady increase through most of the 1990s and early 2000s, and then it careened, roller-coaster-like, into a steep decline over the last decade. The slide has been especially notable in the past few years, with women increasingly targeted by cyberbullying.

That came across with startling clarity when, in 2016, *The Guardian*, a British publication, analyzed its own commenting section, running the numbers on the 70 million comments left on its site. It found that while the majority of regular commenters were white men, every one of the *Guardian* writers who received the vilest abuse was either female or a minority. Indeed, of the ten writers who were targeted with the most vitriol, eight were women. The other two were black men. The ten writers subjected to the *fewest* attacks, meanwhile, were all men.

The *Guardian*'s analysis prompted a "so what?" shrug among my female colleagues in the media. Who among us hasn't experienced it? My daughter once wrote a college term paper on the disrespect and derogatory language directed at women online. She later allowed me

to read it—and I found to my dismay that every one of the examples she cited were references to me. My heart sank. Is this what my children were reading on the Internet? I'd tried my hardest as a parent to teach them to respect others, and to be open to different points of view. What must they think when they saw these abusive comments, written by strangers, directed at their own mother?

In a *Vox* piece headlined "*The Guardian* Study's Hidden Lesson: Trolls Reinforce White Male Dominance in Journalism," writer Amanda Taub warned that the outsize levels of abuse aimed at women online could shut down female writers, who may shy away from significant issues. Taub, who herself has written on hot-button topics, including the Israeli–Palestinian conflict as well as feminism, has been a frequent target herself. As she wrote about the online trolls who have attacked her, they have

> elaborate fantasies for how I should be raped or maimed or killed in order to "teach me a lesson" about why whatever I've written is so wrong. I've received recommendations that I should be sodomized with a gun, that I should be raped by a thousand men, that I should be raped and murdered by terrorists, and that I should be handed over to ISIS to become another journalist murdered on camera—and those are just the ones I happen to remember off the top of my head, not a complete list.

Taub noted that that kind of abuse means female writers are "left as they are now, with the choice of bearing the abuse or changing their own behavior to avoid it."

Digital bullying disproportionately targets not only female writers, but women of any age or occupation. A 2014 Pew survey found that men who have Internet enemies get called names. But women are "uniquely likely to experience stalking and sexual harassment," as well as physical threats.

The virtual bullying of women is the digital analog to real life. The majority of women—as much as 81 percent, according to a recent survey—have experienced some form of sexual harassment, ranging from verbal abuse to sexual assault. Yet for years, women have been loathe to report harassment for fear of retaliation, or of being smeared themselves. Researchers have shown that company grievance procedures like hotlines frequently backfire, largely because victims are afraid of punishment. Even after the #MeToo movement exploded in 2017, and despite the well-publicized firings of powerful men since then, the majority of workers who experienced harassment said in a recent survey that they didn't report the abuse for fear of being branded a "troublemaker."

Their fears are often well founded. Film producer Harvey Weinstein wasn't ousted from his company until the *New York Times* and the *New Yorker* ran exposés revealing thirty years of alleged sexual harassment and assault. Ultimately, the list of women who said he had harassed them included such A-list stars as Gwyneth Paltrow and Angelina Jolie. His victims were either paid off, or intimidated into silence by his power to make or break careers.

Similarly, at Fox News, it took years for sexual harassment allegations inside the company to result in the ouster of its top leadership. Until then, the company attacked the women who complained, even hiring a private investigator to dig up dirt on them.

When former Fox anchor Gretchen Carlson accused then-boss Roger Ailes of sexually harassing her, Fox publicly turned on her. Ailes was terminated only after twenty-five other women came forward. Just months later, when star anchor Bill O'Reilly was accused of sexual harassment by multiple women, the company again blamed the victims, dismissing their allegations because they hadn't called the company complaint hotline. O'Reilly too was ultimately fired, but only after the *New York Times* revealed that he and the company had already paid $13 million to five women to set-

tle harassment suits. Sexual harassment claims ultimately cost the company $45 million.

As with Gretchen Carlson's situation, the more powerful the woman is, the more likely she is to face abuse and sexual harassment. A University of British Columbia study concluded that women who "deviated from traditional gender roles—by occupying a 'man's' job or having a 'masculine' personality" were especially vulnerable to attacks.

••

EVEN WOMEN WHO don't experience overt harassment are familiar with the subtle digs and lack of respect that are part of daily life. Every woman knows how it feels to be marginalized, ignored, interrupted, and simply not taken as seriously as the guy sitting right next to her. That's the reason why #MeToo has gained such momentum. These incidents are wearying, difficult to fight, and the steady drumbeat of them can be debilitating.

Back in Boston, Dr. Merrill was experiencing this herself. She had decided to pursue general surgery rather than orthopedics. Not because orthopedics was "for boys," but because it is focused primarily on mechanical issues—pinning bones back together—while she preferred medical issues that involve the entire body. Yet female general surgeons are also a minority, and she soon ran up against familiar barriers.

She chafed at the casually patronizing comments from others. There was the medical-device representative who patiently explained to her that she should pursue breast surgery, because it allows a woman "'to raise a family and children.'" Dr. Merrill responded in frustration, "Yes, breast surgery is a great specialty. It allows a surgeon, male or female, to actually cure cancer."

As she progressed in her career, she noticed the binary descriptions of female doctors as either too assertive and demanding—the

dreaded "bitchy"—or too "meek." "Why are these my only two options in the professional world?" she wondered. "Why can't a strong and assertive woman be championed as a man would for the same decisions?"

She progressed to becoming a senior surgical resident, but still found herself constantly trying to modulate her tone as she walked that perilously narrow path. "I feel like when I tell someone to do something, it comes across as me being bitchy, as opposed to when a man does it," she told me. "I try to overcompensate by being super, super nice."

The steady accumulation of slights prompted her to finally write a blog post, describing those instances and others. "We are still nowhere near where we deserve to be in the field of surgery or medicine," she wrote, citing the grim statistics: women accounted for just 21 percent of full-time medical school professors and 15 percent of department chairs—a percentage that, for orthopedic surgery, fell to zero.

Once Dr. Merrill finished writing the post, she hesitated. She had intended to submit it to a well-read medical blog, *KevinMD*. But now that she had committed her thoughts to the page, she feared that she was making a mistake, that perhaps she would face a backlash from female as well as male doctors.

"Would my female colleagues agree with my experience?" she wondered. "Would they appreciate me highlighting the bias we face or do they just want to continue doing their jobs without raising a 'fuss'? And my male colleagues, would they accuse me of complaining or playing the victim?"

She took a deep breath and pressed the "send" button. Then, with no small amount of trepidation, she sat back and waited.

At just about the same time, *Science* magazine's latest issue landed on newsstands. Its career advice column, which regularly answered reader questions, carried an eye-catching headline: "Help! My

Adviser Won't Stop Looking Down My Shirt!" The query came from a young female researcher. How, the researcher asked, should she deal with a male supervisor who constantly stared at her breasts?

The advice columnist, Caltech faculty member Alice Huang, had just the answer:

> *The kind of behavior you mention is common in the workplace . . .*
> *I suggest you put up with it, with good humor if you can . . . His*
> *attention on your chest may be unwelcome, but you need his*
> *attention on your science and his best advice.*

Dr. Merrill, reading the column, was stunned. Here was another woman raising the same kinds of issues she had just written about in her piece. And yet this woman was being told—by a female scientist, no less—to be quiet and put up with abuse. You're getting no respect? No problem, the columnist was advising. Just let it slide, and be happy you're in the room.

Dr. Merrill feared the respect gap not only wasn't shrinking; it seemed to be growing wider. "Every time I turned on the news, there was something about this disparity between men and women, or a new study showing women are perceived to be not as smart as their male counterparts, even if they're smarter," she told me. "I thought, wow, it's everywhere."

••

ACROSS TOWN AT Harvard Medical School, another physician was watching the respect gap play out in the headlines. Augustus A. White III is a professor of orthopedics, a giant in his field. Now over eighty years old, he has had a legendary career as a surgeon, writing textbooks on the biomechanics of the spine that became the gold standard in medical schools across the country.

But I reached out to Dr. White because of his expertise in an

entirely different arena: discrimination. I had read his searing book on the topic, *Seeing Patients: Unconscious Bias in Health Care*, an examination of how thirteen separate groups—including blacks, Asians, the obese, and the elderly, as well as women—are subtly discriminated against by physicians.

Dr. White is gracious and even-keeled, one of those people who, when you speak with them, makes you feel as if you are their sole concern in the world. Just listening to him, it seemed, could lower your blood pressure or quiet a panic attack. His equanimity becomes that much more astonishing once you understand his own history.

The issue of bias, Dr. White told me, resonates on a deeply personal level for him. His grandparents were born into slavery. He himself was born and raised in Tennessee, in the heart of the Jim Crow South. Both of Dr. White's parents were college graduates, a rarity in those days for African Americans. But his physician father died young, so to support him, his mother took a job as a school secretary, ultimately working her way up to become a teacher.

Young Gus managed to get a scholarship to a Northern prep school, then to Brown University, where he played varsity football and lacrosse—and was one of just five black students. He subsequently became the first African American graduate of Stanford University's medical school.

Back home in Memphis after college graduation in 1957, he took a summer job at a hospital. All of the surgeons were white; the patients were primarily black. One day, a childhood friend's mother, suffering from uterine cancer, was admitted for surgery. After barking at her in the operating room, "Get on that table, Janet. Be quick about it. We don't have all day," the surgeon botched the incision and kept cutting even as she hemorrhaged. She ultimately bled to death as the horrified young Gus watched.

"Here was this white surgeon treating his black patient the way

he had, without respect," Dr. White recalled. Thus was born "a conviction that we should not be treated this way, that it was simply not tolerable."

That image was seared into his brain, and stayed with him through his years of medical training and his ascendance to the top of his profession. Over time, the kind of overt racism he witnessed receded. But the more subtle lack of respect toward blacks as well as the elderly, the obese, women—anyone out of the mainstream—left a deep impression on him.

Dr. White began speaking out publicly about bias, and in recent years has become a leader in trying to combat it. In medicine, it's literally a matter of life and death. He found, for example, that African-American diabetes patients are more likely to undergo amputations than other groups. Blacks and Hispanics are less likely to be given enough pain medication after breaking a bone. Some surgeons recoil from operating on obese patients.

And women face a host of inequities. When they have heart attacks, emergency workers take longer to get them to a hospital. If a woman's heart attack results from a blockage, she is almost twice as likely as a man to die from it. Women are half as likely as men to be recommended for knee replacement. They're less likely than men to receive kidney transplants.

Dr. White defines the phenomenon of unequal treatment as "cultural illiteracy." It's a condition that can affect any one of us. "Very well-educated people can be devastatingly culturally illiterate," he told me, citing as just one example former Harvard president Larry Summers, who lost his job after suggesting that women may innately have less aptitude than men in science.

Yet even as we spoke, Dr. White was less focused on the problem than on putting forward solutions. Awareness of the issue, he told me, is the key to overcoming it. "I encourage all caregivers, not just young doctors, to treat all patients with the same respect

as your family or your friends. Pay attention to patients, humanize your patients," he says. He stresses open communication, as well, a condition that again "requires respect and rapport. When there is discomfort or dislike on the doctor's side, it can and very often does negatively affect clinical thinking and conclusions."

His is good advice not just for doctors, but for all of us. So is his counsel on what *not* to do. No lecturing. Telling men or women they're wrong isn't the answer.

"Nobody likes to be preached to or criticized," he told me. His words echoed those of others I'd spoken to who have had some success closing the gender gap. When I asked McKinsey & Company's CEO Dominic Barton how to motivate men to care about the issue, he thought for a moment, then said, "One of the things that doesn't work is haranguing people." And Harvard Business School professor Frances Frei warned against "scolding" or trying to catch men in a "gotcha" moment.

Instead, with quiet authority, Dr. White has been urging the medical community, and by extension, the world at large, to acknowledge our own blind spots. As he speaks to groups about the issue, "one thing that's appealing is to [acknowledge] the professionalism of the audience," he explained to me. "Once they understand that we have these hidden biases, they can confront them."

••

THERE ARE SIGNS that the work of men like Dr. White—as well as Ben Barres, Wall Street refugee Polk, and others—is starting to have an effect on closing the respect gap. Dr. Merrill saw a hint of that progress after her blog post about the unequal treatment of female physicians was published.

Expecting criticism, she was instead surprised by a deluge of a different sort: emails, tweets, and comments expressing support, from men as well as women.

At the same time, she watched as both men and women erupted in public outrage over that *Science* advice column advocating that a female researcher "put up with" abuse. The backlash was so severe—prompting the Twitter hashtags #worstsciencecareeradvice and #Don'tAskAlice—that the publication ultimately retracted the piece.

The reaction, to her own piece and to events in the world around her, wasn't lost on Dr. Merrill. She knew now that she wasn't alone, and that not just other women but men were standing up to close the respect gap themselves. She had been so nervous about speaking out about the issue—but now she realized that it was necessary. "The first step in all this is transparency," she told me. "Putting it out in the open is the first step to combat it."

Back when she had pressed the "send" button on her post, she immediately worried that she had made a terrible mistake. It was terrifying to express her thoughts and experiences out loud.

But "by the end of the day, my butterflies had faded, replaced with euphoria and gratitude for the widespread support," she recalled afterward. "The world is taking note of the sexism that exists in the workplace and people are speaking up." Men, not just women, were recognizing the issues and reaching out across the divide to solve those challenges.

As she surveyed the landscape, one thought came to mind: "There may be hope yet."

6

She Deserves a Raise.
But She Won't Ask for It.

The biggest surprise for me when I became a manager was how many men asked for a raise, a promotion, or a bigger office. It came as a shock because I didn't ask for those things myself. Neither did the women I supervised.

The first hint of this alien new world came on the day I moved out from my cubicle. I had spent my career in the open bullpen of a big newsroom. I always loved the energy and excitement and sense of shared purpose of a newsroom. Ideas, inspiration, and bawdy jokes flowed freely across those cubicle dividers. We commiserated when we'd gotten beaten by the competition, celebrated each other's wins, rallied around each other in times of crisis. I learned my trade by osmosis, overhearing the best reporters in the business work the phones to tease information from their sources.

But in my new role as an editor, I would be dealing with confidential information like salaries and performance reviews. I would need some privacy. I was still unpacking in my new office when one of my male colleagues stopped by. Without a word, he began pacing out the perimeter.

"What are you doing?" I asked.

"Your office is two feet smaller than the offices of everybody else in your position. You should complain."

I laughed. Who cared about the size of my office? It was big enough for a desk, and it had a door. It even had a window. I didn't need more than that. I shooed him out and got back to work.

Little did I realize, my male colleague was on to something. The size of my office—or, more to the point, my lack of interest in it—was symptomatic of a larger issue. The other people in my position were men. And men are far more likely to advocate on their own behalf, not just for stuff I considered trivial, like office size, but for indisputably meaningful incentives like salary and other benefits. Just as it never occurred to me to push back about my office, it didn't occur to me that I should negotiate my salary. Not surprisingly, I later learned that the men in my position, those with the larger offices, earned more than I did.

Researchers ultimately concluded what I saw for myself: men are four times more likely than women to ask for a raise—and when women do ask, we typically request 30 percent less than men do, says Carnegie Mellon University economics professor Linda Babcock, coauthor of *Women Don't Ask*. That leads, by her estimate, to as much as $1.5 million in lost income over the women's careers.

The gap is closing somewhat among younger women, who are more likely to ask for raises and are more likely to be the family's primary breadwinner, but women are still far from parity when it comes to negotiating pay. An Australian study of 4,600 employees found that while women were as likely as men to ask for raises, they were 25 percent less likely to receive them.

Advice books tell women that we need to demand what we deserve. The problem is, we don't. That's a major reason for the stubborn gender pay gap. More than a half century after President John F. Kennedy signed the Equal Pay Act of 1963, the gap between what men and women earn has defied every effort to close it. And it can't be explained away as a statistical glitch, a function of women preferring work in lower-paying industries or choosing to take time off for kids.

American women earn less than men in almost every profession. One analysis of 446 occupations found that women are paid less than men in 439 of them.

Claudia Goldin, a labor economist at Harvard, has crunched the numbers and found that female doctors and surgeons, for example, earn 71 percent of what their male colleagues make, while female financial specialists are paid just 66 percent as much as comparable men. In Silicon Valley, women earn 40 percent to 73 percent less than their male counterparts.

Researchers have calculated that women one year out of college earn 6.6 percent less than men after controlling for occupation and hours, and that female M.B.A. graduates earn on average $4,600 less than their male classmates in their first jobs. A comprehensive study, Behind the Pay Gap, found that even after accounting for different occupational choices and hours worked, there was an "unexplained" wage gap of 7 percent for women one year out of college, which grew to 12 percent within a decade. By one estimate, the average woman needs to work twelve years longer than a man just to get to even with his earnings.

Nor is the gap fully explained by women stepping back after they have kids. Multiple studies have shown that women who don't marry or have children face a career gap that they simply can't overcome. A Catalyst survey that followed ambitious business school graduates in the U.S., Canada, Europe, and Asia, for example, found that women who didn't take time off still didn't receive the same opportunities as their male counterparts.

And pity those who do choose to take time for family; they are disproportionately punished. Female M.B.A.s who leave the workforce for eighteen months and then return, for example, earn on average 41 percent less than their male colleagues.

The solution should be so simple. If the root cause for the gap is that women don't negotiate, then we should get over ourselves and just ask for what we are worth, already. A whole genre of books geared

to women has pushed us to do exactly that, from MSNBC host Mika Brzezinski's *Knowing Your Value*, to *Nice Girls Don't Get the Corner Office* by Lois P. Frankel, to Gail Evans's *Play Like a Man, Win Like a Woman*.

So why don't we? Part of the reason is we don't actually *know* what we are worth. Through a quirk of biology and culture, we undervalue ourselves. What's more, even if we do realize our value and then ask for it, we often suffer consequences of another sort. People find us bossy, or uncompromising, or difficult. They don't want to work with us.

It's perilous territory to suggest that women and men are different in that way. It's a small step toward suggesting that one is "better" and the other is "worse." But to eliminate the gender gap, we need to recognize the fact, as uncomfortable as it may be, that men and women are wired differently. And in some ways, women are programmed from birth to value their personal contributions less.

Recall from chapter 1 linguist Deborah Tannen's finding that boys learn to play with one another by competing against each other, and trying to "one-up" each other. They play to win. Girls, on the other hand, are much more drawn to games where cooperation is key. Observing children play, she noted that girls who overtly jockey for status are punished or ostracized by the group. Those girls aren't "nice." They pay a steep social cost. They learn early that if they want to be liked, they need to get along and not suggest they are better than, or "worth more" than, any other member of the group.

That appears to translate directly into girls—and women—valuing their personal contributions less than boys value theirs. An experiment with children using Hershey kisses as "currency" provides a startling example. Researchers gave first graders a simple task, and then asked how many Hershey kisses they should receive for completing it. Boys "paid" themselves far more than girls paid themselves. When the researchers repeated the experiment with fourth, seventh, and tenth graders, this time using cash, they saw

the same results. In every grade, the girls paid themselves less, by as much as 78 percent.

The syndrome continues into adulthood. Female entrepreneurs, who have the power to set their own salaries, nevertheless pay themselves less than male entrepreneurs. Name any task, and women will value their own work less than men value theirs. Social psychologists Brenda Major, Dean McFarlin, and Diana Gagnon asked men and women to evaluate college applications from incoming freshmen and then set their own compensation for completing that task. Both men and women rated themselves equally in terms of how they performed. Yet the men paid themselves 63 percent more.

All of us—men and women alike—are prone to stereotyping. In sociological terms, women are considered an "out group," with less power than men, who are the "in group." In plain English, that means women hold a lower place in society, along with other "out groups," like minorities, who also statistically earn less than white men. In practical terms, that means women, as well as men, have internalized that women are worth less than men are.

Linda Babcock and fellow researchers eloquently illustrated this paradox in a famous experiment using the game Boggle. Researchers asked participants to play four rounds of the word game, for which they were told they would be paid between $3 and $10. Afterward, the participants were given the minimum $3. "Is three dollars okay?" the researcher asked. Eight times as many men as women responded no and asked for more. For another round of the experiment, researchers simply handed participants the $3, without asking if it was okay. Yet 13 percent of the men still asked for more.

You can probably guess how many women asked for more. Zero.

That's what I was seeing in my own office. Male reporters had no problem putting their hands up for promotions or asking for raises. They shrugged it off if they were denied and, like the male Boggle players, kept asking for more anyway.

Women, though, virtually never made those demands. They waited to be recognized for their excellent work. Carol Frohlinger and Deborah Kolb of Negotiating Women, Inc., a training and consulting firm, have dubbed this the "tiara" syndrome—the idea that women expect that their good work will be recognized, and that they will be rewarded for it accordingly.

For much of my career, like other women, I too awaited my tiara. My bosses knew I was a hard worker, always expressed appreciation, and gave me regular raises. It didn't occur to me that others were asking for, and receiving, more. I was grateful for what I already had.

The very few times I did push back, I usually didn't succeed. One boss early in my career told me he couldn't pay me more that year because I would "max out" and he wouldn't be able to give me a raise later. Whatever message these men were trying to convey, the one I took away was simple: I was being pushy and ungrateful.

All of which researchers could have predicted without even meeting me. Business management and organization professor Lisa Barron studied salary negotiations by asking business school students to act as job applicants in mock interviews. She found that the "job seekers" fell into two groups: one that believed it was up to them to determine their own worth, and another that believed the company should decide what to pay them.

She expected to see some difference in responses by gender, but even she was startled by the results. The first camp, those certain that it was up to them to decide their value, was overwhelmingly male, at 85 percent. An almost identical percentage of women, 83 percent, fell into the second camp, figuring it was up to the company to determine their compensation.

In other words, men and women evaluated their worth in diametrically opposite ways. The men believed that they knew what they were worth—and that they had the power to get it. They had control over their destinies. The women, on the other hand, not only didn't

know what they were worth, they weren't comfortable putting a dollar value on their own contributions. They believed it was up to others to decide.

The more time I spent as a manager, the more I saw that disparity for myself. Not that I was clever or wily enough to change my own behavior. I couldn't bring myself to "act like a guy." For years, I had watched as male colleagues sought out job offers that they parlayed into raises; in essence, they were rewarded for not quitting. I didn't play that game, even though I saw that it worked for them.

Once, I turned down a recruiter on the phone when he called to ask if I might consider a job at another news organization. I hung up and went back to work, not bothering to mention it to anyone else. The recruiter's next call was to one of my male colleagues, sitting just a few desks away. He promptly marched into our boss's office, explained he had received a prestigious offer, and then emerged to proudly announce that he had gotten a big raise because of it.

I wasn't necessarily wrong to hold back. Women who do ask for raises can be penalized for it. Women and men alike are more likely to look negatively at a woman who asks for more money than they are at a man making the same request. In a series of experiments, Babcock, along with Hannah Riley Bowles and Lei Lai, asked participants to evaluate job candidates who negotiated for a raise. When reading a written account of the negotiation, participants of both genders judged women far more harshly than men. In another experiment, participants viewed a videotape of either a man or a woman negotiating for a higher salary. This time, while women reacted negatively toward both, male evaluators reacted more negatively to the women.

As the researchers concluded, "Sometimes it does hurt to ask."

What's more, even when women do negotiate a raise, they are rewarded less than men. In one study of 205 graduating business school students, women were just as likely as their male classmates

to negotiate for their starting salary. Yet the women saw gains that on average were 59 percent lower than those negotiated by the men.

Employers—women and men alike—may not consciously realize it, but they expect women to be satisfied with lower pay than men. That in turn sets up women for a career-long lag that increases exponentially with time. By starting out with a lower base, even if those women and men get equal percentage raises throughout their careers, the salaries of the women will never catch up with those of the men.

As the gap continues to grow, women fall farther and farther behind. One study found that the chasm starts to widen at age thirty-two, when men disproportionately begin being promoted into management jobs. Crunching the numbers from Census Bureau data, the National Women's Law Center found the average woman will earn $418,800 less than the average man over a four-decade career—a figure that jumps to close to $1 million for African-American women and even higher for Latina women. The pay gap not only shows no sign of shrinking; it actually grew in 2015. At the rate we're going, it will take 117 years for women to reach pay parity with men.

The pay gap, like other types of bias, is often invisible: it is explained away by other factors. He's older, or he came from a different company where his salary was higher, or he has more potential. Many men, and some women too, argue that there isn't a pay gap at all. If the gap is invisible, though, we can never hope to close it. You can't fix a problem if you don't see it in the first place.

When Glassdoor surveyed 8,254 adults in seven countries, the majority of women and a significantly larger majority of men said there was no pay gap at their own company. In Switzerland, Canada, France, and Britain, about 1 in 10 men said women didn't *deserve* to be paid as much as men. And in the U.S., 15 percent of women surveyed said they would apply for a job even if they knew women were paid less than men. The women *expected* to be valued less than men.

Those findings echo the Catalyst study, which looked at what happened when ambitious, driven, female M.B.A. graduates followed the same career playbook as men. The women let their bosses know they were ready for stretch assignments. They were clear about their career aspirations. They made sure to build a relationship not just with their boss, but the boss's boss. None of it worked. The women still earned less.

"This study raises the question, 'Is the problem really that women don't ask, or is it that men don't have to?'" said Catalyst president and CEO Ilene Lang.

••

COMPLICATING MATTERS IS the culture of silence surrounding salaries. There's a real taboo that prevents us from having a frank, open conversation about what I make or you make. That works against women who do try to negotiate. They aren't aware of what male colleagues earn. Nor do they feel empowered to ask the men directly, lest they be perceived as greedy or grasping.

Some senior women have taken matters into their own hands, sharing their own salary information with younger employees. Another emerging tactic is to prohibit companies from asking job candidates about their previous salary, in order to break the cycle of underpaying women when they switch employers. Massachusetts, New York City, and Philadelphia have all passed legislation doing just that. It's too soon to say how effective those measures may be; one study found that women who don't disclose previous salaries are penalized with lower offers—while men who don't disclose that information get a pay boost.

In an encouraging sign, men as well as women are starting to push back, to shatter that silence. Companies like PayScale, Inc., Salary.com, and Glassdoor, which publish salary databases, can arm women with information about what others in their position

earn, providing the ammunition they need to ask for fair compensation. High-profile women, like actresses Jennifer Lawrence, Robin Wright, Patricia Arquette, and Scarlett Johansson, have brought the issue into the open and emboldened others.

Lawrence famously kicked off the conversation in 2014 after Sony Pictures was hacked and she learned that she earned less than her male costars for the film *American Hustle.* Like many women, she at first blamed herself. In an essay for LennyLetter.com, she wrote that when "I found out how much less I was being paid than the lucky people with dicks, I didn't get mad at Sony. I got mad at myself. I failed as a negotiator because I gave up early . . . I didn't want to seem 'difficult' or 'spoiled.' At the time, that seemed like a fine idea, until I saw the payroll on the Internet and realized every man I was working with definitely didn't worry about being 'difficult' or 'spoiled.'" Subsequently other actresses and high-profile women, including members of the champion U.S. women's national soccer team, have spoken publicly about being paid less than male peers.

While outspoken Hollywood actresses are helpful to the cause, the salary figures they are talking about are so massive that they don't apply to most of the rest of us. Still, the thinking behind their actions does. All of these women cited data to support their case. The same strategy can work for women in any profession, at any level. If enough of us do so, it will no longer "hurt to ask."

Recently, I participated in a breakfast panel about women in the media, discussing the issues and research around pay and promotion. The next day, I heard from a young woman in the audience who worked for a public relations firm. At work after the event, she had received her annual performance review, which offered glowing praise along with an unexpectedly puny raise.

Instead of swallowing her disappointment, as she had done in the past, she pushed back. She explained that her compensation didn't

reflect her contributions. She marshalled the facts she had learned from the panel, and the information she had gleaned about male colleagues who earned more than she did. Her supervisors quickly sweetened her compensation package.

Clare Klemmer, a twenty-six-year-old advertising employee, deployed a similar strategy to negotiate for a nearly $20,000 raise. When Klemmer interviewed for a job at a new firm and was asked about her salary expectations, her first instinct was to answer: "Whatever." Instead, she pushed herself to ask for $75,000, an increase of about $10,000 over her current salary. She was invited for a second interview, and seeing that the company was eager to hire her, upped her ask to the "$80,000 to $85,000" range. "What I was really saying was, I'll take $80,000 but if you want to show me how much you want me, you'll give me a little more," she later explained. When an offer came in, at $80,000, she took a deep breath and pushed one more time: "Make it $82,000 and I'll come over and start right away." She feared she had pushed too hard. But ten minutes later, she got a one-word answer: "Yes."

In Klemmer's case, she didn't come up with that strategy on her own. She got counseling throughout from an expert: her boyfriend, who was simply offering her the tools he would naturally have used himself. Without his advice and his pushing her to ask for more, she admitted, she would never have done so on her own.

And that points to how crucial men are as our allies. When we work together instead of at odds with one another, the gap can disappear. That's what happened at Salesforce, a cloud computing company. Mark Benioff, chief executive of Salesforce, thought he already was paying women equally—until two women in his organization approached him to tell him otherwise. At their urging, the firm performed a gender wage gap audit. It ended up writing checks to employees for $3 million to rectify the gap in 2016 and an additional $3 million a year later.

Benioff went public with his company's wage gap. "I wish I could rewind time and go back and put that women's equality issue into the culture from the beginning," he said ruefully to CNN interviewer Poppy Harlow. "Every CEO needs to look at if they're paying men and women the same," he said. "That is something every single CEO can do today."

In the end, that may well be the most effective approach of all. Indeed, if we're truly serious about closing the gender wage gap, there is something that can be done about it: require companies to publish wages. Shining some much-needed sunlight on the gender wage gap could make a difference for every one of us, men and women, right now.

Almost half of all states have introduced legislation along those lines. Among them is California, which passed a fair pay act requiring men and women to be paid equally for "substantially similar" work. Tech firms Intel, Apple, Salesforce, and SpaceX are among those that have instituted and publicized wage gap audits, as have retailers like Gap Inc.

President Obama introduced a similar federal rule, but it and other gender-equality initiatives were rolled back by the Trump administration, after business executives argued that collecting the data would be too expensive. Notably, three-quarters of top Trump staffers are male, and the median wage gap in the White House more than tripled, to 37 percent, in the first year of the administration.

Wage-gap audits in other countries have proven remarkably effective. After Quebec introduced fair-pay legislation, Montreal's McGill University found that 2,100 current and former employees had been underpaid; the university spent at least $19 million to close the gap. Austria, Belgium, and Britain have passed similar legislation. The wage-gap disclosures will "create the pressure we need for change, driving women's wages up," then–prime minister David Cameron said of the U.K. measure when it was passed in 2015.

Indeed, when the BBC published salary data in 2017, revealing that most of its highest-paid stars were white men, the news sparked an outcry, including a demand by Prime Minister Theresa May to equalize pay. A few years earlier, in 2014, when the consulting firm PricewaterhouseCoopers had voluntarily released its gender pay gap data in Britain, simply saying the number out loud "created much more momentum internally" to close it, Sarah Churchman, who runs the firm's British diversity and inclusion efforts, told me. There's something about publicizing an embarrassing figure, putting it on public display, that is highly motivating when it comes to fixing the problem.

PricewaterhouseCoopers's analysis showed that most of its 15.1 percent pay disparity (compared with a Britain-wide gap of more than 19 percent) reflected a lack of women in senior jobs. It subsequently doubled the percentage of women promoted to partner.

The firm's executives were also stunned to find a bonus pattern that favored men. The analysis showed that men who were passed over for partnership were routinely offered retention bonuses to keep them from quitting. Women weren't. Churchman believes that's because men often threatened to leave, while women typically decided to keep their heads down and work harder. That behavior reflected a familiar phenomenon: guys who are rejected typically believe that they are right and whoever rejected them is wrong. Women, on the other hand, take rejection as a deeply personal flaw that they must work to overcome.

There's a strong argument to be made for transparency not just for women, but for introverted men, minorities, and other underrepresented groups, who face many of the same obstacles. African-American men earn less than white men, for example. A *Harvard Business Review* analysis found that controlling for education, black men in turn outearn both white and black women.

Closing the gender gap is an expensive proposition, to be sure.

But the evidence suggests it more than pays for itself. For starters, about 20 percent of large companies now train employees to recognize unconscious bias, spending billions of dollars to try to stamp out unintentional discrimination. Paying for a salary analysis is cheaper and potentially more effective. Evidence also suggests that less secrecy about pay results in greater employee loyalty and lower turnover.

What's more, closing the gap provides multiple financial benefits over time. As we've already seen at companies from Tupperware to Kimberly-Clark, adding women to work groups leads to smarter decisions and improved financial performance. An analysis of 800 businesses found that retailers with relatively more women than their competitors see as much as a 46 percent increase in revenue over retailers with fewer women, while hospitality companies with more women post a 58 percent higher net profit. Economists estimate that simply paying women equally could add $4.3 trillion to the American economy.

••

IN MY OWN field, the gender wage gap has been remarkably slow to close. In 1991, when I was a young reporter at the *Wall Street Journal*, an analysis by the union that represents reporters and copy editors found that women at the company earned just 76 percent of what our male colleagues were making. A full twenty-five years later, a similar analysis through 2016 found that female staffers still were paid less than 85 cents for every dollar a man earned.

The results were similarly stark at other news organizations. A 2016 analysis of the *Washington Post* salaries, for example, found that women earned 83 cents for every dollar earned by their male colleagues.

Paradoxically, women are just as successful as men—in some cases more so—and are very comfortable advocating on behalf of anyone other than themselves. This is likely because that behavior jives with

how women are "supposed" to act. It's another way of being selfless and caring for others.

In my own experience, I always prided myself on going to bat for others, fighting for their raises or promotions, even though I never felt comfortable doing so for myself. I always thought I was the only person who was a warrior on behalf of others but a wimp when it came to advocating for myself. Apparently, I had plenty of company—but only among women.

In one study, men and women were asked to negotiate the terms of a job offer. Half were asked to negotiate on behalf on themselves. Half were asked to negotiate on behalf of a friend. The difference between men and women was striking. For the men, it didn't matter who they were advocating for: regardless, they negotiated an average starting salary of $49,000. For the women—well, when they negotiated on behalf of a friend, they equaled the men, demanding $49,000. But when they advocated on behalf of themselves, they were doormats. They requested an average of just $42,000, almost 17 percent less than the men. A similar study with experienced male and female executives found the same results.

Other studies have found that women get better results than men—as long as they are advocating for someone else. In one, students were asked how much they should be paid for a particular job, or how much someone else should earn for the same work. Female students paid other people a whopping 48 percent more than they would pay themselves. Men, on the other hand, paid others 20 percent less than they rewarded themselves.

I often advise women to imagine that they are advocating for someone else when putting themselves forward for a promotion or a raise. Think of yourself in the third person, I'll tell them. What are her qualifications? Why does she deserve a raise? How would you make the argument? Most women can answer all of those questions easily.

I thought I came up with this clever strategy on my own. But it

turns out I was reinventing the wheel. Scientists have already documented this approach. In one study, students were asked to write letters asking to be paid themselves, or advocating on behalf of someone else. Women made lower requests than men on behalf of themselves—but requested more than the men when advocating for someone else.

As perplexing as those results are, they also shed light on the solution. They lay bare the key to fixing the gender wage gap. We all need to advocate on behalf of others, and to urge friends and colleagues to push for themselves. Plenty of men have already taken up the challenge. Steve Boehm, who led eBay's global customer service team, for example, encouraged women on his team to negotiate for raises when they moved into new positions.

"It doesn't mean you always get what you ask for," he said, but he tries "to not have that as a one-sided conversation."

••

THE LANDSCAPE IS remarkably similar when it comes to promotions. Men are far more likely than women to raise their hands for a bigger job, whether they're ready for it or not. As one senior executive told me, if a job opening has five criteria, a woman with four of them won't apply—but "a guy will have one of the five and will say, 'Give the job to me!'"

That goes for even the most ambitious women. Virginia Rometty, IBM's CEO, has said that when she was offered a promotion early in her career, she responded, "You know what? I'm not ready for this job." She reconsidered only after she went home that night, and her husband told her that a man would never think that way.

Over the years, I've noticed the same dynamic. One of the most disconcerting challenges I've faced as a manager is when someone—and in my experience, that someone is *always* a woman—turns down a promotion. When a plum job comes open, plenty of men apply,

including some who aren't nearly ready for it, not even close. Yet these men end up advancing at a far faster rate than more qualified women.

The question is: Why are women so hesitant to raise their hands? It's especially perplexing because studies have shown that women are actually *more* ambitious about their careers than men when they first enter the workforce. A Bain & Company study found that 43 percent of women aspired to top management early in their careers, versus 34 percent of men. Yet within two years, the figure for women plunged, to 16 percent, while for men there was no change.

Conventional wisdom holds that either these women focused on family instead, or that they lacked confidence. But the women in the study cited other, more troubling factors: they didn't see role models, they didn't fit in, and, perhaps most critically, they didn't get support from supervisors, who were largely male. Support from supervisors, that feeling that someone has their back, is a critical factor. Without it, women are not only less likely to raise their hands, they are less likely to be in consideration for promotion.

For male supervisors—and female supervisors too—the key is to make sure that women like these are in the conversation in the first place. You'd be surprised at how often they are ruled out. Not because there's some sort of evil sexist conspiracy, but because bosses make assumptions about women that they rarely do about men.

Sometimes, when a great opportunity arises, one supervisor will suggest a terrific female candidate, but others will shake their heads and say, "She'll never want it." Over the years, I've heard it all: She has a new baby. She won't move. She doesn't like to travel.

To which the answer should be: "Let's ask her. Let her make the decision." She needs to know she is in this conversation, she is being considered for this opportunity, even if she doesn't choose to take it. Kimberly-Clark adopted this policy after it brought more women into senior leadership roles. More than half of the employees it pre-

viously assumed would never want to relocate for a new opportunity in fact did.

Too often, though, that message never gets delivered. Women feel overlooked and frozen out. A survey of thirty thousand men and women by McKinsey and Lean In found that the majority don't consider their company to be a meritocracy, and 25 percent of women believe gender has held them back. The survey also found that at every level of an organization, women are 15 percent less likely than men to get promoted.

Part of the challenge is the lack of mentors for promising women. Women hear endlessly about how important it is for us to have professional mentors in order to succeed. It's become a mantra. In fact, we've heard it so often, over so many years, that it has become something of a professional crutch. As Sheryl Sandberg has observed, "searching for a mentor has become the professional equivalent of waiting for Prince Charming."

Unfortunately, the Prince Charming scenario rarely works out. Male supervisors are often loathe to get too chummy with female subordinates—and vice versa. One of the most fraught relationships you'll ever find is between older male executives and up-and-coming women. The reality is, a senior male executive is far more likely to strike up a friendly, mentoring relationship with an up-and-coming man. Two men can have a beer after work. No one raises an eyebrow if they travel on business together. But a man mentoring a young woman has to be careful doing any of these things. It *does* raise eyebrows. It looks like dating, or, if the man is married, something much worse.

One study found that 64 percent of male senior executives "are reluctant to have a one-on-one meeting with junior women," and that half of junior women feel the same way: they "likewise avoid seeking out such contact." A survey of more than five thousand adults found the majority of women and almost half of men said it was "inappro-

priate" to have dinner or drinks with someone of the opposite sex other than their spouse. Another study by three top business schools found that professors are far more likely to mentor white men than they are women or minorities.

And when researchers from the Ewing Marion Kauffman Foundation interviewed 350 female entrepreneurs, the majority said "lack of available advisers" was a primary obstacle to their career advancement. It's perhaps no surprise, then, that women are hesitant when it comes to seeking out mentors. KPMG surveyed more than three thousand professional and college-age women, and found the overwhelming majority didn't feel confident seeking out a mentor or asking for access to senior managers.

Men, meanwhile, face no such barriers. Glen Mazzara, the television producer, notes that up-and-coming men "will use the 'brotherhood' to access (senior) men, to make themselves more familiar, and that's the way they raise their status." Male bosses, he says, "have to be cognizant of that, and you have to either shut it down or allow women the same access."

Even when women do snare mentors, it turns out those advocates are far more effective for men.

That's because women's mentors typically offer advice. But men's champions act as sponsors, with the power to get men promotions and new jobs. There's a world of difference between mentors and sponsors. And that's a crucial advantage for men.

There is a way to overcome the mentorship trap. Frank Dobbin, the Harvard professor, surveyed diversity programs at 829 companies over thirty years, and concluded that they "have failed spectacularly." As he noted, "The problem is that we can't motivate people by forcing them to get with the program and punishing them if they don't."

Yet he also pinpoints three ways in which companies are able to bust biases and help women and other underrepresented groups succeed. In particular, he has found that formal mentoring programs

make a measurable difference. Formal programs, created and overseen by individual organizations, take away the social awkwardness of men and women seeking out one another. What's more, formal mentorship programs give both mentors and mentees a common set of goals to accomplish, and make those goals clear to the rest of the company. It's a lot harder for gossip and tongue-wagging to flourish when mentorship is as built in to the system as ID cards and taco day at the company cafeteria.

Deutsche Bank created one such program after digging into the reason why so many female managing directors were defecting to competitors. The answer, it turned out, was that the women felt they were at a dead end where they were. The bank's new program paired women with executive committee members and gave them more visible assignments. A third of participants were promoted within a year.

When Sun Microsystems created a similar program, it found that the mentors benefited as much as the mentees. Over a seven-year period, employee retention rates for both rose substantially, saving the company $6.7 million it would have had to invest in hiring and training replacements. The Sun and Deutsche Bank results mirror those elsewhere. Research by Catalyst found that women who find mentors through formal programs receive about 50 percent more promotions than those who find mentors on their own.

Even without formal programs, there are multiple ways to mentor promising young employees. I take a page from my own mentors, all men. Very often the mentor/mentee relationship evolves through social contact. My own mentors navigated around this one beautifully. Rather than going out for a night on the town or golfing (and to be clear: you don't want me anywhere near a course, unless it's miniature golf!) they would suggest dinner with spouses, or business lunches, or, after I had kids, family outings. These provided a great way to have sustained personal contact without any raised eyebrows or officer chatter.

Simply listening to women, engaging them in conversation, is a good start. When Bob Moritz became the leader of PwC's New York office, he embarked on a "listening tour," hosting dinners for female partners, so that he could understand the "nuances" between their views and those of men. While both genders were ambitious, he found that women were especially eager for multiple paths to advancement, more flexibility in their careers, and ways to interact with clients beyond golf outings. (Apparently, I'm not the only one who desperately wants to steer clear of the links.)

Harvard's Dobbin has pinpointed two other solutions, beyond formal mentorship programs, that also make a measurable difference for women: diversity managers and diversity task forces. Neither one of these is terribly surprising, since any company motivated enough to create those positions would have had to make diversity a priority in the first place. But the special sauce in creating these positions is transparency—not just making sure employees are aware of the company's goals, but ensuring that they can see the results.

The big accounting and consulting firm Deloitte first tried this tactic in 1992, as it watched promising young female professionals flee at an alarming rate. Although half of its hires were female, most of them left before they'd reach partner level. So Deloitte created an internal task force that required every department to monitor its progress in hiring and retaining women. The percentage of female partners grew from 5 percent to 21 percent by 2015.

That year, Cathy Engelbert was named Deloitte's first female CEO. One of her signature moves was to implement paid family leave for up to sixteen weeks, and up to six months for new mothers. She leaves work to coach her daughter's basketball games, and lets everyone know it.

"I didn't have any women role models," she told me. It wasn't until she became a high-profile CEO that she realized that she could *be* the role model. "I was amazed at how externally important that was. That was a big aha moment for me."

Her experience points to how essential it is for senior management to really believe in all of this, not just give it lip service. Executives need to talk about diversity goals, and their commitment to women, loudly and often. And then they need to act on them. It's telling that when McKinsey and Lean In surveyed more than a hundred companies, the overwhelming majority reported that gender diversity was one of the CEOs' top priorities. Yet less than half of employees agreed.

For managers, another effective strategy seems blindingly simple: when jobs do come open, insist on a diverse slate of candidates. In 2002, after a devastating report showed that black coaches were less likely to be hired and more likely to be fired by the National Football League (NFL), it adapted what's called the Rooney Rule, named for former Pittsburgh Steelers owner Dan Rooney, who chaired the NFL's diversity committee. The rule stipulates that the NFL must interview minority candidates for every coach or other senior opening.

Why not have a Rooney Rule for women and other underrepresented groups in hiring too? Indeed, tech executive Steve Boehm did just that when he was with eBay. Almost half of eBay's employees are female, but less than a third of its senior executives are. So he required corporate recruiters to recommend female candidates for job openings.

You'd think this would be a rather obvious idea. It isn't. "Unless you specifically require recruiters to bring you diverse slates of candidates, they will tend to bring you people that they've seen before, that look a lot like you," he told me. "We had some senior openings where we went for months without having a woman surface in the candidate pool. We literally had to stop the process and let the recruiter know."

The key in every one of these solutions is that men and women are on the same side, pursuing the same goal. It isn't us versus them. It isn't men being dragged into a fight that they feel isn't their own. And in each case, senior leadership is not only aware of these efforts but

has made diversity a highly visible goal. It also helps when diversity is baked into the incentive system—not just as a pat on the head, but as a measurable goal with a financial reward for success.

All of those roads lead back to the same place: trust. Women are especially attuned to behaviors that speak to lack of trust, accustomed as they are to garnering less respect than men. That's a major reason they don't raise their hands for raises and promotions in the first place; they don't feel that they have the support and trust of those above them.

It's impossible to overstate how important it is for bosses to let others know you trust their judgment, you value their contributions, and then give them the autonomy to do their jobs. They may not perform a task exactly as you would, and they may make mistakes, but they need to know that you have faith in them—to perform, to improve, to learn from missteps, as all of us have had to do.

Supervisors who have confidence in their employees, and who have a clear vision that they articulate over and over again, create a framework in which everyone is rowing in the same boat, in the same direction. That's when women as well as men feel empowered to raise their hand for promotions, eager to help steer the organization toward the future.

••

AS MUCH AS women have done to advance the cause of equal pay and promotions, we simply won't achieve equality without men taking up the mantle too. The men I met who have adopted this cause as their own cite a variety of motivations. Each arrived at this point through his own particular path.

One of the most high-profile yet bittersweet efforts to even the playing field was spurred, unwittingly, by a woman named Lori Irving. A social psychologist and professor at Washington State University, she was considered a pioneer in the study of self-esteem. An

anorexic as a child, she grew up to become one of the nation's foremost experts on one of the thorniest issues facing young girls and women: the entanglement of eating disorders with media depictions of women and their effect on girls' self-worth.

Tragically, in 2001 Irving died suddenly of an undiagnosed heart ailment while nine months pregnant with her daughter, who also did not survive. Her death was a sudden and devastating loss for her field, and even more so for her family. It left a particular mark on her heartbroken older brother, Blake. A fine arts major who specialized in typography, he made his way to San Francisco, where he ended up working at Yahoo and Microsoft.

"She was a very inspirational professor, a super cool lady, funnier than hell. She lit up a room . . . You'd follow her anywhere," he recalled. When she passed away, "my pledge to her was to do as much to forward the empowerment of women in my field as she was trying to do in hers."

More than a decade after her death, in 2013, Irving emerged in a new role, as chief executive of GoDaddy, the web domain registration company. The irony runs deep. You probably know of GoDaddy as the company behind perhaps the most obnoxiously sexist ads ever created. Every year during the Super Bowl, for almost a decade, GoDaddy commercials would feature women in as little clothing as possible, almost always surrounded by gawking men. If there was a line between cheap and sleazy, GoDaddy pole-vaulted right over it.

There was the 2011 spot featuring race car driver Danika Patrick, apparently naked, that made the *Daily Beast's* list of "The Five Most Sexist Super Bowl Ads Ever." There was the 2013 commercial in which supermodel Bar Refaeli shares a long, sloppy, noisy open-mouth kiss with "Walter," the nerd, in an excruciating close-up; that ad was apparently only accepted after two other versions were rejected by network censors as inappropriate. The company's commercials were so reviled that they inspired a movement, Breakupwithgodaddy.com, urging a boycott of the company.

But Irving, with his sister in mind, set about changing the culture. First he threw out the advertising campaigns. Then he began hiring women as rapidly as possible. GoDaddy's internship program increased from 14 percent to 40 percent female among technical roles, though the workforce itself is still overwhelmingly male. Irving helped fund a documentary about the challenges facing women in technology, *CODE: Debugging the Gender Gap.* GoDaddy created a women's interest group, which attracted hundreds of members—almost half of them men.

"Can I be a feminist? Why not?" Irving mused.

Irving has since become one of the most outspoken male executives advocating for women, and in particular for pay equality. In addition to instituting a wage gap audit, GoDaddy now analyzes incoming candidates' salaries to ensure that women don't remain underpaid when they join from other companies.

"We call it 'pay it backwards,'" he told me—the phenomenon of a woman who is underpaid at a previous job bringing her low base along with her to the next job. "It's the right thing to do . . . We can make this change right now, and have a positive impact."

GoDaddy's sexist past has been hard to shake. Irving, who planned to retire at the end of 2017, continued to face skepticism; when he spoke at a prominent conference for women in technology, he was pilloried on social media, his efforts dismissed as insincere pandering. He pushed on regardless.

"If you don't create advocacy among men, and awareness, the problem will never go away," he told me. "I think on the one hand, women would like to solve it [themselves], and on the other, having male advocates that are trying to help matters a great deal."

Irving is proof that we can indeed close the gap, one man at a time. I recently looked for the Breakupwithgodaddy.com website. It was gone.

7

Blind Auditions: Solving for Bias, Emotion, and Other Stuff You Can't Control

One of my closest childhood friends, Melanie Kupchynsky, is a gifted musician. Her father, a music teacher, first handed her a pint-size violin when she was four years old. By the time we were in elementary school, she was performing solo concerts up and down the East Coast.

Her dad began teaching me the viola when I was ten years old. I was no match for Melanie—woe to my parents, my sisters, and our dog Skippy, who had to listen as I scratched away! But I worked hard, and Melanie's dad, a remarkable teacher, groomed me to be good enough to join a string quartet with Melanie and her talented little sister Stephanie, also a violinist.

Throughout our childhoods, our quartet roamed around performing anywhere we could. We played at museums, colleges, music conventions, hospitals. One day you might find us at a national conference of educators, premiering a quartet written for us by a celebrated composer; the next we might be dressed in Colonial costumes, struggling to be heard over the carnival barkers at a street fair. On weekends, we honed our performance skills at a local nurs-

ing home, where the elderly residents would stroke our hair and kiss us and tell us we reminded them of their grandchildren.

In college, I continued to study and to play with the student orchestra. But I quit soon after graduation. My job as a reporter in New York City didn't leave much extra time for practicing. By the time I got married a few years later and had a couple of kids, my viola lay forgotten, buried in the back of a closet.

Melanie, on the other hand, was destined to become a professional musician. In 1989, not long after she graduated from conservatory, Melanie was granted an audition with the Chicago Symphony Orchestra. Chicago is one of the greatest orchestras in the world. The most famous musicians on the planet have performed with it, from cellist Yo Yo Ma and violinist Itzhak Perlman to *Star Wars* composer John Williams. It's won sixty-two Grammy Awards and counting.

It also, like other symphonies of its stature, used to be made up almost entirely of men. For most of its history, dating back to its founding in 1891, conductors chose musicians they knew. Auditions were occasionally as casual as stopping by the maestro's hotel room for a cocktail.

By the 1980s, though, the Chicago Symphony and most of its peers had bowed to charges of sexism and switched to "blind" auditions, in which musicians play behind a screen. Before her audition, Melanie received a very specific set of instructions. She was told to enter through a basement entrance of Orchestra Hall, so that none of the judges would see her. She was given a number—23, out of 250 violinists auditioning for just one spot!—so that judges wouldn't know her name. When it was her turn to take the stage, she not only played behind a screen, but walked onstage on a carpet so that conductor Sir George Solti and the orchestra members who judged her from the audience wouldn't hear the telltale click of high heels.

Melanie played brilliantly, and ultimately won that coveted spot. Other women began winning auditions as well. The Chicago Symphony's method of eliminating bias was so striking that economists descended on it—and on the country's four other premier symphonies, all of which also introduced blind auditions—to gain a better understanding of how to combat employment discrimination. They found that women went from fewer than 5 percent of all musicians in those five symphonies in 1970, to 25 percent in 1997, the year of the study. Today, those numbers are edging closer to 50 percent.

Melanie was fortunate to experience a real-life experiment in eliminating bias. Ever since, executives and companies have been trying to figure out how to replicate those ideal conditions. They've appropriated tools from computer labs and neuroscience experiments, from dating apps like Tinder and from comedy-show writers' rooms, and even from a study of the epic Enron financial scandal, to search for just the right formula that will result in purely rational employment decisions.

Some companies are taking cues, quite literally, from the symphony. Firms including Bloomberg, Dolby Laboratories, and BBC Digital have experimented with filling technical jobs through a "blind audition" in which applicants complete a test that's evaluated by a hiring manager who doesn't know anything at all about the applicant—not sex, age, schooling, or name.

The audition process they used is the brainchild of a software entrepreneur, Kedar Iyer, who was motivated by his own experience. He studied electrical engineering in college in India, but couldn't get in the door to interview with the tech companies he coveted because they required a computer science degree. He knew he could code as well as his computer science classmates, but nobody would give him a chance to prove himself. Finally, frustrated, he lied about his major. It worked. He got invited to a prestigious interview, where he

sailed through a coding test. Unfortunately, he also all but got kicked out of school when his career counselor found out.

The subterfuge may have backfired, but it had a novel side effect: it inspired him to cofound, in 2012, a company called GapJumpers that uses software to conduct blind auditions for digital and technical jobs. Applicants take an online test that doesn't reveal gender, age, or education. For example, a candidate for a social-media editor position might be asked to create Instagram posts pegged to Memorial Day for a particular brand. The work samples, with no identifying information attached, are passed along to the client company's hiring managers. The managers then decide which applicants to invite for an interview.

The process has proven a boon to nontraditional candidates in technical fields, including women, the disabled, and minorities. Iyer has calculated that four times more qualified applicants are actually invited for interviews than with a typical résumé-screening process. And of those, the majority hired are female. "We wanted to solve a broken hiring system that didn't value performance," he told me, "that [instead] valued the labels attached to their background, or their resume."

As encouraging as those results are, GapJumpers so far has focused only on technical jobs that don't require interacting with other people. Other companies are tiptoeing into these waters, but they also tend to be focused on technical roles.

Yet most of us work in jobs that require some degree of human interaction. And chemistry—how one fits in, in the culture—remains an undeniably important component in choosing among equally qualified applicants. So the big question is: Can blind auditions work for the rest of us?

••

TO FIND OUT the answer, you need to travel beyond the symphony hall and far from Silicon Valley, to take a peek inside the New York City writers' room of a television comedy show.

Full Frontal with Samantha Bee debuted in 2016. The satirical news show's host hadn't set out to be a stand-up comic. She was supposed to be a lawyer. Born and raised in Toronto, she was, as she recounts in her autobiography, *I Know I Am, But What Are You?*, an "exceptionally quiet" child, the living definition of the term "indoor kid."

She spent a peripatetic childhood pinballing back and forth between divorced parents, and was raised largely by her grand-mother. She was a good student, though she did take a brief teen-age detour into hellionhood with a high school boyfriend who liked to steal cars. Still, she made sure to keep up her grades: after they skipped class a few too many times, she persuaded the boyfriend to smash her hand with a rock so she could be excused from final exams, thus preserving her grade point average.

"I am still a Catholic schoolgirl, and I like my gold star," as she put it in a *Rolling Stone* interview.

The appeal of the courtroom, however, was no match for the lure of the stage. Bee snared a role in a traveling children's theater (her highlight: wearing a sexy, cleavage-baring outfit as the star of *Sailor Moon*), and supported herself with odd jobs, including as a techni-cian at an erectile dysfunction clinic and as a blackjack dealer in an illegal casino, before joining up with three other women to create a comedy troupe, the Atomic Fireballs.

In 2003, when *The Daily Show with Jon Stewart* came to town, friends twisted her arm to audition. Bee wasn't sure she was ready. Like a lot of women, she had a confidence problem. Research has shown that women won't raise their hand for a job unless they feel they are 100 percent qualified, while men eagerly raise their hands if they have 60 percent of the required qualifications. What's more, an analysis published in *Harvard Business Review* found that 22 percent of women—almost double the percentage of men—don't apply for jobs because they're afraid to "put myself out there if I [am] likely to fail."

Bee herself was in that camp. "I had to be kind of brow-beaten into applying because I didn't think I was good enough," she said. But she

nailed the audition and landed a role as the show's only female correspondent.

Late-night comedy shows are notoriously male dominated, veritable hotbeds of testosterone. That's why it surprised me to learn that most of them already use blind submissions to hire writers, with applicants identified by numbers instead of names. It's similar to the process that my violinist friend Melanie experienced with the Chicago Symphony, except rather than playing Tchaikovsky and Brahms, these applicants supply jokes and gags.

But typically, only the first round is blind. After that, the show's producers meet the applicant. And women have rarely made the cut. Even though *The Daily Show* was created by two women, for example, longtime host Jon Stewart at one point had only one female correspondent—Bee herself. Competing late-night shows were just as guy-centric, often with one woman in a writers' room along with a dozen or more men.

After a spate of scathing press in 2010 about this lack of women, the late-night shows scrambled to try to hire more, but protested that they couldn't find enough female applicants. That trend has continued. Even John Oliver, who made a concerted effort to bring in female writers to the staff of HBO's *Last Week Tonight,* and who uses two rounds of blind auditions instead of one to try to improve the odds, has just two women on his staff of ten as of this writing.

Part of the problem is that writers encourage their friends to apply, leading to the same talent pool of guys raised on the *Harvard Lampoon,* with the same comic sensibilities, dominating most writers' rooms. Indeed, researchers have found that people tend to hire others who essentially replicate themselves. They gravitate toward people who look and sound like them. Lauren Rivera, a professor with Northwestern University's Kellogg School of Management, conducted 120 interviews with employers, including law firms, banks, and consulting firms. She found that hiring executives overwhelmingly chose

candidates who were "culturally similar to themselves in terms of leisure pursuits, experiences, and self-presentation styles."

Perhaps just as significant an issue in the comedy world is that professional comedy writers—an overwhelmingly male group—already are familiar with the secrets of how to put together a polished audition packet, using a rigid, almost ritualized format.

"It's such a basic thing, but the format in which you receive scripts is so specific in this world," Bee has said. "If you don't nail the format, your package is at a total disadvantage because it's apparent you don't work in comedy and nobody wants to read it. It's like turning in your thesis handwritten."

So when Bee landed *Full Frontal*, she and her executive producer, Jo Miller, set out to level the playing field further, determined to create a truly blind audition. They didn't want a writers' room populated by the same people with the same voices. Nor did they want other women to face the same obstacles they had endured earlier in their careers.

So Miller created a detailed instruction packet for applicants. It not only provided step-by-step instructions for submissions, it also supplied applicants with the script format. Every application that landed on Miller's desk looked exactly the same. There was no way to tell not just men from women, but professionals from amateurs.

The results were striking. When *Full Frontal* launched in February 2016, its writing staff was split evenly between men and women, and about 25 percent of its writers were minorities. Some were already experienced professional writers, but others most definitely weren't; one came from a job at Maryland's Department of Motor Vehicles.

"I have literally filled my office with people who have been underestimated their entire careers," Bee said. "To a person, we almost all fit into that category. It is so joyful to collect a group of people who nobody has ever thought could grasp the reins of something and f—ing go for it."

The show launched with the slogan "Watch or you're sexist." Yet Bee herself is the first to say she still hasn't cracked the diversity problem. There are plenty of hilarious women and others from underrepresented groups, and she wants to find them.

"It's not like we fixed diversity," she says. "It's a mandate for the show to always be moving the needle forward."

••

OTHER KINDS OF companies, well beyond technology and TV writing, are also starting to adapt elements of blind hiring. There's even an app for that: Blendoor is sort of like a Tinder for potential employees, who can swipe right on a job posting, and apply without giving away telltale details like age, gender, and ethnicity.

Blendoor's founder, Stephanie Lampkin, an African-American woman with an engineering degree from Stanford and an M.B.A. from MIT, created the app in frustration, after she made it through eight rounds of interviews at a major tech firm, only to be told her engineering background wasn't "technical enough." She bristled each time tech firms blamed their miniscule numbers of women and minorities on the lack of available talent coming up through the pipelines.

"I knew from my own experience that wasn't the case," she said. "And I wanted to create a platform that could use data to reveal it's not just a pipeline issue."

Her goal is to expand the app beyond tech into other industries, including health care and sharing-economy companies. Similar efforts are underway across multiple industries. A Chrome extension called Unbias strips names and photos from LinkedIn profiles to encourage gender-blind recruiting. Interviewing.io allows employers to mask applicants' voices during the interview process, while Talent Sonar, a tool for hiring managers, masks applicants' genders and suggests interview questions that focus on skills.

Companies in all sorts of fields are experimenting with this kind of "de-biasing" software. Some rely on a skills test. Researchers have shown that skills tests and structured interviews with specific skills-based questions are more effective than interviewers' intuition.

The key, of course, is applying that test equally—and enforcing it. When Northwestern's Rivera observed the process at one firm, she found that when male prospects failed a math test, the hiring team shrugged it off, but when women and minorities failed, their test results were used against them.

But overcome that bias, and the results speak for themselves. A Harvard Business School study found that when employers use a test to measure applicants, and stick with the results rather than overriding them and going with their gut, the employees they hire are more successful and stay longer.

Unilever and Mercer are among those that have begun using a gender-neutral tool to test potential employees. Morgan Stanley says it now uses a gender-blind system to award accounts, to avoid favoritism that might leave women with lesser accounts. Compose, a software company owned by IBM, eliminates identifying information when it screens job candidates. So-called diversity technology has emerged as a tool for human resources (HR) departments in companies to screen applicants without regard to gender or race.

The practice is spreading around the globe too. Employers in European countries, including Sweden, France, the Netherlands, and Germany, have experimented with blind résumés to screen applicants, and found that they hired more equitably as a result. In France, for example, a government test involving a thousand firms found that women received higher callback rates with blind résumés than without. Australia created a similar pilot program that includes twenty-nine companies and institutions. In the U.K., major companies including HSBC, Virgin Money, and KPMG have adopted

the practice, eliminating names and sometimes education from résumés.

Even in the best of circumstances, none of this is easy. As Rivera found, most of us relate to others like us. We naturally gravitate toward the person who went to the same college, or roots for our favorite sports team, or who listens to the same kind of music. People like us make us feel better—about ourselves and about them.

That's been true forever; it's the premise of the 1952 classic *How to Succeed in Business Without Really Trying*, in which the young striver J. Pierrepont Finch pretends to have gone to the same college as the chief executive as he climbs up the ladder. It's no coincidence that the musical based on the book still resonates today. (Well, most of it does; not so much the song "A Secretary Is Not a Toy.") But those kinds of emotional affinities rarely result in picking the best candidate.

As behavioral economist Iris Bohnet has noted, it's hard to give up human judgment. Our emotions override rationality. Hiring managers "are overconfident about their own expertise and experience, and they dislike deferring to more structured approaches that might outsource human judgment to a machine."

Even when the machine is right. Consulting firm McKinsey & Company, which has been at the forefront of trying to create a more equitable workplace, offers multiple programs to mentor women, flexible schedules to accommodate new parents, and sets hiring targets for women. Even so, when it pitted a computer program against human recruiters to evaluate twenty-five hundred résumés, the computer chose more women than the humans did.

"We found the machines were 10 percent less biased toward women," McKinsey's leader, Dominic Barton, told me—despite the fact that most of the recruiters themselves were female. "We may be knocking people out that we don't want to."

••

BLIND HIRING, OF course, applies to only a small fraction of us. So women have taken it on themselves to invent all sorts of other creative ways to sidestep bias. Some have gone so far as to mask their gender. There's a long history of women passing as men, from Joan of Arc in the fifteenth century to writer Charlotte Brontë, who in the nineteenth century published under a masculine pen name. A modern-day equivalent is Erin McKelvey, who, when she didn't get any bites from prospective tech employers as a new college grad in the mid-1990s, changed her first name to "Mack" on her résumé—and was rewarded with a 70 percent response rate. She landed a job within weeks.

More recently, the two female founders of art e-commerce startup Witchsy invented a male cofounder, who they named, quite literally, "Keith Mann." The women were often treated dismissively by web developers and other outsiders, but not Keith. "It was like night and day," said cofounder Kate Dwyer. "It would take days for me to get a response, but Keith could not only get a response and a status update, but also be asked if he wanted anything else or if there was anything else that Keith needed help with."

Entrepreneur John Greathouse wrote a piece in the *Wall Street Journal* in which he actually urged women to use their initials to obscure their gender. Women, "are you properly curating your online first impression?" he asked, helpfully adding that "if you are a woman raising capital, you might consider not including photos of your team." The response to his piece was so vitriolic that he later tweeted out an apology for his "dreadful article . . . I told women to endure the gender bias problem rather than acting to fix the problem."

His last point, about not fixing the problem, is correct. It identifies an important caveat: blind hiring alone isn't a panacea. It can end up masking a problem, rather than fixing it. If the hiring is equitable, but the workplace itself isn't, the system is still broken.

After former Uber engineer Susan Fowler detailed a culture of

sexual harassment and retaliation in a blog post, for example, for-mer attorney general Eric Holder led an investigation that resulted in recommendations including use of blind résumés. Yet none of those recommendations alone could transform a "bro culture," where, when Fowler reported harassment to the HR department, the men were defended and she was shunned. Or where then-CEO Travis Kalanick jokingly referred to his company as "Boob-er" because it helped him get women.

"All the HR Suggestions in the World Can't Change Uber's Soul," as the headline in *Slate* put it.

Ultimately, Kalanick resigned from Uber. The company hired a new CEO and brought in Frances Frei, a Harvard Business School professor who was involved in gender-equality efforts there, in a new role overseeing leadership and strategy. Shortly after she joined, Frei told me, "We're already a different organization. Uber wasn't a great place six months ago, though today it's a freakin' awesome place." Not long after our conversation, Frei left the company. The follow-ing month, in March 2018, Uber agreed to pay $10 million to settle a discrimination class-action suit filed by women and people of color.

•••

IT'S HARD TO fix the problem and achieve equality in hiring, of course, if women simply don't apply. And surprisingly, that is still often the case. Employment ads may throw up the first barrier. We've come a long way from the days when classified ads were divided into "Help wanted—male" and "Help wanted—female"—a practice that wasn't outlawed by the Supreme Court until 1973.

Still, certain words that you'll frequently find in job descriptions have a dog-whistle effect, attracting men while subtly steering away women. The words and phrases press emotional buttons in us, and we respond accordingly.

Textio, a tech startup with clients including Starbucks and Microsoft, found that a job listing that uses words and phrases

such as "proven track record," "hard-driving," "rock star," or even "extremely" is more likely to attract men, while phrases like "a passion for learning" attracts women. Textio's software singles out the offending phrases and suggests gender-neutral alternatives.

When *Fortune* magazine used Textio to analyze thousands of Walmart job postings, it found that more than half skewed toward male applicants. On a sliding scale of seven levels, from "very feminine" to "very masculine," 26 percent of managerial postings fell into the supercharged macho top stratum of "very masculine."

Trying to democratize ads, a female programmer created an app called Gender Decoder, which calls out words that are seductive to men—like "challenge" and "analyze"—versus those that subtly suggest the position is for women, like "support" and "empathy." As someone who has hired a fair share of people, I was curious about how I would rate. I'd already learned I am unconsciously biased against working women like myself; would that bias translate into job recruiting as well?

So I used Gender Decoder to analyze a job posting that I had written. The twist was, I had written it with a particular woman in mind, someone I thought of as my ideal candidate to fill a senior role. Would the ad skew female? Would I be at least gender neutral?

Not even close. The app determined that my posting was "masculine coded" and "it risks putting women off applying, but it will probably encourage men to apply." My error, according to the app, was the posting's greater emphasis on leadership than on more "feminine-coded" words like "collaborative" and "understanding."

As it happens, I hired a woman for the post anyway. And that points out the shortcomings of a software solution. As interesting an exercise as it is to try to scrub the language of "gendered" words, it also can unintentionally exacerbate the worst kinds of stereotypes rather than wiping them out. The woman I hired told me specifically she was drawn to the job because the description emphasized leadership, not in spite of it.

••

BLIND HIRING PRACTICES and "neutral" employment ads may not be perfect, but at least they're a start. When done right, as with blind auditions, they get results. That's because at their best, they strip not just bias out of the process, but emotion too.

The role of emotion can't be underestimated. It not only is an out-size factor in hiring; even if we do get the hiring right, it can be the thing that trips us up once we're actually working together. It's at the heart of the missed signals, the knee-jerk reactions, and the mis-communication between men and women that can taint our inter-actions with one another. Indeed, as I reported for this book, the role of emotion consistently emerged as one of the most confounding challenges that is thwarting efforts not just to equalize hiring and the workplace, but to communicate with one another in everyday life.

To try to comprehend why—is there a physical difference between the sexes, something hardwired into us?—I looked to science. In the past decade, our understanding of the biology as well as psychol-ogy of gender has expanded in ways we couldn't have imagined back when women first started entering the workforce in large numbers in the 1970s.

Scientists can pinpoint the differences in men's and women's brains that lead to miscues between the sexes. Computer scientists are studying emails to learn how that translates into different com-munication styles in the modern age. One researcher, perplexed by inconsistent results in an experiment with mice, found that labora-tory mice react with fear to male lab assistants—or even to the men's T-shirts—which changes their body chemistry and creates anxiety. No similar experiment has yet been tried with humans, but you can't help but wonder if results would be similar.

These scientific discoveries first tell us that no, we aren't crazy,

that there truly is a biological divide between men and women that gets in the way of communication. The differences don't affect intelligence, but they do have a meaningful impact on how men and women interpret each other's behavior—or don't.

Consider the case of women crying. When I meet with executives around the country—asking men what flummoxes them most about their female colleagues—they almost inevitably mention tears. They dread them.

Cardinal Health's Paul Gotti, for example, has been in the forefront of trying to recruit more women into his traditionally male field. Even so, a while back, he noticed that when he gave performance reviews to employees, he treated men and women differently. With men, he was candid, straightforward, and comfortable in offering them advice on what they needed to do to improve. With women, he felt uneasy. He was leery about being so candid, and wary about criticizing them. To his dismay, he realized that he wasn't being fair in his performance reviews. He was going easier on the women.

It wasn't that he held the women to a lower standard, he explained. It was for a wholly different reason: "I didn't want them to cry, to feel bad."

I was puzzled when Gotti told me this. He was afraid of crying? I admit it, I weep over Hallmark commercials, and you don't even want to see me at the end of *Beaches*. My daughter and I once stumbled across a rerun of the famous weeper and melted into tearful, drippy-nosed puddles, crying in each other's arms, to my husband's endless amusement. But I have rarely cried in the office. I haven't seen too many other women cry at work either.

Not long after speaking with Gotti, I mentioned our perplexing conversation to my friend Jonathan, an editor who has been managing journalists for two decades.

"Yes!" he exclaimed. He had the same fear. He had even begun

a new policy when he needed to have a tough conversation with a female subordinate. Now, he makes sure there is a second woman in the room, both to give him a reality check on his own behavior and to provide moral support to the other woman.

"It happens all the time! Women cry and I don't know how to handle it," he told me. "I always try to make her feel better, but I end up making things even worse."

Inadvertently, I had touched on a third rail of gender relations in the office. According to one blog, crying is one of the "10 things women do that absolutely terrify men," right up there with talking about their periods. Another counseled, "A crying woman is every man's kryptonite." A Reddit thread on the "Ask Men" section included the topic: "Men of Reddit: Is it scary, annoying or sad when a girl cries over you?" (Both "scary" and "annoying" had plenty of votes.)

It's ingrained in popular culture too, the reason why the most famous line in the 1992 film *A League of Their Own,* comes when Tom Hanks, as Jimmy Dugan, coach of an all-female baseball team, reams out a player who begins to weep: "Are you crying? Are you crying? There's no crying in baseball!"

Books and advice columns for men are riddled with angst over women who cry. Barbara Annis and John Gray, coauthors of the book *Work with Me: The 8 Blind Spots Between Men and Women in Business,* identify emotional displays as one of the major challenges men face. Weeping is awful at home or on a date, and if anything, even more horrifying at work. If a woman starts sobbing at the office, a man wants to get the hell away. He wants to flee.

It turns out, though, that there's a biological reason behind this fear. Scientists have found that women are wired to cry more frequently than men—and young women are ten times more likely to cry at work than men over forty-five, according to Anne Kreamer, who conducted a poll about emotion in the workplace for her book *It's Always Personal.*

But she also found that when women do weep at the office, it's not because their feelings are hurt, as men like Gotti and my friend Jonathan assumed. It's because they're pissed off. They're frustrated. They're furious.

None of which is apparent to men. "Let me tell you about my trouble with girls," explained Tim Hunt, a renowned scientist and Nobel laureate in medicine to a room full of science journalists. "Three things happen when they are in the lab: You fall in love with them, they fall in love with you, and when you criticize them they cry."

His comments sparked a firestorm of protest and a new meme, #distractinglysexy, with female scientists tweeting photos of themselves in full lab-coat-and-goggles regalia. So fierce was the reaction that Hunt was forced to resign as an honorary professor at University College in London.

Yet his sentiment, as tone deaf as it was, is more common than you'd think. According to Jill Flynn, of the consulting firm Flynn Heath Holt, the issue isn't simply that men don't know how to react to women who cry. They're also afraid of getting in trouble with the "diversity police" for speaking harshly, or of women being "too high maintenance, or she'll ask a million questions." As a result, "men are scared to death to give us feedback . . . They'll let women run astray and off course and be fired before they'll take the chance to give them feedback."

And that's the problem with the fear of tears. When men go easier on female subordinates, the women don't get the feedback they need. What's more, if those men are relentlessly and blandly positive, those comments are discounted by all concerned. And as we've already seen, the feedback women *do* get is often a critique of their personality—that they're "abrasive" or "emotional"—rather than constructive criticism that would improve their performance. So women don't get the guidance they need to progress—nor do they get credit when they've succeeded.

Studies have found, for example, that women in the energy business receive less criticism than men. So do women working in England's National Health Service. In one particularly revealing study, scholars analyzed performance evaluations at a Wall Street law firm. They found that women received more positive comments ("excellent!" "awesome!") than men. But despite stellar evaluations, only 6 percent of the women—versus 15 percent of the men—were mentioned as potential partner material. It's pretty clear women who cry have a good reason to be angry!

Women's careers suffer as a result. An Australian consulting firm that studied performance review conversations found that when both participants were men, the sessions were relaxed, collegial, with frequent use of the pronoun "we" and discussions about the employee's prospects. When the manager was male and the employee female, though, the sessions were uptight; he tended to focus on her performance, not her career development, and to more frequently use the pronoun "you."

Compounding the issue, Howard Ross, the management training expert and author of *Everyday Bias: Identifying and Navigating Unconscious Judgments in Our Daily Lives*, has found that among his clients, men tend to overrate themselves in performance reviews, while women underrate themselves. Women also tend to give credit to their team, while men take personal credit for the team's work.

Add those factors together, and a woman whose performance is equal to that of a man is at a disadvantage, receiving less useful feedback, less support, and enjoying less rapport with the boss than the guy in the next cubicle.

The irony is, just as women are penalized for showing emotion, men can score points for doing so. In a telling *New York Times* article about women in Hollywood, male studio executives criticized director Catherine Hardwicke, whose films include *Twilight*, for being "overly emotional."

As Hardwicke noted in the piece, she had previously worked

for twenty directors, most of them male, and "I was on the set to witness firsthand a range of sometimes atrocious emotions—well-documented firings, yellings, fights between directors and actors, hookers, abusive things, budget overages, lack of preparation. A man gets a standing ovation for crying because he's so sensitive, but a woman is shamed."

Scientists have pinpointed several biological explanations for this puzzling behavioral paradox. Laboratory experiments have found, for example, that when women cry, it actually changes men's body chemistry. A recent study from Israel's Weizmann Institute of Science concluded that when men so much as smell tears, their testosterone levels fall. That's terrifying for men on a professional level.

Judith Orloff, a psychiatrist and author of *Emotional Freedom*, has called testosterone "a key power hormone that gets corporate executives in warrior mode." Without that testosterone, they lose their competitive edge. She said that when a woman cries, "it's threatening hormonally. Studies have associated lower testosterone levels in men with feelings of failure."

Not only are men's hormones on the fritz when a woman cries, so are their brains. One intriguing study has shown that men are able to "read" emotions of other men by looking at their faces. But they are unable to easily decipher emotions on the faces of women. The women were simply a mystery to them.

For the experiment, German scientists asked men to view photographs of women's and men's eyes, and then describe what emotion they telegraphed—for example, was it "distrustful" or was it "terrified"? The men could quickly and correctly grasp the right answer when looking into the eyes of men, but were frequently baffled by those of women. The scientists theorized that the disconnect dated back to prehistoric days, when cavemen needed to make snap judgments to evaluate whether another man was a friend or an enemy. They didn't have the same biological imperative to interpret women.

This experiment explains so much. No wonder men are so fearful of saying the "wrong" thing to women. They aren't sure not only what to say, but also how to evaluate a woman's reactions. They have no idea what the hell she's thinking. She's a mystery. Any word they utter could be a trap. Their fear is, biologically speaking, justified.

Thus, when a man like Paul Gotti, or my good friend Jonathan, was confronted by a crying woman, a 200,000-year-old instinct kicked into gear. It tripped their "fight or flight" mechanism. They wanted to get away.

The good news is, once men recognize it for what it is, they can override it. Once Gotti became aware of his own fear of women crying, for example, he began double-checking to make sure his evaluations of female employees were as candid as those for men. They should have the feedback, he said, "so that they can grow too."

••

SOME OF THE most intriguing research into this paradox is happening right now at the University of Pennsylvania. Over the past several years, scholars there have peered inside the skulls of around a thousand men and women using sophisticated new imaging techniques. The researchers weren't looking for gender differences when they began this project. They were instead attempting to evaluate the brains of young people to see if there is an early marker for psychiatric disorders. To their astonishment, they found that ordinary male and female brains are wired in virtually opposite ways.

"It was a fairly amazing finding," researcher Ruben Gur explained when I met with him at his hospital office. "First we thought we miscoded something in the program. Most sex differences are more subtle."

Dr. Gur ushered me into a subbasement deep below the hospital, where a young man was lying silently, face-up, inside a high-powered

MRI machine that scanned his brain using a sophisticated technique called diffusion tensor imaging. On one of the dozen computer monitors in our observation booth, images flickered to life, providing a map of connections inside his skull, akin to creating a Google Map of his brain.

To me, those images looked like indecipherable squiggles. But to Dr. Gur's colleague, a computer scientist turned computational neuroanatomist named Ragini Verma, they read like a novel. Dr. Verma, a computer vision and math whiz who earned three advanced degrees in her native India, started her career coding facial recognition and expression analysis for the film industry. Now she uses those skills to turn these squiggles into 3-D renderings of the brain. "I'm fascinated by gender differences," she told me. "It's the content of Sunday morning conversations over mimosas with my girlfriends."

In her lab, Dr. Verma has used such scans to construct a 3-D image that shows the pathways that connect the different regions of the brain. When these 3-D images first sprang to life, this is what jumped out at her.

Ragini Verma

Women's brains (like the one on the right in the picture on the previous page), on average, had multiple connections between left and right hemispheres, which control logic and intuition. The female brain map looked like an especially intense version of the kid's game Cat's Cradle. That cross-hemisphere wiring suggests women are able to engage and connect to various parts of the brain simultaneously.

But men's brains (as seen on the left), on average, were wired in an entirely different manner, with connections going from front to back. There was almost no connection between left brain and right brain. This suggests that on average men are predisposed to focus on a single task at a time.

Her findings showed with startling clarity why so many studies have found women are better multitaskers than men. "What it means is that while I'm talking to you, I can work on my laptop, and finish a project, and think about which pair of shoes to buy in the evening, " as Dr. Verma put it to me.

The two types of brains are "complementary. It shows that the best outcome is if they (men and women) work together and complement their skills," Dr. Verma said.

At the same time, though, the different wiring also suggests that "men and women are perceiving each other differently. Our perceptions of the environment are different. It means that everything will affect you differently. How I react to things will be different than how a man reacts. People should accept there will be differences."

••

IN THIS DIGITAL age, the disconnect in how we interpret one another is that much more fraught. There are even more opportunities for misunderstandings and crossed communication wires. For the most illuminating research on that score, we can thank Enron.

In late 2001, one of the biggest financial scandals in history blew up when Enron, a once-mighty energy giant, collapsed in spectacu-

lar fashion. The Houston company had been hailed for its brilliance in oil trading, its top executives celebrated in glowing magazine profiles and rewarded with massive payouts.

Glitz and glamour and over-the-top spending were its credo. Its chief executive, Kenneth Lay, bought himself seven homes, including an extravagant $10 million Aspen showpiece that was one of four he owned in the pricey ski-resort town. The company set aside $1.5 million for an employee holiday party, and not once but twice rented a live elephant for internal meetings. The spending free-for-all seemed limitless—right up until a whistleblower exposed the enterprise as a massive financial fraud.

In the aftermath, government investigators swooped in. Among other evidence, they gathered 600,000 internal email chains. It was a treasure trove for journalists, who descended with glee in search of juicy tidbits, like the $590,000 of company cash spent on a sculptured light switch.

More than fifteen hundred miles away, Andrew McCallum was celebrating for a different reason. He's a computer scientist at the University of Massachusetts, Amherst, who studies social networks. He was trying to learn how groups of people communicate by email. Unfortunately, nobody wanted to give him access to their accounts. So when he stumbled across a news item about the massive Enron email cache, it was as if he had received a gift from the research fairies.

"When I read about it, I thought first of all, 'Gosh I feel sorry for the innocent people at Enron who have personal emails,'" he recalled. Unfortunately, nobody wanted to give him unfettered access to their accounts. "But in the same breath, 'Oh my gosh, email researchers across the world will rejoice!'" He promptly paid the federal government $10,000 for the entire database.

Computer scientists have been having a field day slicing and dicing the data ever since. On a rainy summer day, I met one of them, a Columbia University graduate student named Vinodkumar Prabhakaran. Vinod, as he is known, is an expert in a growing field known

as computational sociolinguistics research. It's a mouthful, but basically it means applying computer learning to understand language and social trends. Vinod had a very specific interest in getting his hands on the Enron emails: he wanted to probe the differences between how men and women communicated digitally with one another.

His research tapped into one of the key questions in our digital age. The way we text and email one another has added a degree of complexity in the relationship between the sexes. Scholars are only just beginning to understand the consequences. For example, men tend to write direct, short emails. To women like me, a brief, flat email can look unfriendly at best and hostile at worst. I'll read all kinds of motivations into it: *Is he angry at me? Does he think I've imposed on him? Is he resentful?*

More than once, I've shown an email to my husband to get his opinion. His inevitable response: *He's fine. He isn't angry.* So far, my husband is batting a thousand.

Women in emails tend to be chattier, friendlier, and far more likely to apologize for troubling you, or to thank you multiple times for doing something you were supposed to do anyway. When I write emails myself, I find myself double-checking them before I send them, to make sure I'm not completely debasing myself. Usually I force myself to at least erase an extraneous exclamation point or two.

No matter what topic a woman is writing about to a man, if she apologizes and hedges, she is sending one overriding message: She is the supplicant. He is in control. If she's too friendly toward him, on the other hand, the way women often are toward each other—I often get emails and texts signed with *xo*'s from other women in business—she'll look like she's got other intentions.

Meanwhile, a man who writes assertively, even to a woman who is his boss, is sending another message: He doesn't like her. Or he is challenging her authority. Or he doesn't respect her. Neither the

man nor the woman may intend to be sending those signals. But that's how they are interpreted.

As he studied the emails, Vinod found an even more perplexing wrinkle in how men and women communicate. Flipping open his laptop, he showed me how he had created an algorithm comparing language used by men to that used by women. His goal was to identify what are known in his trade as "overt displays of powers"—outright commands, with no softening language like apologies or hedging.

After he built the algorithm, he fed the Enron emails into it. Perhaps not surprisingly, he found that men used powerful language far more frequently than women. But he also noticed something quite peculiar: female executives routinely downplayed their power, avoiding direct commands. While men might say, "Come to my office now," the women would say, "Would you mind stopping by my office?"

Most intriguing, he found that the higher a woman ranked, the less powerful language she used. She would actually downplay her authority, make herself more of a supplicant, and seem to work extra hard to not remind others of her power. Just like in real life, where powerful women dye their hair blond to seem less threatening, powerful women try to diminish their digital personas.

These women may not have realized what they were doing, but they were making themselves smaller and less threatening. As they climbed the ladder and increased their authority, they seemed at pains not to flaunt it. Vinod theorized that this was because as women rise in power, they are less liked. "Women tend to hold back in order to not be perceived as pushy," he told me. "You don't want to be called 'bossy.'"

Even when you are the boss.

••

SCIENCE AND RESEARCH are helping to clarify the gender gap, which ultimately will help us close it. With each new discovery, men and

women alike are learning how to better understand one another, to eliminate the confusion and mixed signals. We are inching closer toward that "blind audition" ideal, where we can strip emotion out of hiring decisions and work together while understanding our differences rather than fearing them.

Still, progress is maddeningly slow when you consider that the blind audition concept was invented more than three decades ago, and yet here we are, still striving to achieve that perfect goal. My friend Melanie, when she auditioned for the Chicago Symphony Orchestra violin section back in 1989, didn't realize how ahead of the curve she was.

As the holidays approached, I visited with Melanie in Chicago. Before a concert one night, she let me tag along with her to the ladies' locker room, deep in the basement of Chicago's famed Symphony Center. With its benches and lockers, it could have been host to a college soccer team or the WNBA, except for the strains of music in the air and the strikingly different contents in each locker—formal outfits and priceless instruments.

Melanie is at home here. She has now performed with the Chicago Symphony Orchestra for almost three decades. When her three children, including twins, were born in quick succession, she sometimes found herself onstage in her concert black with spit-up in her hair. Her colleagues have become her family, supporting her through the best of times and the worst, including the deaths of her beloved father and younger sister.

Each year, the Chicago Symphony goes on tour. With her colleagues, Melanie has performed in China and Russia, in Japan and the capitals of Europe. Often when she's on the road, she will take in a concert from that city's own orchestra. One of the most memorable, she recounted as she pulled out one of the multiple formal black outfits hanging neatly in her locker, was the first she attended by the Vienna Philharmonic.

Like the Chicago Symphony, the Vienna Philharmonic has a storied history. Founded in 1842, it grew out of the royal ensembles that performed the music of court composers like Haydn, Mozart, and Beethoven. In the nineteenth century, it premiered classical works by Brahms and Bruckner. The first time in history that concertgoers heard the hauntingly beautiful strains of Tchaikovsky's now-legendary violin concerto was at a Vienna Philharmonic performance.

But as Melanie watched the concert, she was immediately struck by something strange on the stage. The symphony was a sea of men in tuxedos. She strained to look. Among the more than 120 members of the orchestra, there were no women. Zero. No one who looked like her. It was an odd sight, one she wasn't prepared for.

There's a reason why the symphony was all men. The Vienna Philharmonic was perhaps the last remaining major orchestra in the world to adopt blind auditions. Instead, performers were chosen by their peers, almost all of whom are men. The first woman wasn't accepted until 1997.

Even after the Austrian government reduced its funding in protest in 2011, the orchestra still resisted. Almost as if to spite the government for meddling in its sexist ways, at the philharmonic's first concert of January 2012, only two female musicians sat aside their male colleagues. Every year since, it's been something of a sport at the annual New Year's Day concert for regular concertgoers to count the few women onstage.

As Melanie watched the orchestra perform that day, she couldn't help but think of her own experience. She and her female colleagues have helped to make the Chicago Symphony Orchestra one of the greatest musical ensembles in the world.

Indeed, even as we spoke, the women's locker room in the basement of the concert hall was a hive of activity, as a crowd of female musicians changed into their concert dress, unpacked their

instruments, checked their iPads, and gave last-minute instructions to the babysitters back home. One of her colleagues pulled out her phone to show me photos of her daughter, another talked about her son's school science project. The women around us, virtuosos all, were casually tuning up priceless instruments between bites of pre-concert salads they'd brought in Tupperware containers from home.

These women weren't giving a thought to gender in their daily work. They didn't have to. They would soon file onto the stage with their male colleagues, where they were to perform a concert including the music of composer John Williams, conducted by Williams himself. The phenomenon of blind auditions that economists had studied several decades earlier was in full bloom. The blind auditions had worked. The results were clear, right in front of me.

But at the same moment, across the ocean, there was still a stark reminder of what life would have been like if the Chicago Symphony and others hadn't introduced blind auditions all those years ago. These women wouldn't have been here. The ladies' locker room itself wouldn't be here. These remarkably talented women might be giving music lessons to children in their living rooms. If they were really lucky, maybe they'd be in the audience tonight.

As if to underscore the fact, half a world away in Austria, the Vienna Philharmonic was rehearsing for its annual New Year's Day concert, a televised extravaganza that's viewed by 50 million people in more than ninety countries. It wouldn't be long before the curtain would rise on that signature event. And when it did, on that New Year's Day, astute audience members scouring the stage, searching through the musicians seated there, shook their heads in disbelief.

These were 125 of the most talented musicians in all of Europe. The very best of the best.

Onlookers could spot just five women in the entire ensemble.

8

Invisible Women: The World's Greatest Untapped Resource

One of the smartest people I know is Carol O'Keefe. Carol and I met as freshman-year roommates, and remained loyal "roomies" for the rest of our college years.

If you had read our college applications, you would have reasonably concluded that we had nothing in common. I was the nerdy violist from New Jersey who worked on my high school newspaper and couldn't so much as connect a tennis racket to a tennis ball. Carol, from rural Maryland, was the superstar athlete who, despite topping out at less than five foot three on a good day, was the varsity captain of almost every female sport in her high school, including basketball.

We were certain that the college dean had put us together in the same room as some sort of cosmic joke. But the joke was on him. We became fast friends and remain so to this day.

For years, Carol and I lived our lives in almost eerie parallel. Immediately after graduation, she married her college sweetheart, Regis. I was a bridesmaid at their wedding, where their first dance was to the *Muppet Movie* love song "Rainbow Connection." Then she and Regis headed off to Boston, he to finish medical school and she to start law school.

Neither came from well-off families, and as a young couple they barely scraped by. When I visited them, we shared a dinner of plain spaghetti in their tiny apartment with its crooked floors. Then I helped Carol make a stack of peanut butter sandwiches that we brought in a brown paper bag to Regis, who was making his hospital rounds. He couldn't afford to eat in the cafeteria.

Meanwhile, I was living in New York City, where I was a cub reporter for the *Wall Street Journal.* I was earning a pittance myself, sleeping in the living room of a tiny apartment I shared with my roommate, an investment banking trainee who made more money than I did and could afford the bedroom. A few years later, I married my husband, Tom, a boy I'd also met in college. Carol was one of our bridesmaids, gamely wearing the hideous pink polyester lace dress I picked out for her.

As Tom and I settled into married life, so did Carol and Regis, who relocated to Rochester, New York, so that Regis could complete his medical residency. Carol worked long hours at a law firm, sometimes arriving at 6:00 A.M. I was working long hours myself, first as a reporter, and then as a daily advertising columnist for the *Journal.*

The trajectory of our lives continued in tandem when, in our late twenties, Carol and I became pregnant at the same time. We both worked straight through nine months, refusing to vacate our desks until the last possible moment. We were determined to protect our hard-earned professional status, to show that we could do it all.

But after Carol's son Patrick and my daughter Rebecca were born, our lives diverged. And in the years since, the paths we've taken provide a kind of road map for what companies can, should—and shouldn't—do to keep working mothers from falling off a professional cliff.

Our trajectories illuminate one of the biggest yet least-recognized issues facing corporate America. It's an issue that, if handled in a commonsense way, could supercharge the economy and immeasur-

ably improve women's lives. It's a simple fact, but one that seems lost on many working moms, and even more so on most companies: kids grow up.

More to the point, when those kids do grow up, you've got a cohort of millions of women who are just as ambitious and smart and passionate about work as they were before they had children—probably even more so. Yet they remain stubbornly invisible to employers. These women are perhaps the single greatest untapped resource in business today.

When we talk about working mothers, we tend to focus on moms of babies and young kids. The emphasis is on maternity leave, parental leave, and parenting young children. Those are critically important issues. But much less attention has been paid to the other end of the spectrum, to mothers of older children. Some have been out of the workforce for several years or even a few decades, and desperately want to come back. Others may have continued working, but dialed back while their kids were young and were "mommy tracked" in dead-end jobs, yet are now ready to rev up again.

There's a compelling case to be made that this is where we need to train our efforts next: on these women, who want to reenter the workforce or revitalize stalled careers. Not just young moms fresh off maternity leave, but experienced older women who have been sidelined for years, yet who have a multitude of talents and the ambition and smarts to dive back in.

Reengaging these women doesn't just help them; it helps all of us. Having more women in the workforce is perhaps the single best accelerator for the U.S. economy. If more women worked, the U.S. could add an eye-popping $2.1 trillion to the gross domestic product over the next two decades, according to the McKinsey Global Institute. Half of all states would see their GDP spike by more than 10 percent, the report found.

The same is true elsewhere in the world. In 2013, Japanese Prime

Minister Shinzō Abe launched what he called "womenomics," a program to jump-start the country's stagnant economy by encouraging more women to enter the workforce. Around the globe, a McKinsey report estimated that if women participated as fully as men in labor markets, it would add an astonishing $28 trillion to the world economy.

A key to any of this growth is to make the working world hospitable not just to young mothers, but to older ones too—those whose kids have grown and who are eager to jump back in to the workforce, if only anyone will hire them.

I'm embarrassed to admit it took me too long to figure that out. When I did, it was men—my own male bosses—who showed me the way.

••

OF COURSE, WE all know, intellectually, that kids eventually turn into grown-ups. But who's thinking about that when you're up in the middle of the night, for the forty-seventh time in a row, with a crying baby? It seems you are in the middle of a never-ending maelstrom of dirty diapers and doctor appointments; as they get older, you're overwhelmed with teacher meetings, playdates, homework, soccer games. Balancing that with a job is guaranteed to be impossible. High-potential women frequently take themselves off the fast track, not imagining a time when they will want to get back on.

That was the case with my friend Carol. After Patrick was born, she was eager to spend time with her new baby. Plus, she and Regis knew they wanted a big family. So she negotiated a deal with her law firm: she would work half days, for half pay. It seemed like an ideal arrangement. Her law firm had no part-time policy, but she was a smart, savvy lawyer. Her work was valuable. It seemed like a perfect solution for everyone.

I took the opposite approach. I loved my job, and feared I would

no longer be taken seriously once Rebecca was born. So after a few months of maternity leave, I resumed my grueling pace. I rarely got home before 8:00 P.M., and sometimes much later. Tom had an even more punishing schedule as a junior lawyer.

We wanted Rebecca to grow up as we had ourselves, with family meals together, so we came up with a ruse: "dinnertime" was whatever time Mommy and Daddy came home. That's why you'd frequently find us eating takeout fried chicken at midnight. It was an excruciating juggle. I had to plan for weeks in advance to make it to a birthday party or a "Mommy and Me" class—the one where our babysitter typically played the role of "Mommy."

My days and nights were filled, mostly, with guilt. I felt guilty at work and guilty at home. No matter where I was, I wasn't doing enough for the other part of my life. At work, I was a slave to deadlines. At home, I missed first steps, first words, first friends.

My working-mother guilt is familiar to anyone with a child. I fully realize that I am more fortunate than the majority of parents. My husband and I had access to quality day care, which so many parents do not. I was able to sneak away from the office occasionally for pediatrician appointments and, in later years, for ballet recitals and back-to-school nights. People with hourly jobs or inflexible schedules—including many fellow parents at our kids' elementary school—don't have that luxury. Many of them could never so much as meet the teachers, much less make it to the children's annual Halloween costume parade.

Yet even for the most privileged among us, guilt runs deep. I once was invited to lunch with broadcasting legend Barbara Walters, during which I told her how much I enjoyed her autobiography, *Audition: A Memoir*. As a working mother, I said, I was inspired by her book, especially as she described her dazzling career while raising a daughter.

Her reply: "There's guilt on every page."

There's a reason that guilt, even now, remains such a powerful force. Most American moms now work outside the home, yet all of us—including the moms ourselves—can't shake lingering bias against them. A Pew Research Center poll found that 41 percent of American adults say the increase in working mothers is bad, almost double the percentage of those who say it is good.

In the same survey, working mothers gave themselves much lower marks for parenting skills. Yet researchers have found no truth in their self-assessments. In fact, daughters of working mothers earn higher incomes as adults, while sons of working moms spend more time on child care and household chores as adults. And men who were raised by working moms "are significantly more egalitarian in their gender attitudes," according to Harvard Business School professor Kathleen McGinn.

••

YET AMERICAN CULTURE, for all its virtues, builds working-mother guilt directly into the system. There are deeply rooted structural issues in this country that make it difficult, even now and even for those with vast resources, to balance work with parenting. Our policies and politicians do precious little to alleviate it.

America is the only industrialized country in the world that doesn't offer paid parental leave. Think about that. It's an astonishing fact, especially considering that the majority of Americans across the political spectrum support it, right up to First Daughter Ivanka Trump. Even more mind-boggling: when you include Third World and developing nations, the U.S. is one of only two countries on the planet that doesn't offer paid maternity leave—the other being Papua New Guinea.

It's a financial issue, for sure. Companies and politicians worry about the expense, though in California, one of the few states to require paid leave, more than 90 percent of companies reported it

had a positive or no effect on profitability, while in a separate poll, half of American workers say they would prefer more leave to a raise.

Perhaps the more intractable issue is a cultural one. For all of our talk about American values, our societal worship of the family, and for all of the platitudes by politicians of every persuasion about the importance of family, their actions—or lack thereof—suggest the opposite.

And there are signs that the situation for American mothers is getting worse, not better. Countries across Europe and elsewhere offer subsidized child care; many have strengthened parental leave and other family-friendly policies in the past few decades. Not so in the U.S., where most child-care costs fall on parents, and where those costs have skyrocketed by more than 168 percent since the early 1990s.

Meanwhile, for salaried professionals, the average workweek has escalated to more than fifty hours, from forty hours, leaving little time for family. The burden is especially heavy for households headed by minimum-wage workers; child-care costs can eat up 30 percent of their total income. Child care is unaffordable in forty-nine of fifty states, by the U.S. government's own standards. In more than half of all states, day-care centers cost more per year than tuition at a state university.

Not only are child-care costs soaring, but women who have kids take a salary hit. Being a mom literally makes you less valuable. Researchers have found, paradoxically, that men who become fathers are viewed as better workers, while for mothers the reverse is true.

That helps explain why, for example, in academia, fathers with young kids are 35 percent more likely than mothers to get tenure-track positions, and 20 percent more likely to actually secure tenure.

In the U.S. overall, sociologists have found that women experience a financial penalty of 7 percent per child. Even after controlling for years of job experience, the gap is 5 percent per child. The gap exists

in every state, at all education levels; not just professional women, but moms with a high school education who are child-care workers, waitstaff, cashiers, and cleaners earn less than dads who hold the same jobs. The paradox is sometimes referred to as the "motherhood penalty" and the "fatherhood bonus."

One reason behind the gap: mothers are viewed as less committed to their jobs than fathers. Harvard Business School's Robin Ely spearheaded an eighteen-month study of a major global consulting firm. She and her colleagues reported that both men and women endured brutally long hours that made it impossible to balance their lives, and led to burnout by both genders.

"Virtually everyone—women and men alike—suffered from the competing pulls of work and family," the researchers concluded.

But women were penalized for trying to achieve some balance, while men were not. For example, when a woman left the office early, coworkers assumed it was for family reasons. When a man left early, coworkers assumed he was attending a work-related dinner or meeting. What's more, both men and women described the firm's female partners as bad mothers—though male partners weren't considered bad dads.

When you add up the facts, it's stunning but clear: working women in the U.S. actually have a disincentive to have kids. The more children we have, the less we are worth to employers. It's the opposite dynamic of the one I experienced in Iceland, where I met dual-career couples with three, four, even five children. Why not? they told me; the country not only has generous parental leave—paid for nine months, split among both parents—but it also offers heavily subsidized day care.

In the U.S., meanwhile, without parental leave and affordable day-care options, the financial demands on parents are extreme, even for those who are relatively well off. When Rebecca was born, my company offered four weeks' paid leave. I know I was lucky to have that

kind of stability. Even so, we were still paying off my husband's law-school loans. I was absurdly excited to learn Rebecca was breech and she had to be delivered via cesarean section, which meant I got an extra two weeks of disability pay because the C-section was classified as major surgery. When Andrew came along two years later, I chose to have a C-section, in part because of those extra two weeks' pay.

It seems horrifying to me now that any woman would choose major surgery in order to squeeze in an extra few weeks of paid leave to care for a newborn. I hope my own children never have to make that choice. But the lack of government support for parents, combined with the high cost of child care, presents an almost impossible challenge to many women. In one survey of stay-at-home moms, 15 percent said they left the workforce because child care was too expensive.

It's no wonder that mothers feel so stressed out. They earn less for becoming moms in the first place—and then face sky-high child-care costs that can crush working families, and that ultimately drive many women out of the workplace altogether. Add to that the fact that when those women's kids grow older and the women do try to get back in, they find doors are closed to them.

••

FOR WOMEN WHO hang on and stay in the workforce, meanwhile, the balancing act can feel impossible. Two years after Carol and I each had our first children, we each gave birth to a second. I was back at my full-time job within a few months; Carol continued part-time. All right, I admit it: I was jealous of her. She seemed to have figured it all out. She was working half days, and enjoying time with her son and newborn. Meanwhile, I was on a treadmill of guilt, dirty diapers, and sleepless nights. There was no room in life for anything but kids and work. I slept in earrings and a watch, simply to save a few precious extra seconds of time in the morning.

I was missing important milestones in my children's lives too. Just

before I gave birth to Andrew, I hosted Rebecca's second birthday party. I was completely mystified by the proceedings. Our babysitter had planned the party and created the guest list. She had baked the cake. She stood next to me at the doorway so she could introduce me to each one of my daughter's friends, none of whom I had met, as they arrived.

It hit me that I had no idea about how my daughter spent her days, who were the children she loved the most, what were the games they played with one another. I was the saddest mom you've ever seen at a party of happily squealing two-year-olds.

A few weeks later, just moments after I gave birth to Andrew and still groggy from anesthesia, I took an editor's phone call in the recovery room. That's when I realized something had to give. When I got back home from the hospital, I announced to my husband that I wanted to quit. But we couldn't afford it. As it was, we still hadn't finished paying off his school loans. And we were better off than most: the vast majority of women couldn't have even entertained the thought of stepping back. That's even truer today: Americans owe $1.4 trillion in student-loan debt, and the class of 2016 graduated with an average of $37,172 in debt per person, up 6 percent from a year earlier.

I was feeling plenty sorry for myself. But one day, Carol and I managed to find time together on the phone. And then she told me what life was really like for her. She was paid half-time, yes. But her workload remained almost the same. The past year, she told me, she had billed 85 percent as many hours as the full-time lawyers at her firm, while earning half as much.

Her situation wasn't unique. In fact, it's just as likely to be the case today. For her 2015 book, *I Know How She Does It*, author Laura Vanderkam asked part-time working moms to keep a diary of their hours. She found that most put in more than thirty-five hours a week at work. One "part-time" consultant was sometimes working more than fifty hours a week.

"I found that many of those on official part-time schedules work well outside the bounds of them," Vanderkam wrote in *Harvard Business Review*.

••

NEITHER CAROL NOR I had figured out how to balance work and family. But I was about to learn one of the most valuable lessons of my career—from my male bosses. The paper's top editor, Paul Steiger, moved me into an editing job on the Page One desk. At first, I was furious with him. I wasn't ready to stop being a reporter! But he was insistent. And he proved to be right. Page One stories were generally long-term projects, which meant we had a bit more control over our schedules. We weren't as frequently at the mercy of breaking news deadlines.

I found to my surprise that I loved editing even more than writing. On Page One, we edited the three major stories that ran on the front of the paper each day. At the time, we had a crew of about a dozen editors who did nothing but polish those articles into gems. These were pieces that reporters might have spent weeks or even months researching and writing. They were the pride of the paper. We used to call the *Journal* "a magazine on the outside and a newspaper on the inside" because of those carefully constructed stories. In my years as a reporter, I always had more ideas than time to execute them. I found that now as an editor, I could spread those ideas around. I loved working with reporters, and found editing both easier and more enjoyable than writing from scratch.

But just as much as the work itself, I appreciated the relative flexibility of my editing job. My Page One boss allowed me to work at home some mornings, a rare move in those early digital days. That meant that I was no longer a stranger to my children's daily lives.

It's hard to overestimate the psychic benefits of knowing who my children's best friends were, of being able to comfort them if they scraped a knee, and—the greatest luxury of all—of picking them up

from preschool. Every day, we'd share an 11:00 A.M. bagel "lunch" before I'd explain that "Mommy has to go to work, but just until dinnertime"—since they had no concept of time, and "dinner" might be nine hours later.

Researchers have found that work–life balance is perhaps the best indicator of how satisfied women are with their jobs. According to one survey, 93 percent of women who don't feel like they have a good work–life balance are extremely unsatisfied with their jobs. On the other end of the spectrum, the vast majority of women who believe their life is in balance are extremely satisfied.

Carol and I fell on both ends of that spectrum. Just as the studies have shown, my balancing act, precarious as it was, allowed me to have more control at work and at home. I was happier in my job largely because I was happier at home. Carol, though, was not. She found herself working almost the same hours as full-timers, yet her half salary barely was enough to pay the babysitter. She reached a breaking point one night, working late—once again—with two older male partners.

"I don't know if I can do this anymore," she told them. "I've got to go home and make dinner."

One of the partners looked at her quizzically. "Just pick something up on your way home," he said.

"We can't afford it!" she blurted out.

To his credit, the older lawyer explained her situation to the firm's senior partners. Ultimately, the firm paid her retroactively for her extra hours. But Carol had had enough. She stopped overseeing cases, and instead took on research and litigation support projects for the firm. She continued to work as a "research drone," as she laughingly called herself, while her family grew, to four kids in all.

Carol's law firm made it clear she could return, for which she was grateful. But she knew climbing back on the partnership track would

require a punishing and unforgiving schedule. So with each passing year, she fell farther and farther behind the high-powered legal track she had started out on.

Younger lawyers started at the firm, zoomed past her, ended up making partner. Meanwhile, travel sports teams and carpooling and homework took up more and more of her time. Her vision of a powerful legal career, her once-promising professional future, was now a distant memory. Carol kept up that part-time work for eighteen years, hanging on to the hope of a fulfilling legal career. Finally, with four active teens at home, she quit altogether.

My own bosses, meanwhile, wouldn't let me fall off the track— even if I thought I wanted to. I loved my job, but with two young kids, I found my ambitions had changed. My dominant goal in life was now to get home in time for dinner with the kids, not to climb the next rung on the career ladder. Looking back now, I can see I was inadvertently mommy-tracking myself. My bosses, though, didn't see it that way.

After I spent a year or so on Page One, they offered me a promotion to become a bureau chief. I turned them down. I didn't want to lose the precious bit of flexibility I already had. They came back a year later and offered an opportunity for a management role in London. I said no again. Later they offered the chance to run a section of the newspaper. I still said no. For almost five years, my bosses offered me opportunities to advance. Each time, I declined.

Here's the extraordinary thing that I didn't appreciate at the time: they kept asking.

Most women are written off the first time they turn down an opportunity, or certainly the second time. But my bosses taught me one of the most valuable lessons I've ever learned, and that I have tried to carry with me as a manager myself. They were aware that I wanted time with my young children. But they never wanted to make that decision for me. They never considered me to be on the dead-

end mommy track, and as a result didn't allow me to put myself on it either.

After five years, with both children now in school, when Paul Steiger came back yet again and asked if I would be interested in creating a new section of the newspaper—one that ultimately became *Weekend Journal*—I said an emphatic yes.

My bosses were savvy enough to realize something that, at the time, I didn't: kids grow up.

In many meetings at different companies since then, I've heard someone suggest a woman for a plum role and a senior manager reply, "She's great, but she'll never want to move." Or, "She'd be perfect, but she has little kids. She wouldn't be able to travel."

Whether you're a man or a woman, if there's one thing you take away from this book, it is this: Don't decide for her. Let her make that choice on her own. To my bosses' great credit, they never made assumptions about me. Instead they said, "Here's an opportunity. You decide if you want to take it." If not for their foresightedness, I never would have had the opportunity to continue my career and kick it back up to high gear later, when the timing was right to do so.

What's more, don't assume that all women with children want to step back in the first place. Until a few years ago, Bain & Company, a consulting firm, recruited female prospects by spending as much as 70 percent of their conversations talking about flexibility and support for working mothers. The firm found that women resisted.

Like men, they "are joining to be the best and brightest," partner Julie Coffman told me. The firm still stresses its benefits for working women, just not as much. Now it focuses on career opportunities, just as it does for male recruits.

••

WHEN CHILDREN ARE babies, it seems as if those long sleepless nights full of tantrums and ear infections will never end. Time stretches

infinitely before you. But one day you wake up and find those infants are teenagers. You wonder how it all went by so fast.

That's what happened with Carol and me. Just yesterday, it seems, we were meeting for the first time in our freshman dorm. Now, seemingly defying all logic and sense of time, our own children started heading off to college. And Carol was ready to reengage at work.

The problem was, how to go back? She hadn't practiced law in years. But she was a quick study, and a friend helped her land a part-time job teaching a class at a local law school. That was satisfying, but it didn't last long; she had to give it up when she and her husband moved to St. Louis a few years later, for his new position as chair of the orthopedics department at Washington University.

In their new city, this one-time golden girl, the smartest kid in the class with the best work ethic you've ever seen, the woman who earned honors degrees from Yale and Harvard, found herself unknown and, for employers, unwanted. She applied to half a dozen different positions online.

She got zero replies. "Not a word. Not one word."

••

THE SAME SCENARIO has played out for so many women. In a poignant essay for the online tech magazine *Model View Culture*, Seonaid Lee, a physicist who stepped back to raise her kids, lamented that she was now "invisible" at age forty-three:

> *Stopping out or shifting to a part-time position is seen as failure, a sign that the person is not qualified for the work. Not only do colleagues left behind wind up believing this, but the person who has left does as well . . . We, who have stopped out, or walked away, or changed careers, presume that returning would be impossible.*

Lee took the specific steps career experts advise, including completing a program intended to refresh women's technology skills. It wasn't enough.

"I am repeatedly cautioned that I'm likely to have difficulties because of my age," she wrote. "My question is, why? I'm a far better developer than I was at 27. I can think more clearly and I have more experience to bring to my work. I can prioritize, juggle responsibilities, make reasonable estimates and meet deadlines. Yet my age and my non-linear work history, rather than being assets and a sign of creativity and resilience, are seen as non-starters."

She has plenty of company. So many women have renewed energy and ambition when their kids get older or leave for college. "Here's what working mothers are told again and again: The early years of your kids' lives are going to be tough. Suffering from sleep deprivation while trying to establish your career and get your kids off to a good start in life is no piece of cake," Wall Street veteran Sallie Krawcheck wrote in *Fortune* magazine.

"Now, here's the working mom secret they don't tell you: This empty-nest moment can be a career renaissance for women."

Unfortunately, too few companies and top executives are aware of this potential "career renaissance" that's there for the taking. Indeed, a 2005 study found that just 40 percent of women who try to return to full-time professions after raising children succeed in doing so; most find that their jobs, professional status, and work relationships have disappeared. What's more, a study of U.S. unemployment found that in 2012 to 2013, women over fifty made up half of all the long-term unemployed in this country—defined as those out of work for six months or more.

These women want to contribute. They've got the skills to do so. Yet just as they are ready to rev up their careers, to dive in with all the energy they had as a fresh college grad—only this time with the maturity and judgment that comes with experience—they are left behind. Ignored. Forgotten. They're the invisible women.

••

IT WILL TAKE men as well as women, working together, to change that dynamic, to take advantage of the untapped resources staring us right in the face: those millions of women struggling to stay on the career track or to climb back on it.

As a manager, I try to be vigilant on this front. I do my best to continue to offer opportunities both to parents of young children who may not raise their hands for new challenges, and to those who stepped back to focus on kids but are now ready to dive back in. I remember what I learned from my own male bosses: Just keep asking. Keep offering opportunities. Don't make the decision for her.

I know what a difference it made for me.

My husband and I are empty nesters now. We work as hard as ever—maybe harder. But this time there's no guilt. There's joy in pursuing careers that engage us. There's delight when we spend time with our kids. I am more grateful than ever to my male bosses who, two decades ago, understood far better than I did that this day would come.

Carol, meanwhile, continued looking for work. She taught herself coding through an online course. She sent out résumés. She was powered by all the energy she once expended on raising four kids. She had experience and hard-earned wisdom.

"I'm going to be so much better at everything so much more quickly than others would be. I should be hired immediately," she told me, months into her search. "I'm going to hit the ground running at whatever I do. I don't care what it is."

Yet employers still weren't biting. She sighed. "It's humbling."

••

THERE ARE A few encouraging rumblings of change. Dozens of companies now offer "returnships," for both men and women who have taken time off. Structured somewhat like internships, they offer training and ease participants back into the working world.

Goldman Sachs kicked off the idea in 2008. It offers a paid ten-week-long program for people who have been out of the workforce for more than two years. Other financial firms, including Morgan Stanley and Credit Suisse, have since jumped in with their own programs.

A mini-industry has sprung up to help, including iRelaunch, which has worked to create returnship programs with companies including General Motors, IBM, Johnson Controls, Caterpillar, Ford, and Johnson & Johnson. A nonprofit called Path Forward, launched in 2016, places returnees for stints at tech companies like GoDaddy and online educational platform Coursera.

The concept is spreading worldwide. Some twenty-three companies in the U.K. now offer similar programs; about 90 percent of the people who enroll are female. Meanwhile, organizations like ReBoot Career Accelerator offer workshops and seminars to women who are trying to return to the workplace.

These programs are still new, with a mixed track record. "Proceed with caution," warned a report on CNBC, the business network. Even the most selective of them don't necessarily lead to jobs. The Goldman Sachs class of 2013 chose 19 participants out of 1,000 applicants—yet only about half were ultimately offered positions at Goldman itself. But at least programs like this are a start.

More college placement centers are also getting involved in helping older alumni of both genders who have lost jobs or been out of the workforce for a long period of time. Many of these schools retooled their career placement efforts after the 2008 financial crisis, in order to help alums whose jobs had disappeared. When the University of Chicago School of Law offered a day of career counseling in 2009, the program filled up in twenty-four hours. Schools including the University of Michigan now offer career counseling to alums at any stage of life; it even offers career services and workshops specifically for women, through its Center for the Education of Women.

But if we are to truly address this challenge, it will take more than career counseling. It will take transforming workplace culture, reengineering it in ways that offer multiple paths to success.

One practical solution was proposed by a former consultant named Paulette Light. A classic overachiever, armed with degrees from Columbia and Harvard in addition to a Wharton M.B.A., she worked hundred-hour weeks and traveled frequently before she had the first of her four children. But finding it impossible to manage work and family, she quit, joining the 43 percent of high-achieving women who drop out after having children.

"Leaving the workforce was not easy for me," she later wrote in *The Atlantic*. "I spent many a mommygroup crying in the bathroom . . . I mourned my career, and the role where people listened to me, where there were right answers."

She volunteered, even starting a preschool and cofounding a synagogue. But she was eager to get back to work, and tried to do so as soon as her youngest entered kindergarten. Yet almost immediately, she hit a roadblock. Researching potential employers, she found plenty that offered lactation rooms, adoption assistance, and other perks for young moms—all of the modern-day accoutrements that are in line with our tunnel-vision focus on new parents. None of these companies, on the other hand, offered the kind of flexibility that mothers with older kids might need. Ultimately, she gave up, and cofounded her own company, MomStamp, a platform where moms can trade recommendations for providers like babysitters and summer camps.

Yet even as she builds her own company, she sees a clear solution that should be available to women like her, or anyone who steps back temporarily from a full-time career: project-based work, with clear deliverables and deadlines.

"If you want high-achieving mothers back in the workforce, don't give us an office and a work week filled with facetime, give us some-

thing to get done and tell us when you need it by," she wrote. "Consider the management, negotiation, budgeting skills we gained in our years out of the workforce and the skills that many of us never lost." Among other projects, she suggests returning parents could "do strategic analysis, build financial models, write legal briefs or PR pieces, generate blog posts or plan corporate conferences."

"Bring back the 43 percent into the workforce," she continued, in a cry to corporate America. "Help us add value—you just have to structure the job so that we can."

••

UNTIL CORPORATE AMERICA comes around and adopts these new ways of working, women like Light, locked out of the careers they once dominated, unable to fight their way back in, have little choice but to start all over again, often in entirely different fields. Like her, some go on to start their own businesses, what Krawcheck calls "third act" careers. Krawcheck herself, after being ousted from a high-profile senior position at Citigroup, went on to found Ellevest, a financial services firm for women with the slogan "Invest like a woman. Because money is power."

Other women turn toward philanthropy, like my friend Kathy Soll. Before she had kids, she ran a home furnishings design and licensing company. But after Jesse and Lauren were born, she became a full-time mom. Years later, when Lauren was in high school, Kathy looked toward the empty nest looming before her and knew she wanted to go back to work. But how? There was no clear path for women like her.

"What job would I do? What kind of company? I had no idea," she recalls. Ultimately, she began volunteering with an organization devoted to public service for kids. That led her and a friend to launch their own nonprofit, Teens for Food Justice, which teaches New York City youths to become urban farmers. It now employs an expanding staff, and operates student-led farms in city schools, each of which

grows twenty-two thousand pounds of fresh produce a year. "The idea of building something with meaning was what I thought about," she told me. "I wanted to build something that outlasts me."

Kathy had the skills and determination to forge her own path. She wanted to create something new. But highly skilled women like her who want to join existing firms wouldn't get even a first glance by most employers. And even those who do succeed in creating a "career renaissance" will likely never regain their lost earning power. If they have a spouse who can cover the financial loss, or they have saved up from lucrative earlier careers, they have a cushion. But many women, especially those who are divorced, widowed, or no longer partnered, don't have that option.

••

AS FOR MY friend Carol, she continued her search, determined to find work, facing rejection or something far worse—silence. Being ignored.

Finally, six months into her search, she got a bite and landed a contract job at a law firm as a document reviewer—the lowest of the low among lawyers. Months later, the firm hired her as an associate. She's starting from the beginning all over again, even retaking the bar exam. But she's delighted with what she's got, telling me—in a sentence that has probably never been uttered before in history— "I'm having a lot of fun working on foreign exchange fraud cases!"

Carol's employers were smart to hire her and fortunate to have her. But at a time when women earn more than half of college and advanced degrees, when they are trying desperately to bring those skills to a marketplace where such skills are badly needed, why should it be so difficult? The fact is that by working together, men and women can and must attack the heart of the problem, starting with lousy maternity-leave policies, bias against working moms, and loss of earning power if they leave the workforce temporarily,

and culminating in the inability to get back on track when they do return.

By working together we can put smart policies in place to counter every one of these challenges. We can offer opportunities to women who may be stagnating on the mommy track. We can create flexible, project-based jobs for women—and men—who want to stay connected to the workplace. We can hold our companies accountable for paying moms and dads equally.

Each of these strategies has been proven to work, to get results. We simply need to keep pushing, to implement them more widely, and ultimately to transform the workplace culture in a way that will benefit men as much as women.

I'm thrilled that my brilliant friend Carol has finally landed back where she belongs. But there are tens of thousands of women like her still out there. Every day, more women are returning to the job hunt. They bring wisdom and judgment to spare. They are our best hope at growing the economy. They may well be this country's greatest untapped resource. And yet they still struggle for far too long, and fail to find meaningful jobs far too often.

It's about time to make the invisible woman visible again. Together, we can.

9

The Next Generation: The Harvard Experiment

On a chilly November day, I traveled to Cambridge, Massachusetts, to the hushed campus of Harvard Business School. Passing by empty tennis courts, I found my way to the Spangler student center. I was here to meet with members of a new men's student group called, unironically, the Manbassadors. The name is hilarious, but the goal couldn't be more earnest: to support gender equity at work and at home.

By now, I had watched as symphony orchestras, companies, even entire countries, experimented with every way imaginable to narrow the gender gap. Blind auditions. Bias training. Quotas. There seemed to be nothing they hadn't attempted. And yet the gap still stubbornly yawns between us. The problem, as was becoming increasingly clear, is that by the time most of us reach the workplace it's already too late. Bias is established long before we ever get our first jobs.

That's what brought me to Harvard. The school had posed an intriguing question: What would happen if you tried to start the clock earlier, to eliminate biases before letting students loose in the world? In search of a solution, the school had launched one of the most ambitious experiments yet in social engineering.

In 2013, writer Jodi Kantor chronicled the beginning of this grand plan in the *New York Times*. Several years earlier, Harvard

Business School had upended its curriculum, changing courses and requirements, with an audacious goal: to create an environment that would eliminate gender bias and encourage success for its female graduates—and its female faculty.

The experiment meant blowing up an ingrained social and academic culture. Class participation counted for 50 percent of grades, yet discussions were typically dominated by men. At night, to blow off steam, some of the men played a drinking game rating female classmates on a scale of "F——, Marry or Kill."

To change things up, Harvard installed note takers in class, in part so that professors wouldn't forget when a woman had spoken up. It introduced a new course called "Field" that required group problem-solving rather than focusing on individual contributions, which often seemed to favor men. Students got coaching on how to raise their hands, to make sure that women and introverted male students didn't get lost in the crowd. Harvard worked as well with female faculty, who were far less likely than their male peers to get tenure.

The experiment succeeded in some ways: women participated more in class and won more academic awards than before. But by one important measure it failed: some of the men rebelled. One described it in the *Times* as "patronizing." Echoing the older male executives I had met who bristled at diversity training, some students complained that the gender message was "shoved down our throats."

I was curious, though, about what had happened since. Was the experiment ultimately a success? Would the lessons the school taught its students stick with them in the workplace? Or would they be forgotten? In short, could early intervention, exposing students to a meticulously designed curriculum intended to even the playing field, pay off for everyone?

••

YOUNG MEN HAVE played an outsize role in the misogynistic "bro cultures" of Silicon Valley and Wall Street. Yet there's also ample evidence that on the whole, their generation of millennials has a more equitable view of the world than that of their elders.

Millennial men, between the ages of eighteen and thirty-five, are more likely than those in other generations to favor an egalitarian relationship between husbands and wives. What's more, when Deloitte asked millennials of both genders what qualities were most important in a career, the top choice was "good work/life balance," outranking more conventional aspirations like opportunities for promotion, leadership, and even deriving meaning from work.

In part this is because the men, largely children of working mothers, have a different perspective than that of their fathers and grandfathers before them. In part it's because the women, raised on "you go, girl" huzzahs, won't put up with it any other way. And perhaps most of all, it's because of the twenty-four/seven work culture that has burned out men and women alike. Seeing how their parents work, attached to their devices and at the beck and call of their offices, young adults are saying enough.

I've noticed the phenomenon myself. Years ago, when one of my colleagues took paternity leave, our coworkers were astonished—and skeptical. They were pretty sure he was just goofing off or maybe stealthily looking for another job. Back then, when I interviewed men for job openings, they never talked about wives or children; the topic simply didn't come up.

Fast-forward to now, and virtually every young father I interview for openings stresses the importance of family time. Almost all tell me they need to discuss a potential new position with their wives— ironic, considering that few women these days would dare suggest they need to check about a job with their husbands.

Nor do the female job candidates I meet explain the intricacies of how they split child care with their spouses, as the young fathers I

interview often do. It's the men, not the women, who ask if they will have the flexibility to spend time with their children, to coach soccer, to occasionally work at home. For the men, it's a point of pride. For the women, it's still considered a sign of weakness.

That attitude is even stronger for the youngest adult men, those eighteen to twenty-five. They overwhelmingly disagree with the notion that men should be the breadwinner and women should take care of the home. This isn't just a Harvard phenomenon. Nor is it one that is unique to business schools or to highly educated men. It signals a generational shift, among men from every walk of life, that may well have a profound influence on gender relations going forward.

To see how it's playing out—and to get a sense of whether those attitudes will stick—I hurried up the stairs to a second-floor conference room to meet with the Manbassador leaders. As the group's stated mission—to engage men "in a productive, ongoing conversation about gender issues"—suggests, on the whole, Harvard Business School (HBS) students are a self-serious lot. Professors, and the school's own website, state unequivocally that their goal is to create future global leaders.

"Our mission is to educate leaders who will make a difference in the world," one of the deans told me. The school's "definition of leadership is about making others better as a result of your presence, and having it last after your absence."

Several students described a social life that is as intense as any of their studies. Romance is calculated, with an almost artisanal obsession for detail. "By date three, they had to decide whether this was their life partner or not," one recent male grad explained. "It's the type of personality drawn to HBS." The students approach their clubs just as purposefully. Each class of about nine hundred is broken into ten sections, and in each section those students vie to become representatives of various clubs—including the Manbassadors.

The group's origin dates back to a conversation between two friends. In 2013, then-student Tara Hagan noticed that the men on campus sometimes had trouble relating to their female classmates. Women are still a minority at business schools. They made up just 41 percent of HBS students in 2016—and that figure itself was a historic high. Hagan was particularly struck by a comment made by one of her close male friends.

"If you're a man, you've never talked about gender before," he had told her. "But what is my role? What am I supposed to contribute? I don't know what to say. I'm afraid of being politically incorrect."

Hagan realized that, while HBS may attract students with great test scores and enormous ambition, the men here were in one respect no different than men anywhere else: they were scared out of their wits to talk about gender. From that revelation came the spark of an idea: create a club affiliated with the women's student group, but made up of men.

It was a eureka moment. Still, even Hagan, who became one of its founders, was uncertain the idea would work. "I was scared," she acknowledges. "I was afraid . . . people would think it was lame."

She needn't have worried. The day of the school's club sign-up fair, she arrived with nothing more than a laptop and a poster. By the time she left, a hundred people had signed up.

Not long afterward, thirty male students gathered in a classroom. One by one, they spoke up, going around the room to explain why they were there. One had watched as his mother struggled at work. Another saw that his sister didn't have the same opportunities as he did. It gave Hagan chills as she heard each classmate tell his tale. The Manbassadors had arrived.

The club has gained considerable traction since then. These days, about 40 percent of HBS's male students join the Manbassadors, and the movement is spreading. In the last couple of years, similar men's groups have formed on other business school campuses, including at

Wharton, Stanford, Columbia, UCLA, Duke, the University of Chicago, and the University of Michigan.

The group hosts events, like work–life balance conversations, with prominent HBS graduates and their spouses. Its members identify themselves with tastefully understated gray Manbassadors T-shirts. The first version of the shirt was hot pink, emblazoned with Thomas Jefferson's quote "Men of quality are not threatened by women of equality." But "no one wore them," Hagan told me. "That was a lesson," she said. "Baby steps."

Inside the conference room, I was greeted by one of the Manbassadors' cochairs, Sam Travers. Soft-spoken and serious, wearing a maroon sweater over his plaid button-down shirt, Sam had worked at the Department of Defense before coming to Harvard. He was also among the minority of students who were married. His wife was in law school, and one of the issues the couple discussed frequently was how they would someday balance work and family.

"Before HBS, I wouldn't have thought to join a women's advocacy network at work," he told me. But the discussions with his wife, along with his previous job experience, where "I was lucky to have female mentors and managers," made him more aware of the issues facing women. "So coming to HBS, I was excited to see a community of men and women who can talk about these issues, about work–life balance."

Sam is similar to many millennial men in that, like others in his generation, he expects to have an equal marriage with his wife and a balanced life for them both. Sam and other male students I met were confident that those ideals were within reach.

At job interviews, Sam told me, he always asked about paternity leave policies. His wife "is told this information as part of the standard package for female applicants," he said, yet prospective employers were often surprised by his question. "I've had people give me credit for asking, and they say, 'Your wife must be proud of you.'" He couldn't figure out why there's such a double standard:

"There's no such thing as a man's or a woman's issue. Everything is interconnected."

Sitting beside Sam was another Manbassador, Matt Simpson, fashionably bearded and sipping takeout coffee. Matt, like Sam, had a female boss before he entered business school, in his post-collegiate job at a consulting firm. Through her, he learned "issues I wasn't aware of," like pressures his boss felt to "keep it all business." He was astonished "that a woman who was that great a leader would feel pressure to 'act like a guy.'" It made him realize "there's little things men don't pick up on . . . little subconscious behaviors, like men are more likely to listen to another guy . . . Just being aware of it makes you more mindful."

I was struck by how easily Sam and Matt spoke about gender, far more easily than most older men I knew. They weren't self-conscious or hesitant. They volunteered that they had become attuned to small slights, like women being interrupted in discussions. They talked about commonsense actions they now took, like calling out when a woman's idea was attributed to a man. Unlike their elders, they didn't reflexively gag and turn ashen when the topic turned to gender.

"Here, I've been able to help engage. It doesn't have to be a formal thing," as Matt put it. "You can talk about it with your buddies having a beer."

The men were certainly sincere. And yet, as optimistic as they were about this new world, the truth is that neither HBS nor the business world it trains its students to conquer has caught up with them. That became clear when a female classmate joined the conversation. She noted that in one of her classes, the discussion revolved around making technology so simple "your mom or sister or grandma" could use it, while in another, hypothetical business leaders were described "using male pronouns."

The latter reflects an unfortunate reality: only 9 percent of HBS case studies—the course material students read about real-life

executives—focus on female leaders. That trend holds true across all top business schools; one analysis found that 90 percent of business-school case studies are about men.

Both Sam and Matt fully expected to become leaders as they went forth into the world, just as HBS was preparing them to do. And when they got there, they told me, they would remember the lessons learned here. They expected to be great bosses . . . to the women who will work for them.

"When I think of opportunities three, ten, twenty years out of HBS," Sam reflected, "improving gender equality will be a huge part of making sure the women I've mentored will be able to succeed."

••

THE STUDENTS SEEMED so sure of themselves. I wondered if their professors were as optimistic. So taking leave of the Manbassadors, I headed toward the office of Robin Ely, a senior associate dean who runs the school's Gender Initiative. The initiative, created in 2015 as a center for research on female leadership, is Harvard's flag in the sand. It's a shout-out to the world that it is serious about closing the gender gap. If anyone could take the temperature of gender relations on campus, it would be Ely.

A petite woman with spiky blond hair and pink glasses, Ely ushered me into her office, comfortably crammed with overstuffed bookshelves, award plaques casually propped against paperbacks, and an unwieldly pile of papers obscuring her desk. A scholar of race and gender relations, she has studied everything from masculinity (by observing men on drilling rigs) to women's leadership programs. Her latest research was on the "double bind" women face: the more competent and powerful a woman is, the less she is liked.

Ely herself is quite powerful—though it's been a long road to get there. When she first landed at Harvard Business School in 2000, she planned to teach a course on diversity. No one signed up. Students

didn't want to talk about race and gender; they were at HBS to learn to be successful, to crush the competition, to win—not to take lessons in sensitivity training.

Frustrated, Ely rethought her approach. She hit upon a new idea for a course. This time, she included some of the same material about diversity, but cloaked in a different guise. Her new class was about "power and influence." It became an overnight sensation.

"I'd throw in issues of race and gender," she said, laughing.

Still, she had a hard time engaging students more deeply than that. They didn't see how getting ahead bore any relationship to diversity. "Nobody was picking up on it, or beating my door down like in other places, wanting to have these conversations," Ely said, recalling her frustration. "Why aren't we talking about this? I can't get anybody to bite in terms of the topic."

Since those early days, the atmosphere has "really changed dramatically," Ely told me. The steps HBS has taken have helped, she said. The proportion of female students has grown, and a quarter of students are ethnic minorities. But there's more to it than that. "Part of it is the zeitgeist. Clearly the world was wanting to have a conversation."

Even so, Harvard Business School's faculty still remains overwhelmingly male. Women make up only about a quarter of the school's professors. Female junior faculty often fare poorly, and turnover among them has been alarmingly high. A 2012 faculty climate survey found that male faculty members were far happier than their female counterparts.

Women have been so lacking—in classrooms, in case studies, in academic leadership—that in a 2015 meeting with female alums, Dean Nitin Nohria apologized, saying women at times had been "disrespected, left out, and unloved by the school." The school needed to walk the walk itself if it had any hope of trying to transform the culture for its students.

A few years ago, Frances Frei, a senior associate dean, dug into the dismal female faculty numbers herself. She found, to her consternation, that HBS was hiring men at twice the rate of women. What's more, it was promoting those men at twice the rate of the women, and making lateral hires of men from competing universities at *ten times* the rate as for women.

Drilling down behind the numbers, she found that one major problem was that women were disproportionately rejecting offers to join Harvard's faculty in the first place. Often they cited family issues, such as having a trailing spouse who needed to find a job in a new city, or having a young child and being unable to travel for research.

The unequal rate of promotions was perhaps even more troubling. At first Frei suspected unconscious bias against women. But her analysis revealed a surprise: the male scholars were publishing more frequently than the women, with more citations of their work, making them objectively more qualified for promotions. In an environment where "our sport is writing," as she pointed out, if you don't write, you don't win. The men were simply better qualified than the women.

"On the one hand, I was like, f——!" she said of her findings. "On the other hand, I was deeply relieved. I was like, let's ask the question: Why are men more prepared than women?"

What she found was that the men were no smarter or better prepared than the women—but they were far more confident when it came to submitting papers. Women kept trying to make their work better; they never felt it was quite good enough. The men suffered no such illusions. When they submitted papers, the men welcomed the feedback and review process as a way to improve their work. Not so the women; if their papers weren't perfect, they felt they were being a burden.

You wouldn't think *any* faculty members at HBS would suffer from

a lack of confidence. The place holds itself in such high regard that it borders on—some would say crosses the line into—arrogance. Yet Frei's findings at HBS reflect what researchers have discovered about women everywhere else. Numerous studies have concluded that men are overconfident about their own abilities, while women are under-confident about theirs. A study of trial lawyers, for example, found that female lawyers are less satisfied than male lawyers with their arguments to juries, regardless of results.

In academia, that tendency is even more pronounced. Academic citations are considered an important measure of influence. But a recent study found that men frequently cite *themselves.* By pumping up the number of citations, they create the illusion of widespread recognition, and increase their perceived level of authority and influence. That translates directly into professional recognition and rewards. The tactic has grown over the last two decades, with men citing themselves 70 percent more frequently than do women.

Meanwhile, if a paper is rejected, it hits women far harder than men. Researchers have found that women, even those who have made it to the pinnacle of academic success at HBS, need more out-side affirmation of their value than men do. KPMG commissioned a study of more than three thousand professional women and college-age women. It found that when it came to self-esteem and a woman's estimation of how she was performing, a boss's praise is more mean-ingful than even a raise or a promotion.

Lack of praise—or worse, rejection—can be professionally dev-astating. And as journalists Katty Kay and Claire Shipman noted in their book *The Confidence Code*, "confidence is more important than ability when it comes to getting ahead."

That's exactly what was happening at HBS. "Women were such perfectionists that they wouldn't send their papers out," Frei said, "or if they got a little bit of bad news, they faded away."

So now, HBS leaders are on the lookout for the syndrome. They

jump in early to encourage female academics to publish. The school also installed video cameras in the back of classrooms, so that professors could review their teaching and catch their own misfires—annoying ticks, or a boring stretch when they lost the room—and learn how to make improvements.

Ironically, though, the recordings ended up helping male professors—while hurting female professors. For the women, it made them "that much more self-conscious," Frei said. "It derails her teaching. It turns out it's a terrible idea for many women, and made it worse."

I can relate. I once was asked to substitute as an anchor for a cable television news program. In advance, network trainers taught me to read a teleprompter, taping the sessions so I could review them before I went on air. A male friend was also asked to substitute, and given the same training. He spent an entire week scrutinizing and deconstructing his tapes. Meanwhile, I couldn't bear to look at mine. I still haven't. You can guess who performed better on live TV.

HBS also provides one-on-one coaching for professors who need to improve their classroom performance—but that too sometimes has the reverse effect. In the business school's cafeteria, a haven of paneled walls and honeyed wooden tables, I sat down with Meg Rithmire, one of the most popular young professors at HBS. With shoulder-length blond hair and wearing horn-rimmed glasses and a slouchy sweater, she could easily be mistaken for a student. A specialist in the Chinese economy, she was an acknowledged star among the older professors with whom I spoke. As we chatted, she munched on an apple and explained that she was putting the finishing touches on a book. She had just returned from a research trip to Asia, which HBS had helped make possible by arranging for her husband and baby to travel with her.

But she also was highly aware of her female peers who hadn't had the same degree of immediate success—and she noted that even if they

recover after a rough start, it's hard for women to overcome that first impression. "I have friends who did poorly the first year, then phenomenally," she said. "But in the eyes of their department, they're still not a player." That too is true for the rest of the world; women's mistakes are noticed more, and remembered longer, than those of men.

Another issue for female faculty, she noted, is that women are expected to mentor other women, whether or not their skill sets, teaching styles, or academic specialties line up—which in turn takes time away from research and publishing. "I don't have the time to be a mentor to every woman in the office," she said.

"There's a weird thing: there's a lot of discussion about mentorship. When I was in grad school there was a movement to have every woman have a woman mentor," she added. "I thought that was hilarious. Why? You should have a professional mentor."

Rithmire is critical of the "Lean In" movement, which encourages women to support one another. It's "done more harm than good," Rithmire said. "The expectation is women have to take care of one another—and meanwhile, my male colleague is publishing articles."

The time that women spend mentoring other women, or sitting on multiple departmental panels because there are so few women to choose from, hurts them professionally by taking precious hours away from their core jobs, in her view. "In finance, academia, business, law, we're being judged on our productivity during our reproductive years," she said, as we rose to leave. "It isn't going to be solved by a bunch of women leaning in."

Rithmire echoed a frustration I've heard from other women in a variety of industries. Senior women are so scarce that they are often tapped to sit on every committee, to represent their organizations at conferences, to be the public face for recruiting, and to mentor other women. All of which prevents these women from actually doing their jobs.

That, in turn, points up how essential it is to include men if we are to equalize the workplace. Men can be mentors as well as women, and men can advocate just as forcefully for equality. Women simply can't do it all on their own. By putting the burden on the very few of them to be the symbol and the savior of all women, we can unwittingly set them on a path to failure.

••

ON THE TRAIN back from Cambridge, I reflected on those conversations. The school had succeeded, somewhat, in leveling the gender playing field. But ultimately, is Harvard Business School's approach working? Perhaps HBS's recent graduates, those who had been fully indoctrinated into its gender-leveling approach, could provide some answers.

And so, back to New York City I went, in search of graduates from the class of 2013, the one so vividly profiled in the *Times*.

I soon found my way to Jennifer Braus. Trained as an engineer, Braus was an all-American soccer player in college, and one of the few among her female Harvard classmates to choose a career in finance.

In a class already made up of stars, Braus was a standout. After graduation, she was one of the few students in her class—and the only woman—to attract a financial investment from two professors who backed her to start a highly competitive "search fund," a pool of money with which to identify and acquire companies. Search funds are the shiniest, most prestigious brass rings a grad can grab. Simply attracting funding means your backers have rock-solid confidence in you. It's the fastest way to run your own business as an owner and chief executive officer. She and her husband promptly moved to Seattle, where she began searching for a business to buy.

As far as she was concerned, Harvard "did a pretty good job" at maintaining gender equality while she was there: "I never felt dis-

respected, and felt that everyone was very professional and my professors were excellent."

But the real world has been a different story. Running a search fund means dealing with business brokers, intermediaries who represent companies that are for sale. And the brokers, almost all of them men, have sometimes left her speechless with their comments.

"One guy asked me if my husband knew what I'm doing," she told me. Others assumed her husband was in charge, asking in surprise, "*You* are going to run the business?" When they learned that yes, she was, they'd ask, "'What's your husband going to do?' I say, 'Look, you don't ask that for anyone else.' Why is everyone so concerned about my husband?"

She added, "I've asked my male peers, and never once was anyone asked if their wife is going to help run the business."

Then there's Kunal Modi, who was class copresident back then. As a student, he had written the *Huffington Post* piece urging men to "man up" and participate in the fight for gender equality at work, at home. and at the ballot box. As he wrote at the time, "Men, just as equally as women, must take ownership of these family issues, which are core to American economic competitiveness."

After graduation, he became a management consultant. He told me the school's focus on gender equality did indeed stick with him. "Men need to do more to step up. Men have a real stake in this personally. We won't be the type of husbands and fathers we want to be if we aren't cognizant of these issues."

Still, as hard as he has tried to hold on to those ideals, reality keeps getting in the way. Sometimes he notices the unintentional slight—the woman being cut off in conversation, or her ideas credited to a man—but it's tricky when you're the new guy, not the boss: "It's hard for a junior woman or man at work to say to a senior executive, 'That thing you said is boneheaded.'"

Modi remains hopeful, he told me, but he sees how much work

remains to be done. By his estimate, "Ten percent of guys are totally onboard and supportive. Ten percent of guys are going to be Neanderthals and boneheaded. We've got to figure out the 80 percent of guys in the middle, who generally are for creating equal environments, where talent rises to the top. How do we reach them and help them understand that the status quo is a biased one?"

I'm reminded of something Frances Frei had told me earlier. There's still sometimes a disconnect, she said, between the bubble of Harvard Business School and the world outside its walls. She admitted some students are jolted when they leave HBS with the best of intentions and come smack face-to-face with reality.

"How dare you make it such a great cocoon!" some former students scolded her. "You didn't prepare us for the harshness of the world."

It's an almost impossible conundrum. Harvard Business School is relentlessly focused on its stated goal, of creating the leaders of tomorrow. What it isn't focused on is the more immediate issue: creating the junior employees of today.

How do you expect your students to change the world when they aren't in charge? How do they empower others when they have no power themselves? The realization hit me: Harvard and other schools need to prepare not just for leadership down the road, but for how to navigate, and change, the real world right now, as—dare I say it—junior staffers. It has yet to crack that code.

Frei was sure HBS was on the right path. She was certain she saw a change in her male students that would last beyond graduation.

"Oh yes," she said emphatically, when I asked whether the lessons of HBS will stick. "I'm a crazy optimist, but I do believe in ten years, gender won't be the obstacle to meritocracy that we're obsessed with now. Something else will take its place.

"The reason I'm optimistic," she added, "is I see the millennials. They are different than any group I've ever seen. Gender doesn't occur to them. They aren't self-conscious about gender in a way that every other class was conscious of their gender. They're conscious

about many other things, but gender doesn't seem nearly as high on their list."

I'd like to believe that these men and the younger men coming along behind them will bring about meaningful change. At the same time, the evidence so far suggests that millennial men's youthful idealism will fade with age and responsibility. The forces of the culture we live in are powerful and difficult for a single generation to transform.

As these young men grow older, marry, have children, and take on mortgages, their attitudes change. A study by the Families and Work Institute found that just a third of millennial men without kids think they should be primary breadwinners—but that figure spikes to 53 percent for those who have kids. And a study published in *American Sociological Review* found that while both young men and women have egalitarian views, they change their attitudes when faced with inflexible workplaces and lack of family-friendly policies.

At Harvard Business School, male grads so far have trod an exceedingly traditional path. A 2014 survey found that half of its male millennial grads still expect their careers will take priority over that of their wives. What's more, two-thirds assume their wives will deal with the kids, taking on the majority of child care. Yet only a minority of their female classmates agree with either of those assumptions—a potentially explosive land mine for both men and women down the road as they marry and have children.

I saw an inkling of that gender divide while on campus. The investment clubs were still almost all male. Few female HBS grads end up in the lucrative and presitigious world of venture capital. And the business leaders who visit the campus only reinforce the gap. One new grad told me about the finance executive who came to lecture his class and told them point-blank that "if you're a woman and you want to have a baby, it will be hard to be a banker at this bank."

••

THE HBS CLASS of 2013 that Kantor wrote about in the *Times* is now well on their way toward the leadership roles the school groomed them to obtain. Brooke Boyarsky, who was one of that year's standout students—a George F. Baker Scholar, awarded to the top 5 percent of students in the class, and chosen by her peers to speak at graduation week—went on to become a consultant at McKinsey. Looking back on her time at HBS, she is philosophical about how lasting the emphasis on gender will be.

"The group of people who would have been passionate about these issues have gone on to be more passionate, and many are men," she told me. "I can say my male friends at HBS who I now work with . . . they have been huge supporters. The men have stayed involved, which is a good sign."

But she is realistic. "HBS isn't a miracle. I don't know that it made everyone a warrior for women."

••

HER WORDS GOT me thinking back to the Manbassadors. With the club now fully established, I wondered how its original founders were faring. Surely, they'd still be activists. After all, they were the most vocal students, the ones who led the way in the pursuit of gender equality.

So I searched out Tara Hagan, whose conversation with a perplexed male friend helped spark the club that sparked a movement.

After her 2014 graduation, Hagan had joined a large advertising agency. When we spoke a year later, she told me her male boss was terrific. Of course there were times when he used male pronouns by default, as if assuming everyone of importance is a man. But she didn't feel it was her place to point that out.

"At HBS it's about making you better leaders, so being inclusive makes you a better leader," she said. "But if I'm in advertising, I can't necessarily say that understanding diversity is going to make a

better ad product. It's harder to tie in. I can't say, 'Let's use female pronouns because that will win us an award.'"

And what of her activism on behalf of gender issues? "In HBS it's cool to brand yourself as a feminist," she said. "At work, I'm pretty sure women are feminists. But I feel like I shouldn't broadcast it, because it could be off-putting to my coworkers."

Then she told me something that left me wide-eyed with surprise.

"I don't even tell my coworkers I did Manbassadors, because it's so weird," she confessed. "Part of me is torn. [With] all this experience at HBS, I should go into the corporate world" and bring along that sensitivity to gender issues, "but it's kind of intimidating."

The corporate pecking order simply doesn't lend itself to the kind of conversations fostered at HBS. At school, "you're all peers. There's no set hierarchy," she explained. "Whereas in a corporate structure, you're new on the job and you can't really change a culture of a corporation. It's tougher in the workplace."

••

MILLENNIALS AND THEIR younger siblings may yet change the dynamics between women and men. But as Hagan and her colleagues have already found, it will take hard work. Despite the best efforts of Harvard Business School, the future business leaders of tomorrow are still running splat into the brick wall of institutional sexism of today.

To effect real change, these young men and women will need to shed the bad habits of their elders, and stay focused on breaking the cycle of unequal pay, promotions, and respect. They will need to work together to keep pushing for family-friendly policies and to fight for equality, at work and at home.

For her part, Tara Hagan is still trying to do just that.

Two years after our first conversation, I checked in with her again to ask if workplace culture had progressed. Not so much, she

admitted. "It's just insanely hard to get real change and improvement at the top."

Yet she also told me about strategies she has devised that are making a difference. She works with simpatico clients who feel as strongly as she does about diversity. She uses humor to defuse sexist behavior. And she is already mentoring the next generation. That's what gives her hope for the future.

"I have a handful of awesome women on my teams," she told me, "that I'm grooming, that I see growing. They're awesome."

10

The Best Place in the World to Be a Woman?

"Woman"
When all has been said
When the problems of the world
Have been weighed gauged and settled
When eyes have met
And hands been pressed
In the sobriety of the moment
—some woman always comes
To clear the table
Sweep the floor and open the windows
To let out the cigar smoke.
It never fails.
ICELANDIC POET INGIBJÖRG HARALDSDÓTTIR (1983)

I crane my neck up toward the top of the monolith in front of me. Inside a tall glass cylinder rising up from the floor, suspended in clear fluid, is what must be the world's largest penis. Erect and standing on end, it's taller than I am.

I glance to my left and then to my right. Everywhere I look, there are more of them. Huge ones, medium-size ones, tiny ones, hung

from the walls, hanging from the ceiling, and sprouting from the floor. It's a forest of phalluses.

I shake my head, bewildered. Is this a hallucination? A delusion born of jet lag?

No. It's Iceland. I'm in what is billed as the world's only penis museum. It boasts 285 specimens, from the massive sperm whale member in front of me down to tiny hamster and field mouse appendages. There are ancient carved phalluses behind glass, lampshades and bow ties made out of whale foreskins, and letters hanging on the wall from men who have proudly pledged their organs to the museum after they die. One case prominently displays silver casts of more than a dozen human penises, with a photo above that helpfully identifies their owners: the Icelandic National Handball Team, pictured (in uniform, thankfully) after winning the silver medal in the 2008 Beijing Olympics.

Perhaps it's fitting that this museum is in the heart of Reykjavik, the country's capital. Iceland remains one of the most masculine cultures in the world. This is a country that takes its Viking roots seriously, from the axes in the souvenir shops to the statue of explorer Leif Erikson standing guard over the brazenly phallic tower of the Church of Iceland.

On the way in from the airport, I had been mesmerized by the harsh landscape of pocked black rock stretching for miles beyond the bus window. It turns out Iceland's terrain of volcanoes and geysers is so rugged, so otherworldly, that Neil Armstrong and his fellow Apollo astronauts trained here before walking on the moon.

The people I meet here are at least as tough. I'd found myself in the museum—officially the Icelandic Phallological Museum—only after ducking in to escape the freezing rain and gusting winds. The Icelanders strolling the streets didn't seem to notice. Not one carried an umbrella, an accessory that is apparently a mark of humiliating weakness. The pleasant young clerk at the hotel front desk had

shooed me outside half an hour earlier, assuring me, without irony, "It's a beautiful day for a walk."

Yet I'm here because Iceland by some measures is the best place in the world to be a woman. For eight consecutive years, the World Economic Forum has ranked it the number-one country on the planet for gender equality. That puts it ahead of 144 other countries, including the U.S., which came in a disappointing forty-fifth, well behind Rwanda and Burundi.

Iceland's men are famously supportive of feminism. When the United Nations introduced an initiative called HeForShe in 2014, to enlist men to support women's equality, Icelandic men trumped those of every other nation. One in 20 of them—some 35,000—signed on, a percentage that, if replicated in the U.S., would work out to about 16 million men.

I had to travel here to understand why. How did this tiny island nation figure out how to solve a problem that has bedeviled the rest of the world for centuries? Are Icelandic men different than men everywhere else? What secrets might they impart?

Most of all I wanted to know: What does true gender equality feel like?

The curious thing about this number-one ranking, I couldn't help but notice, was the speed with which it happened. Iceland and other Nordic countries have long clustered in the upper reaches of such lists. But Iceland leapfrogged over the others quite quickly to claim the top spot.

Perhaps, I thought, it could show the rest of the world how to transform a culture, and to do so swiftly. Maybe it had finally cracked the code of how the rest of us can make great strides to close the gender gap too. After all, Iceland had begun its race to the top of the gender-equality rankings only after 2008.

It turns out that date was no accident.

••

IN SEPTEMBER 2008, the world economy crashed. The meltdown was the worst since the Great Depression. In the U.S., the stock market plunged. The banking system was forced to its knees. People's retirement savings were wiped out, their jobs lost, and their homes suddenly worth less than the mortgages that they could no longer afford to pay anyway.

But if there was anything that could make Americans feel a tiny bit better about the crisis at home, it was the thought that hey, at least we weren't Iceland. Because in Iceland the damage was far worse.

No country crashed harder than Iceland after the crisis. That's because no country behaved so insanely before it. Convinced that they could do anything Wall Street financiers could do, a nation of fishermen and sheep farmers became international bankers and currency traders.

"Business Vikings," they were called, with pride. They donned bespoke suits from London, collected gorgeous girlfriends who wore furs and jewels instead of snow boots and parkas, and plowed their Range Rovers—once a rarity in this land of humble compact cars— through Reykjavik's narrow streets.

They were virtually all men. Young men.

"They were all heroes in the eyes of Icelandic people. We had the 'geniuses' that were conquering the world," Jón Steinar Gunnlaugsson, who was a Supreme Court justice during the boom years, told me when I visited him in his modest post-crash law office, near the waterfront. He sounded almost wistful. "Maybe one of the reasons for this tragedy in the Icelandic economy was those guys were too much tough guys."

When Icelanders talk about the boom years, you encounter that kind of muscular imagery a lot. Conquerers. Vikings. Marauders. The banking system was like a "Viking ship," as a government report described it. "Icelanders are risk takers. They are daring and aggressive," the country's president, Ólafur Ragnar Grímsson, proudly told an audience at London's tony Walbrook dining club in 2005.

It was a message he repeated in countless talks from Wall Street to London to Asia to the World Economic Forum meetings in Davos. Like Vikings on the high seas, Iceland's bankers were young, energetic, quick decision-makers—and ruthless, conquering everything in their paths. What's more, the bankers not only threw cash around themselves. They lavished it on others, handing out bank loans to almost anyone who asked. The rise of these new Vikings lifted all boats, quite literally.

••

BACK AT MY hotel, after a rain-swept trot from the Phallological Museum, I meet Gunnar Sigurdsson. A grizzled fifty-six-year-old with an impish smile and a wicked sense of humor, he, like most men I meet here, is a fisherman. Or, I should say, *was* a fisherman. When the banking boom erupted, he was able to pursue his real dream: to become a theater director.

He borrowed money and funded a theater company. He borrowed more money and bought a two-bedroom flat in a good neighborhood. He leased a Nissan sedan. He took out his loans in euros and yen, like other Icelanders; the theory was that the value of the Icelandic krona was rising so fast that it was cheaper and smarter to pay off debt pegged to other, less-vaunted currencies. If you were to look at a chart of Iceland's national debt from 2001 to 2008, you would see a pretty much vertical line, shooting straight up.

Gunnar may not have realized it, but his good fortune was the result of a regulation change in 2003, when Iceland privatized its three state-owned banks. Before then, bankers made a tidy but unremarkable living lending to local fishermen, sheep farmers, and the people who sold Icelandic sweaters to tourists. They knew their customers personally. After all, most of them were relatives.

Iceland is home to only about 320,000 people. It's so homogeneous that scientists famously use it as a petri dish for genetic research. We owe pretty much everything we know about Alzheimer's genes and

genome sequencing to experiments done on Icelanders. So many of them are related that there's an app that tells young Icelanders whether the person they're about to hook up with is a cousin.

Before the boom years, Iceland had enjoyed years of peace and, if not exactly prosperity, at least general, congenial comfort. Its citizens are among the most educated in the world, and its health care system is strong. Its paid parental leave policy is extravagantly generous, spanning nine months. It hasn't seen war in centuries and doesn't field an army.

Like other Nordic countries, it's as close to socialism as you can get in the modern world. When I landed at the Reykjavik airport, I noticed that the first-class travelers were herded into the same lines as the rest of us, as if Icelanders want to make sure these rich folks don't get too full of themselves.

But all that changed after the banks were privatized. The country erupted in a frenzy of international financial chest-thumping. Suddenly, the newly private banks could do business with anyone, anywhere. Then—prime minister Davíd Oddson spun visions of international domination. A poet and onetime mayor of Reykjavik, he had become besotted with his free-market heroes Ronald Reagan and Margaret Thatcher. He lowered taxes and freed up trade. Icelandic inflation was soaring—a quirk of the country's massive investment in aluminum smelting—and the country's interest rates were high, shooting well into the double digits by 2007. When the newly privatized banks opened their doors to the outside world, foreign money flooded in, looking to make an easy 14 percent a year. The banks were suddenly floating in cash.

For Gunnar, the timing couldn't have been better. He had spent years scrambling to make a living in a variety of jobs, from fishing to owning a shop that sold videotapes and ice cream. Now, for the first time, he didn't have to worry about money. It was easy to get his hands on cash. Not only was he earning his keep as a local theater

director, he was dreaming up far grander ambitions. Like the bankers, he set his sights on international expansion. He wrote a play and rented a theater in London. Then he set about rehearsing his actors to prepare for his international debut.

His plans seemed modest compared to those of some of his friends. In the U.S., the stock market doubled from 2003 to 2007. In Iceland it didn't double or even triple; it multiplied by *nine times*. Iceland, once known for its equitable income distribution, suddenly had a class of people who were unspeakably, ostentatiously, unimaginably filthy rich.

The owner of a shipping company converted one of his warehouses into a giant party space and hired Elton John to perform for his birthday. A retail magnate named Jón Ásgeir Jóhannesson bought a 145-foot yacht and a $25 million Manhattan penthouse apartment (though he was later sued by potential buyers for equipping it with a cheap Ikea kitchen). A bank CEO, Larus Welding, was so frustrated with bankers demanding he triple their salaries that he told them, "Just stop buying yourselves Porsches and drinking so much booze and you will feel much better; stop changing wives and it will save you a lot of money."

Iceland's bankers were giddy over this endless geyser of cash—and oblivious to signs that they were in the midst of one of the biggest financial bubbles the world had ever seen. In fact, the Icelandic economy was on the brink. By late 2007, there were whispers that the bubble was about to pop. International bankers, regulators, and journalists began asking questions. Around the world, a sense of alarm, of impending disaster, was growing.

But back in Reykjavik, Gunnar, the fisherman-turned-director, didn't worry himself over the rumblings. He trusted Iceland's politicians, who shrugged them off as nonsense. A banker friend publicly dismissed the concerns as "an image problem" that could be solved with "a PR campaign."

Gunnar figured his friends and his country's leaders knew better than those nay-saying foreigners, who probably were just jealous of Iceland's success. Besides, he was too busy rehearsing his actors for their London premiere. He had poured his savings into rehearsal space to go along with the theater rental. All was proceeding just as he had planned.

"I thought everything was going well," as he recalls. "The financial geniuses had everything under control, and the ones saying otherwise were just morons and idiots."

The "morons and idiots," of course, turned out to be right. Gunnar's play was scheduled to premiere on October 8, 2008. As it turned out, that instead was the day Iceland's banks failed. None could withstand the international panic that had followed the collapse a few weeks earlier of Lehman Brothers in the United States.

Chaos reigned. Iceland, the little country that could, suddenly became the ridiculous wannabe that couldn't. The rest of the world had decided that Iceland—unlike, say, Goldman Sachs—wasn't too big to fail. And fail it did, spectacularly. Iceland was effectively bankrupt.

In Reykjavik, Gunnar watched events unfold with growing dread. Desperately, he began reaching out to his backers in London. They stopped returning his phone calls. All of his grand plans, everything he had been working for his entire life, evaporated before his astonished eyes.

Dread turned to panic, and for good reason. In the aftermath of the collapse, the krona crashed. The loans Gunnar had taken out in euros he had to pay back in now-worthless Icelandic currency. Payments suddenly tripled. He turned in the keys to his car. He stopped paying his mortgage. Gunnar's play would never open, shattering his dreams of international acclaim. He would lose every cent of his investment.

Some of his neighbors had it even worse. One infuriated Ice-

lander, his home now owned by the bank, was so angry he bulldozed the place. Newspaper classified ads offered cars for *negative* prices—the owners would pay someone to take the vehicle off their hands. One joker listed Iceland for sale on eBay—Icelandic singer Björk "not included." Starting bid: 99 pence.

In the fall of 2008, when it all came crashing down, Iceland's citizens, a generally pacifist lot, erupted in fury against "stupid thinking." Crowds tumbled out on the streets. Gunnar, his savings gone, his dreams for his theater dashed, his car repossessed, joined the protesters. The mob demanded that the government resign.

To be sure, the demonstrations were carried out in thoroughly Icelandic fashion. Law-abiding protesters pushed double strollers, and at their most agitated threw oranges and bananas. A typical chant went like this:

> *Do we want new ways of ruling? Yes!*
> *Do we want to abolish corruption? Yes!*
> *Do we want peaceful demonstrations? Yes!*

It was around this time that one of the country's few female bankers heard an insistent knocking on her door. Hers was the only bank in the country that had avoided the crazy risks and that was still solvent—thanks to, in her business partner's words, bringing "greater female values into the financial world."

She padded to the door and opened it to find an old man. "I just want some women to take care of my money," he said, as recounted by writer Michael Lewis in his engaging take on the crisis in *Boomerang: Travels in the New Third World*. As Lewis observed, "One of the distinctive traits about Iceland's disaster, and Wall Street's, is how little women had to do with it."

••

AMONG FINANCIAL JOURNALISTS, the gallows-humor joke was that there wouldn't have been a crisis if we had "Lehman Sisters" instead of Lehman Brothers. And it's true, as Lewis noted, the U.S. and Iceland had that in common: women had virtually nothing to do with the disastrous financial bets in either country.

What's more notable, though, is how each country responded. In the U.S., the men who crashed the economy remained at their posts. In Iceland, the men were sent to jail. Women replaced them. Two of Iceland's three banks named women as their new presidents. The entire Icelandic government resigned, right up to the prime minister, the swashbuckling cheerleader of the business Vikings. He too was replaced by a woman, Jóhanna Sigurðardóttir, the first openly lesbian leader of any country in history.

The head of Iceland's Chamber of Commerce, also a woman, spoke for many when she derided the "man-made" crisis as a "penis competition" among bankers.

It was an extraordinary phenomenon. It's as if an entire population rose up, unified, with a single objective: to flush the testosterone out of its system. It flew in the face of thousands of years of history, turning upside down a culture that had always celebrated its bloodthirsty Viking heritage.

The women's takeover was a spectacle the world had never seen. In the U.K., the *Guardian* heralded the move: "After the Crash, Iceland's Women Lead the Rescue." The *Financial Times* declared, "Iceland Calls in Women Bankers to Clean Up Young Men's Mess." In New Zealand, the *NZ Herald* crowed, "Viking Women Fight to Save Nation in Meltdown," while perhaps most pointedly, PBS announced, "Viking Women Aim to End Iceland's Age of Testosterone."

Indeed, Jóhanna's new government called for bringing in a bucket full of estrogen to the male-dominated worlds of business and finance. (Icelanders are referred to by first names rather than surnames.) She wasted no time in drumming men out of some of the most senior positions of power, instituting a quota requiring 40

percent of corporate board seats to be held by women. She created a new arm of the finance department, devoted to "gender budgeting," which is just what it sounds like: an office devoted to making sure the government doesn't spend more money on men than on women.

"Iceland was the first in the world into the crisis, but we could be the first out, and women have a big role to play in that," said Halla Tómasdóttir, one of the founders of a female-led bank. "It goes back to our Viking women. While the men were out there raping and pillaging, the women were running the show at home."

The women in charge of the country convened a group of experts to get to the bottom of the financial crisis—Icelanders called it the "truth commission." And then, in an astonishing move, they brought in a couple of female gender-studies professors from the local university to assess what role gender played in the crash. In what may well have been a first in any country's history, Iceland's government actually studied whether macho posturing led to its economic meltdown. Its conclusion can be summed up in one word: yes.

What's most remarkable about this wholesale transformation is that it only gained traction after that initial flush of power. Almost nothing was untouched by the new "feminization." What started out as a crackdown on reckless bankers spread into every corner of the culture.

In 2010, Iceland banned strip clubs. It announced a plan to crack down on hard-core Internet pornography. A woman was named for the first time as the head of the Church of Iceland. And in 2010—five years ahead of the U.S.—Iceland, which had already permitted civil unions, formally legalized gay marriage. The prime minister was among the first to wed.

When I arrived in Iceland, I suspected that Iceland's situation was a fluke. I was certain it was a case in which a country gripped by mass financial madness before 2008 had traded it in for a mass-hysterical compulsion to purge itself of everything manly.

But as my visit wore on, I realized that this was no passing fad.

Perhaps what surprised me most is that the men I met were at least as supportive of the move toward "feminization" as the women.

Certainly for Gunnar, it was a welcome development. "Icelandic sagas are full of women," he tells me later that week, as we drive along Reykjavik's main thoroughfare. "Look at the stories about the famous Vikings, [who] were mainly killing each other when they were sleeping. But behind those guys in the sagas were strong women."

If anything, he wishes the women had gotten even further. "I think it's wrong," he scowls when I mention Iceland's number-one ranking in the World Economic Forum analysis. "We are a long way from equality."

Momentarily distracted, he points out a beautiful home that we're passing, on a bluff overlooking the harbor. That's where Ronald Reagan and Mikhail Gorbachev first met in 1986, he tells me.

"Beautiful," I murmur.

"It's haunted."

"What?"

He turns onto a side street. "Iceland has 350,000 people, but 500,000 elves and 250,000 trolls and a million ghosts, so we are actually very crowded," he says with satisfaction.

Soon we pull up to Kaffivagninn café, a rough-hewn wharfside coffee shop. Fishing boats bob in the background and big groups of fishermen are gathered around long wooden tables.

Ensconced at a corner table is fishing boat captain Arthur Bogason. He's a big, muscular man, well over six feet tall. He's been working on fishing boats since he was fourteen years old, except for a brief interlude as a competitive power lifter in Dayton, Ohio. He's sixty years old now, but still looks like he could dead-lift a few hundred pounds without breaking a sweat.

Arthur isn't here to talk about bankers (whom he dismisses as "elves, because being an elf in general language is being kind of

stupid"), nor is he interested in opining about fishing. He wants to discuss, instead, the gender wage gap. In Iceland it hovers at around 18 percent, similar to the gap in the U.S.

"I have never been able to understand this, and find it still so stupid that I lack words," he says. "I have a big problem understanding why women who work the same job as men don't get the same salaries. I support gender equality with all of my heart."

As he speaks, I'm starting to understand a singular aspect of Icelandic culture—and in particular, of Icelandic men. Almost every man I meet shares the same view: it doesn't matter what some pencil-pushers at the World Economic Forum in Switzerland say about Iceland being number-one in gender equality, Iceland is still not remotely equal enough for women. The men are as fervent believers in this narrative as the women.

As it happens, my visit coincides with a conference marking one hundred years of the women's right to vote, granted in 1915. For those keeping score at home, that's five years ahead of the U.S.

The conference is held at the magnificent new Harpa concert hall, a boom-era monument to excess. It's a slightly ridiculous modernist glass-prism concoction commissioned by one of the banking moguls, designed by a famous Icelandic artist, and left half-built after the crash, when taxpayers were stuck with the bill to finish it.

The women I meet at the conference, like the men I've been speaking with all week, aren't satisfied with the progress Iceland has made on gender equality, either. They note bitterly that the first female prime minister has already been voted out of office (her successor not long after our visit will be forced to resign in a financial scandal). The anti-pornography laws have been hard to enforce and widely derided. A *Vice* article labeled the country's anti-porn efforts "asinine." The government is again run by men.

Yet the conference also gives me some insights into how, despite it all, Iceland still trumps other countries when it comes to women's

equality. In part it's a reflection of the famed egalitarian streak that all Nordic countries share. The social distinctions we're accustomed to in the U.S.—you're unlikely to find an American CEO and his auto mechanic at the same dinner party—don't resonate here. Instead, fishermen fraternize easily with financiers.

As if to prove the point, during a break at the conference, over coffee and pastries, I recognize an older woman with short blond hair and flats, clutching her purse and making small talk in the lobby. It's former president Vigdís Finnbogadóttir. No VIP rooms or bodyguards or roped-off areas for her.

Indeed, that evening, I'm one of several dozen conference attendees invited to a reception at the current president's house—Iceland's equivalent of the White House. I'm surprised and delighted, and also concerned about getting my papers in order for the inevitable background check. I know that in the U.S., a White House visit means running a gauntlet of Secret Service checks, cement barriers, metal detectors, and bomb-sniffing dogs.

But this is Iceland. Nobody asks for my papers. And instead of a phalanx of security, we pull up in a bus to a charming former schoolhouse, sitting aside a public jogging path. We walk through the unlocked front door, hang up our coats, and are greeted by a man who turns out to be the president himself, Ólafur Ragnar Grímsson. The Icelanders expect as much. On any given day, they might see him standing behind them in line at the grocery store. "Iceland is Bloomington, Indiana, as a nation," is how a friend describes it.

At the president's house, I have a chance to meet Vigdís, who is funny and profane and reminds me about the long history of strong women in Iceland. On October 24, 1975—almost forty years to the day of my visit—the women of Iceland famously went on a strike. They poured into the street, abandoning jobs, refusing to cook or clean or look after children at home, virtually paralyzing the entire country.

Banks and factories, fisheries, schools, and shops had to close.

Men brought their children to work, armed with candy to keep the kids quiet. It didn't always work; radio announcers were drowned out by the sound of children playing in the studios. The country's economy was brought to a halt. The protest became known as "Women's Day Off," and it changed the political dynamic in the country for good.

Within five years, Icelanders had elected Vigdís, back then a popular theater director, as Iceland's president, a largely ceremonial post, but nevertheless she was the first elected female head of state in the world. During the race, a male opponent had derided her as "half a woman" because she is a breast cancer survivor. The night she won, she shot back, "Well, I'm actually not going to breastfeed the Icelandic nation; I'm going to lead it."

And the gains for women continued. In 2000 the country introduced one of the most liberal parental leave policies on the planet: a government-funded paid leave of nine months, including three months for the mother, three for the father, and three more for whichever parent chooses to use them. Day care is heavily subsidized by the government. Not long after my visit, a female member of Parliament made history by breastfeeding her six-week-old baby while making a speech to the assembly.

None of which stops Icelanders from complaining. As I grab for a *kleinur*—a traditional Icelandic confection that tastes like a Krispy Kreme doughnut, to which I have quickly become addicted—I meet a fellow conference participant, an energetic, fashionably dressed woman named Sigríður Einarsdóttir. She is an Icelandair pilot, a three-decade veteran of the airline, and the highest-ranking female pilot in the company. She helmed the first all-female crew in the airline's history in 1996. Yet she is discouraged. "When I look back, I find so little has changed. Still mostly men are in all manager positions."

Another guest, a gregarious woman named Katrín Anna

Guðmundsdóttir, joins us. Katrín, a onetime spokeswoman for the Feminist Association of Iceland, ran Iceland's gender-budgeting department, which meant she spent her days ensuring that state budget allocations didn't favor men while discriminating against women.

"Iceland is not a female world. We are still a male-centric world," she says. She scoffs at the World Economic Forum ranking too. "Just because we're number one, it just says that the status of gender equality is really bad in the world. It's a testament to how far we still have to go."

I'm puzzled by the contradictions. Iceland is supposed to be the best place in the world to be a woman. Women have achieved great power, and once even commandeered the entire government. And yet everyone I meet, men as well as women, is dissatisfied. Nobody believes that in Iceland the genders are truly equal. The most common adjective I have heard on my trip is "stupid."

The next day will be my last in Iceland. After packing my bags, I head down to the lobby for one last outing with Gunnar. Since losing everything in the crash, he is again stringing together jobs to make a living. He's a tour guide as well as a theater director, political activist, and my translator throughout my visit. Now he has one more friend he'd like me to meet.

We drive to the outskirts of town, to a building that looks like a sad old California strip mall. Inside, up a flight of stairs, we stop in to see Guðmundur Gunnarsson, a burly, bearded electrician who until recently ran the Icelandic electricians' union. He tells me that after the crash, half of his union members went bankrupt. Many lost their homes. They subsisted on cheap blood sausage made from sheep intestines. They were disgusted by the boom-era government, "our president and the Icelandic Vikings that were talking down to the other nations." When it all came crashing down, he adds, "many people said maybe we should let the women be more active in how we control the Icelandic economy."

That's when it clicks for me. Suddenly it all makes sense. I notice something else about Icelandic men: for all their macho posturing, they are remarkably comfortable talking about gender, in a way that American men aren't.

In the U.S., if you utter the phrase "gender equality" you can practically see men physically recoiling, shrinking into a defensive crouch. Not so in Iceland, where the women in Parliament once performed *The Vagina Monologues*—and even Iceland's President Grímsson, the great promoter of the business Vikings, responded by declaring himself a "Vagina Warrior."

Now, in his office overlooking the water, Guðmundur, a solidly built man in blue jeans, doesn't blink when I press him on the subject of women.

"It's no problem for me to say I'm a feminist," he says easily, in his deep, booming voice. He brought up his own six children to be feminists too, he says. He taught his four daughters that "if they don't like what the male is saying, they just get up and say, 'I'm not going to listen to that guy.'"

That's the difference between Icelandic women and American women, he insists. He has a daughter who lives in the U.S., he explains. And when he visits her there, it drives both of them nuts: "American women are likely to sit there and listen to the crap the male is talking about."

It's hard to imagine a similar conversation playing out with an electrician, or almost any other man, in the U.S. On the other hand, I should know by now that Iceland isn't like anywhere else. This being Iceland, Guðmundur's daughter, the one who lives in America, is better known to the rest of us as the singer Björk.

My visit now coming to a close, I think I finally understand why Iceland truly is so hospitable to women, even though Icelanders themselves insist it isn't. The reason this country ranks number one for gender equality, doesn't, it seem, have much to do with the women at all. It's all about the men. The men are agitating on behalf of the

women. The men are as frustrated with inequality as their wives and daughters. The men and women of Iceland are in this struggle together.

I think back to something Arthur Bogason, the muscle-bound fishing boat captain and former power lifter, had said the day before. "Why is it that it's so easy for you to talk about women's issues?" I had asked him. "And how should we women engage American men in this conversation about gender? Men seem so defensive if we bring it up, as if we're haranguing them, accusing them of something awful."

He had stroked his stubble for a moment, looked me square in the face, and then given me some advice to pass along to American men: "I would ask them if the world would end if they get yelled at. So what? Take the goddamn conversation.

"It's based on fear and ignorance," he says of American men's unease. But the conversation "is necessary. It will eventually happen. The sooner they take the step, the better."

Conclusion: The Future Is Now

Teresa Shook, a grandmother from Hawaii, was frustrated. It was November 2016, and she was alarmed by presidential candidate Donald Trump's behavior toward women, most recently revealed in the highly publicized *Access Hollywood* outtake in which he boasted about grabbing women's genitals. Now he had just won the election, notably with a majority of white female voters supporting him. Venting her frustration on Facebook, she came up with an idea. Why not, she suggested, stage a march in Washington, D.C., for women's equality? So she sent a Facebook invitation to a few dozen friends, asking if they'd like to join her. Then she went to bed.

She had no idea that her single post would explode into a movement. Her suggestion caught fire. And the day after President Trump was inaugurated, the Women's March on Washington attracted more than half a million participants, with millions of other women around the world taking to the streets as well.

They gathered not only in U.S. cities like Washington and New York, but internationally, from Paris to Lima, Peru, to Tbilisi, Georgia, to Erbil, Iraq. As many as 5 million people are estimated to have marched in the U.S. and two hundred locations worldwide.

The marches were an extraordinary show of female solidarity. But something else struck me as I watched video feeds of the gatherings from around the world: the men. Untold thousands of them. They had unabashedly joined the marches to voice their support for gender equality. For many of them in the U.S., this wasn't about being a Democrat or a Republican. It was about being human.

"I'm a typical Trump voter, a 54-year-old white guy. But my momma brought me up correctly!" Washington, D.C., marcher Jeff Parker said. Widower Glenn Wallace marched in honor of his late

wife. Alexander McCoy, a Marine Corps veteran, marched because "I've been led by women before—and my big Marine Corps ego survived just fine. It's time the country sees that following a woman's leadership doesn't make a man weak."

And this is why I'm optimistic that despite the issues still confronting women every day, despite intractable issues of misogyny and abuse and an alarming drumbeat of sexual harassment cases, we are closing in on solutions. More men are joining us, reaching across the gender divide to help us close the gap.

These men hail from all corners of the country and the world, and from wildly different political viewpoints. They cross socioeconomic, racial, ethnic, and age spectrums. They're taking steps to close the gap at home, in the office, and at school. They may not be calling themselves "feminists" as the men in Iceland do, but their actions transcend labels—and they are already making a difference.

They are men like Jared Mauldin, a college student majoring in engineering in Washington state. He decided to take a stand after noticing that his mostly male classmates were dismissive of the women in their program.

In a letter to the school newspaper, addressed "to the women in my engineering classes," he wrote, "you and I are in fact unequal." He listed the obstacles women face—being discouraged from pursuing science, being called "bossy," being overlooked by teachers, being considered less qualified and a "diversity hire." He concluded: "When I experience success the assumption of others will be that I earned it. So you and I cannot be equal. You have already conquered far more to be in this field than I will ever face."

The letter went viral, the response overwhelmingly positive. As far as he was concerned, that simply proved his point. "I said nothing new," as Mauldin told NBC's *Today* show. "The distinguishing factor . . . happens to be that I am a man."

Men a few years older than he is are taking a similar stance. One interesting indication came from the *Wall Street Journal*, which,

acknowledging that executive women are frequently asked how they balance work and family, turned the table to ask the same question of twenty-five male business leaders.

As the *Journal* noted, "Work–life balance isn't a women's issue. But it often feels that way."

Some of the *Journal*'s most poignant responses were from men in their fifties and beyond, like fifty-five-year-old Dan Glaser, chief executive of professional services firm Marsh & McLennan Companies, who missed out on the childhood activities of his first two children and redoubled his efforts to make time for attending activities like soccer for his third.

"When you're younger, you have this sense of your own immortality and you'll always be able to catch up. You'll make it up to your kid or you'll make it up to your wife," Glaser said. But "your kids are only young once and you can't get that moment back."

Satya Nadella, forty-nine, the chief executive of Microsoft and a father of three, admitted that "it's a struggle" to balance work and family. "Like if I take my daughter to a lacrosse game, how much time am I on the phone versus actually watching her lacrosse game? I strive for a few moments that I'm doing something with them that I'm actually present."

Younger male executives, meanwhile, are setting a different example. Adam Goldenberg, the thirty-five-year-old chief executive of JustFab, hired an executive coach in order to help him find balance, and ultimately created a plan to make it home for dinner three times a week and block off weekend time to spend with family.

Eric Poirier, the young chief executive of Addepar, marks time off on a calendar that's visible to all employees, noting that he's taking his young daughter to the pediatrician or leaving work at six to have dinner before her bedtime. His reasoning is that it will help employees feel that "they have the company's support" for their own personal lives.

Men like these are helping drive workplace changes that ben-

efit both sexes. Their influence is apparent in multiple ways, most visibly in new perks like gender-neutral paid parental leaves. The practice started in the tech industry, and has since spread to companies, including Ernst & Young (16 weeks), Johnson & Johnson (up to 17 weeks for moms, 9 for dads), and Credit Suisse (20 weeks, though only for the "primary" caregiver). Meanwhile, at last count five states have passed mandatory paid-parental-leave laws, including New York, California, New Jersey, Rhode Island, and Washington, in addition to Washington, D.C.

What's more, like the student Manbassadors at Harvard, older male executives are starting to join organizations in support of their female colleagues. At male-dominated firms from Bain Consulting to the law firm Simpson Thacher & Bartlett to the bank MB Financial, the women's groups are beginning to include men in their meetings.

When I've spoken to mixed-sex groups like these, I'll notice that nod of recognition among the women in the room when I discuss the subtle indignities, the unconscious bias, that we experience. For the men, though, these conversations can be eye-opening, a smack-to-the-forehead moment.

Just in the past few years, multiple organizations have sprung up with the goal of uniting men to champion women. Paradigm for Parity, founded in late 2016 by executives including former DuPont CEO Ellen Kullman, calls for equality in the executive suite by 2030, and offers a "toolkit" of recommended actions. Among them: unconscious-bias training, basing evaluations on performance rather than face time, and providing high-potential women with sponsors who can advance their careers, not just mentors who offer advice. Chief executives of more than two dozen companies—most of them men—signed on in support, including those from Bank of America, Coca-Cola, and LinkedIn.

An equivalent student effort from the Forte Foundation, a nonprofit founded to encourage women to pursue business education,

now invites in men too. It created a "Men as Allies Initiative" for students and faculty who want to create groups for men who support women on campus. The nonprofit Lean In organization, meanwhile, has a #LeanInTogether campaign aimed at bringing in men.

Similar efforts are springing up around the globe. In Australia, the Male Champions of Change organization brings together male executives four times a year to work on issues including gender pay transparency and flexible work schedules; the men also pledge not to participate in all-male panels. Kenya, for its part, has Men for Gender Equality Now. The 30% Club, started by U.K. financial executive Helena Morrissey, signs on top executives who support its goal of increasing the percentage of women on boards. Founded in 2010, it now has spread to six additional countries, including the U.S.

And the United Nations launched HeForShe, aimed at men with the express purpose of supporting women, with actress Emma Watson serving as its public face. "Gender equality is your issue, too," Watson said in a U.N. speech introducing the initiative, imploring the men in the audience to "ask yourself if not me, who? If not now, when?"

Internationally, these men's groups are often focused on curbing violence against women, which has shown an alarming rise in multiple countries from Indonesia to the U.K. In Ecuador, a men's organization called the Cascos Rosa ("Pink Helmets") teaches schoolboys to respect women. Men in Argentina, Chile, and Uruguay have joined protests in support of women's rights. A Burundi men's group supporting women's empowerment, the Abatangamuco, literally translates as "bringing light." In January 2015, HeForShe and the U.N. hosted a "Barbershop" meeting—the first of its kind, an international gathering of men brought together to discuss women's issues. Hundreds of men flew in from countries, including Pakistan, Tunisia, Latvia, and Sweden.

Groups like these are a step in the right direction. But let's be clear: on their own, they aren't enough. For real change to happen,

if we are to transform a culture that has long been molded by and for men, it will take individuals, one at a time, taking a stand, reaching across the gender divide. The wins will come from the accumulation of small, everyday interactions of both women and men.

Wharton professor Adam Grant, for example, has made it a practice to intervene when he hears belittling or offensive remarks about women. Sometimes, he will simply ask a quiet, gentle question: "What did you mean by that?" It's a nonconfrontational approach that often jars men into reflecting on what they've said and why, allowing them to come to their own realization about their behavior. In more extreme cases, Grant takes the offender aside to let him know that others are noticing his behavior and that it is affecting his reputation.

Grant also acknowledges his own hidden prejudices. "One of the things men can do is talk about our own biases," he told me. "Men feel judged when you call this stuff out. If you acknowledge [your own bias], you level the playing field."

Venture capitalist Roger McNamee, for his part, suggests taking one action a day to try to balance the scales. For example, he consciously changed his email style a few years ago to embrace what he describes as a more "female" approach. He begins each missive with a formal salutation ("Dear Joanne"), and introduces his ideas as questions rather than directives, in order to convey collaboration. The idea is "to show respect for the other person," he says, adding, "If enough people do one thing every day, it will matter."

The men whose voices populate this book offer multiple other strategies, writ large and small, that will ultimately move us toward a more equitable world. Men like PricewaterhouseCooper's Robert Moritz, writing about why women are critical to business success. And Brian Welle, teaching fellow Googlers to recognize their own unconscious biases. And Sam Polk, calling out the damaging "bro talk" in the finance industry. And the Container Store's Kip Tindell, speaking about the value female executives bring to decision-making. And

Kimberly-Clark's Tom Falk, tying bonuses to successful diversity initiatives. And Dr. Augustus White III, explaining "cultural illiteracy," and how awareness is the key to treating everyone, regardless of gender or ethnicity, with respect.

Without question, we still have a long way to go to close the gap. Even the most enlightened men, who are earnestly trying to do so, face structural and cultural forces that are hard to overcome.

"The thing I am consistently amazed at is how deep this goes, and even people who are progressive still act in ways that are dismissive and disrespectful toward women," Polk told me. "It takes vigilance. It takes a lot of hard work."

Consulting firm McKinsey & Company's leader, Dominic Barton, the Canadian-born son of a missionary, for example, is one of this country's most outspoken advocates for women. He encourages senior men to mentor up-and-coming women. The firm requires all employees to take unconscious-bias training (it used to be voluntary, but "the people that have the problem, that are biased, don't come," he told me). It even instituted gender-based recruiting targets to bring in more women in entry-level positions.

Barton's ambitious mission is to increase the percentage of female partners to 40 percent by 2020. Yet in 2016, women accounted for just 11 percent of senior leadership. "It's been going in the right direction, but it's not fast enough. We haven't solved it," he acknowledges.

He's still trying. "Men have a critical role to play," he told me. "It can't just be women."

These efforts require courage. Men who defend women sometimes risk not just verbal abuse but violence. The most benign show of support can spark outrage. When an American Jewish professional group, Men as Allies, asked men to pledge not to participate in all-male panels, *The Atlantic* magazine was inspired to invite its readers to do the same. The response was so vicious the magazine had to shut down its comments section.

Men face opposition not just from other men, but from women too. Some women's groups intentionally exclude men, in part to avoid alienating members. "The women's movement remains continuously unwilling to bring men into the fold," as Joshua Reiman wrote in *International Affairs Review*. Yet allowing men to join "would transform their cause from one that is largely by and for women into an all-inclusive social movement."

Nevertheless, these men persist. And they are slowly but surely shattering the stigma around men who are openly supportive of gender equality. They give an insight into what it will take for women—and men too—to convince more men to join them. Their strategies vary, but their message is the same: Women aren't going to solve this problem on their own. Men need to see this as their issue too.

Ultimately, equality for women means equality for men too. We need to expand the definition of acceptable jobs for boys as much as for girls, especially in an economy that increasingly values traditionally feminine values like empathy and collaboration. A female surgeon shouldn't raise eyebrows any more than a male nurse does. As Gloria Steinem has observed, "I'm glad we've begun to raise our daughters more like our sons, but it will never work until we raise our sons more like our daughters."

••

MILLIONS OF MEN have proven that they are ready and willing to close the gap. But many more are potential partners in this cause. The question becomes, then, how can we supercharge these efforts? How do we get more men to understand that this is their issue too? How do we get them to care? In short, how can we bring them into the conversation?

Sometimes, all we need to do is ask. For tech executive Steve Boehm, awareness of the gender gap started with a simple question. Years ago, a colleague asked him if he'd ever spoken with a coworker

from a different background—a woman, or a minority—to inquire what it was like to work at their company. He hadn't. He is the first admit that back then, he hadn't given much thought to the challenges facing women and others from underrepresented groups. But the question prompted him to reevaluate his own attitudes and behavior.

Fifteen years ago, "I thought I was a good guy, I treated everybody fairly," he told me. "Lots of people are like me. They are well-intentioned. But they don't know what they don't know."

Women do know. But we need to go beyond just talking to ourselves. It is time to invite men to join the conversation too.

The men I met in the course of reporting this book—and the women who are working to create an equal society for all of us—give me great hope. From Glen Mazzara ensuring that the women in a television writers' room aren't interrupted, to symphony orchestras showing us every day what an unbiased world looks like, to the scientists peering inside human skulls and the researchers scrutinizing Enron emails, more men are reaching across the gender divide every day.

Without question, this is a nascent movement among men. Right now it's diffuse and largely under the radar. But the people I've met along the way are starting to bring it to the forefront, coalescing around the idea that we need men as well as women working together to close the gap. They are sparking a prominent national conversation.

The men and women I met don't pretend to have all the answers. Nor do I. Life at work, like life everywhere else, is messy. But my travels helped me—and, I hope, will help others—to rethink how we look at each other, and how we treat each other.

Yes, women are still living in a man's world. But every day, more men are reaching across the gender divide. We truly are working side by side, facing forward as we look toward the future, together.

Afterword

When I first began working on *That's What She Said,* I explained to potential publishers that the book was intended for men, as well as women, to help us work together to close the gender gap.

One publishing executive responded definitively: "Men will never read this book."

Thankfully, that prediction has proven wrong. (Also, thankfully, I chose a different publisher.) I hear from male readers daily who are embracing its precepts. Men are realizing that the world has changed, and they need to change too.

That's become especially apparent in the year since this book was published. The #MeToo movement has trained a harsh spotlight not only on sexual abuse, but also on the broader issue of bias against women. Awareness is growing that, while not every woman has been sexually abused at work, *every* woman knows how it feels to be marginalized, interrupted, ignored, and simply not taken as seriously as the guy sitting next to her. It's time to end that cycle.

In some important ways, we've seen progress. The 2018 midterm elections swept a record number of women into the house. In California, new legislation outlaws all-male boards for publicly traded companies headquartered there. Several states over the past few years have extended or lifted the statute of limitations for sex crimes. Companies including NBCUniversal are experimenting with programs like blind resumes and "returnships" to bring back women as well as men who may have left the workforce to care for family.

And some firms singled out for misogynistic cultures are taking aggressive steps to try to rectify the problem. After female Nike employees circulated a survey about harassment and discrimination, the chief executive apologized, a number of senior managers

were fired, and the company gave salary raises to 7,000 underpaid employees. Google's top executives vowed to make policy changes after 20,000 employees staged a walkout protesting sexual harassment. These are nascent steps, and how they will play out isn't yet clear, but at least they are a start.

I've also been inspired by readers who have offered additional creative ideas for closing the gender gap. Some companies are changing up meeting dynamics by rotating the leader, so that it isn't always the same white guy in charge. At least one created a "roulette wheel" that participants spin to choose a different meeting leader, or to mix up the agenda with commands like "start with the last agenda item first," or "all participants must stand." I've also heard of women's employee groups that invite men to their events, so that male colleagues are aware of the issues the women discuss among themselves.

For example, at A. T. Kearney, a consulting firm, senior female executives decided to each bring along a male colleague to a meeting for female employees. Those invitations became "a badge of honor," so coveted that senior men begged to be included, says Beth Bovis, global head of leadership and organization. Both men and women came away with a better understanding of—and an increased comfort level with—one another.

One of the most intriguing potential solutions has been pioneered by a people analytics firm called Humanyze: mandatory paternity leave. The Boston-based company is among the first to not only give both men and women twelve weeks of paid leave, but to insist that men take it. The firm instituted the policy in 2016 because most men don't take leave even when it's offered, for fear it will derail their careers. That message—that having a baby will kill your career—isn't lost on women who *do* take leave.

"Bias plays such a clear role, we decided we are going to say, 'It's not an option. You (men) have to take the time off,'" cofounder Ben

Waber told me. After all, if men and women have to take equal leaves, there's no excuse to penalize either one.

Humanyze executive Jeremy Doyle, the first new dad to be subject to the mandatory policy, told me he never would have taken off that much time if it were voluntary. As it was, he took his leave in several chunks, spread out over the course of a year. Still, he faced the stigma of the "obvious social implications and/or gender expectations that everybody contends with around this." Some people snickered, with "little jabs or jokes," that he must be just goofing off. Others, particularly older relatives, suggested that if he was able to take such a long leave, he "must not be seen as somebody who's important" at work.

In other words, he was treated . . . just like a woman. And in many ways, that's the point. If leave is normalized for new dads as well as new moms, it's difficult to stigmatize either one.

As encouraging as these signs of progress are, they are fragile. If we don't aggressively push forward, we will inevitably fall backward. Frustratingly, in some ways we have regressed since this book was first published. The percentage of female CEOs of S&P 500 firms has declined over the past year, to less than 5 percent. Gender inequality has widened year over year, according to a 2017 World Economic Forum report. In a recent survey, most employees of both genders said they've seen no policy changes in their workplace since the #MeToo movement exploded. Nor has any significant legislation targeting inequity been passed since then.

And backlash against #MeToo rears its head regularly. A movement about *all* women has too often been recast as a political litmus test. A HuffPost/YouGov poll in August 2018 found that 54 percent of Republicans said #MeToo had "gone too far" compared with 9 percent of Democrats. The divide was particularly stark during the October Supreme Court nomination hearings for Brett Kavanaugh, after Christine Blasey Ford testified he had sexually assaulted her in high school. Senator Lindsey Graham declared the accusa-

tions "despicable," while President Trump called them a "hoax" and said, "It's a very scary time for young men in America." The Twitter hashtag #HimToo began trending, casting men as victims in imminent danger of being falsely accused of harassment.

Some male executives insist they'll never mentor a woman or even hire a woman for fear of false accusations. I have no patience for that. It's too often an excuse used by men who weren't interested in hiring or promoting women in the first place. False accusations are rare—estimates range from 2 percent to 10 percent. But an alarming 77 percent of women who have been sexually assaulted don't report it to police, for fear of retribution, ridicule, or not being believed.

Yet there are plenty of men, good guys of all political stripes, who would like to be part of the solution. They simply aren't sure how to go about it. I've lost count of the number of times I've been asked by men, "How do I start this conversation?" My goal in *That's What She Said* is to remove the awkwardness and the fear that these men have about engaging in what is sometimes a fraught topic.

That's why I've added two "cheat sheets" to this edition, one a list of steps that individuals can take right now to help close the gap, and another of changes organizations can make. It's also why I have been spending more time meeting with male leaders and working with male-dominated organizations, from the World Economic Forum to banks and tech firms to the Council on Foreign Relations.

It's important to understand that the inequities we describe in these pages don't only impact women. Much of the research I cite also applies to those in other underrepresented groups—whether race, ethnicity, religion, sexuality, physical handicap, or other qualities that put them in a minority. I've heard from black men, religious minorities, older employees, and even white male introverts who tell me the findings in this book apply to them as well.

When these individuals fall into more than one underrepresented group, they face even further hurdles, a phenomenon known

as intersectionality. As I noted in the book, while women in the U.S. on the whole earn about 80 percent as much as men, that figure is just 63 cents on the dollar for black women and 54 cents for Latinas. When I speak with organization leaders, the term "intersectionality" is often a mystery to them. But when I speak with younger groups of recent college graduates, it is top of mind. This is a primary concern of the incoming workforce—our leaders of the future—and it needs to become a priority for the rest of us as well.

What I've learned, most of all, is that senior leadership of any organization—whether a company, a school, or a government—must *own* diversity. I've met remarkable diversity and inclusion professionals in my travels. But they alone can't change an organization's culture. In corporations, for example, the chief executive and the chief financial officer must understand that this isn't a "soft" skill or a "nice to have;" it's a business imperative.

More than once I've spoken at a company and, afterward, a male executive will say, "Yes, on the one hand, we really care about diversity . . . but on the other hand we have to make our quarterly profits." That's the wrong approach. It betrays a fundamental misunderstanding of the issues at stake. Those two "hands" are in fact one and the same. There is no "either/or" scenario here. Achieving one is dependent on achieving the other. Attaining gender parity and attaining success are the same goal.

None of this is easy. We need systemic changes, throughout society. We've been talking about gender equality for more than half a century, since the Equal Pay Act was passed in 1963. Yet we're still faced with the same inequities, including a startlingly large pay gap. Enough with the talking. It's time for action.

We can get there. This isn't just about giving women equal opportunity. It's about creating a less fractious world with greater opportunities and more successful livelihoods for all of us.

That's why, despite my frustration that so much more needs to be done, I remain optimistic. As I've traveled the country meeting with readers and speaking with organizations, I've witnessed growing recognition among men as well as women that the gender gap isn't a "female issue" or a "girl thing." It's a humanitarian issue. It impacts all of us, and all of us need to work together to close it. And when we do—men together with women—we can, and we will, change the world.

Acknowledgments

I am profoundly grateful to all of those who shared their stories, advice, research, and time. Your generosity animates every page.

This book grew out of an essay I wrote for *The Wall Street Journal's* Review section, headlined "Women at Work: A Guide for Men." I am deeply indebted to editor Gary Rosen for his support and graceful editing.

At William Morrow, my appreciation knows no bounds. Thanks to publisher Liate Stehlik and to extraordinary editor Rachel Kahan, whose every suggestion improved this manuscript (and we made it to the finish line before your due date!). Huge thanks to Sharyn Rosenblum, Lynn Grady, Molly Waxman, and Alivia Lopez, for championing this book every step of the way. Julia Meltzer, Nyamekye Waliyaya, and copy editor Karen Richardson saved me from myself more times than I can count. My thanks as well to Henry Ferris, who advocated for this book from the start.

This book wouldn't have happened without the inimitable Suzanne Gluck, who pushed me during the proposal phase, encouraged me during its gestation, and offered valuable feedback when the manuscript was done. She's also a great friend and kick-ass #momboss who leads the way for all of us. Thanks as well to Matilda Forbes Watson, Janine Kamouh, Lauren Szurgot, and Andrea Blatt.

For her assistance as we sprinted toward the deadline, journalist Michelle Higgins has my eternal gratitude (and lifetime pool privileges for Veloria!). Thanks as well to researchers/fact-checkers Kevin Milian, Taylor Hess, and Nicole Gimpl.

During the course of writing this book, I joined Gannett and the *USA Today* network. My colleagues inspire me every day with their talent, dedication, and creativity. I am grateful to so many of you

whose insights inform these pages and whose support I treasure, including—but not limited to!—early readers Barbara Wall, Brent Jones, and Keira Nothaft, as well as Chrissy Terrell and Markus Williams.

Huge thanks to Roger McNamee for his enormously valuable feedback on the manuscript. My gratitude as well to others who read part or all of early drafts and improved it at every turn, including Sheryl Sandberg, Ragini Verma, Andrew Tisch, Adam Grant, Sallie Krawchek, Katie Couric, Charles Duhigg, Matt Krentz, Melanie Kupchynskey, and Glen Mazzara. My appreciation to Maggie Kneip and Courtney Hamilton for their excellent counsel. And special thanks to my forever-roomie Carol O'Keefe for her wisdom, candor, and friendship.

Finally, I thank my family: My late father, Burton Lipman, and my mom, Diane Lipman, for raising three strong daughters, who in turn have raised two more generations of equally strong and compassionate daughters and sons (and sons-in-law!). To my own kids, Rebecca and Andrew, who are an inspiration to me daily. And to my husband, Tom, who not only lived *with* this book for three years; he has *lived* the book his whole life, as a champion of women in general and me in particular. My love for you is infinite.

Notes

Introduction

xii "Long before my..." Ye May session of ye woman's rights convention. Ye orator of ye day denouncing ye lords of creation (Cartoon). Wood engraving in *Harper's Weekly,* June 11, 1859. Permanent Link: http://www.loc.gov/pictures/item/2005676505/

xii "In an 1875 . . ." *Illustration from Victorian magazine Fun, June 25, 1875.* Series 2, volume 21, page 245. London: T. Baker. Permanent link: http://ufdc.ufl.edu/UF00078627/00026

xii "A recent Harvard..." Dobbin, Frank & Alexandra Kalev. "Why Diversity Programs Fail." *Harvard Business Review,* July–August 2016, https://hbr.org/2016/07/why-diversity-programs-fail

xii "'We beat 'em . . .'" Howard Ross, personal interview, January 2015.

xiii "'I have two . . .'" Wingfield, Nick. "Intel Allocates $300 Million for Workplace Diversity." *New York Times,* January 6, 2015, https://nyti.ms/2kcyIsB

xiv "Misogynistic corporate cultures..." Stanglin, Doug. "Bill O'Reilly Ousted at Fox After Sexual Harassment Investigation." *USA Today,* April 19, 2017, https://www.usatoday.com/story/news/2017/04/19/foxs-bill-oreilly-heading-exit/100639096/; della Cava, Marco. "Uber CEO Travis Kalanick Resigns Amid Mounting Pressure from Investors." *USA Today,* June 21, 2017, https://www.usatoday.com/story/tech/news/2017/06/21/uber-ceo-traivs-kalanick-resigns-report/103060200/; Guynn, Jessica, "Start-up Investor Dave McClure Resigns from 500 Startups." *USA Today,* June 30, 2017, https://www.usatoday.com/story/tech/news/2017/06/30/dave-mcclure-500-starts-sexual-harassment/103334242/

xiv "One out of 5 men" Kaur-Ballagan, Kully. "Three in four women around the world believe there are unequal rights in their country." *Ipsos MORI,* March 7, 2017, https://www.ipsos.com/ipsos-mori/en-uk/three-four-women-around-world-believe-there-are-unequal-rights-their-country?language_content_entity=en-uk

xii "One suggested that . . ." Moritz, Robert E. "White Men: Four Things You Can Do to Advance Diversity." LinkedIn, March 5, 2015, https://www.linkedin.com/pulse/white-men-four-things-you-can-do-advance-diversity-robert-e-moritz

xv "He offered five..." Modi, Kunal. "Man Up on Family and Workplace Issues: A Response to Anne-Marie Slaughter." *The Blog, Huffington Post,* July 12, 2012, http://www.huffingtonpost.com/kunal-modi/man-up-on-family-and-work_b_1667878.html

xv "One of the . . ." Kunal Modi, personal interview, August 19, 2015.

xv "When Catalyst, a . . ." Prime, Jeanine, and Corinne A. Moss-Racusin. "Engaging Men in Gender Initiatives: What Change Agents Need to Know." Catalyst, May 4, 2009, http://www.catalyst.org/knowledge/engaging-men-gender-initiatives-what-change-agents-need-to-know

xvi "When Blake Irving . . ." Metz, Cade. "GoDaddy Isn't the Company You Think It Is." *Wired,* May 26, 2015, https://www.wired.com/2015/05/godaddy-isnt-company-think/

xvi "'We have a lot of men'" Telle Whitney, personal interview, June 16, 2015.

xvi "Wharton psychology professor . . ." Grant, Adam. "Why So Many Men Don't Stand Up for Their Female Colleagues." *The Atlantic,* April 29, 2014, https://www.theatlantic.com/business/archive/2014/04/why-men-dont-stand-up-for-women-to-lead/361231/

xiv "Even one previous . . ." Annis, Barbara, and John Gray. "Do Men Have to Walk on Eggshells with Women." *Work with Me: The 8 Blind Spots Between Men and Women in Business.* New York: St. Martin's Press, May 27, 2014.

xvii "In one survey . . ." Ibid.

xvii "51 percent of men . . ." Prime, Jeanine, and Corinne A. Moss-Racusin. "Engaging Men in Gender Initiatives: What Change Agents Need to Know." Catalyst, May 4, 2009, http://www.catalyst.org/knowledge/engaging-men-gender-initiatives-what-change-agents-need-to-know

xvii "No wonder almost . . ." Covert, Bryce. "About a Third of Women Have Experienced Discrimination in the Workplace." *Think Progress,* August 19, 2013.

xvii "In the male-dominated . . ." Bellstrom, Kristen. "You Won't Believe How Many Women in Tech Say They've Faced Sexual Harassment." *Fortune,* January 11, 2016, http://fortune.com/2016/01/11/survey-sexual-harassment-tech/?iid=leftrail

xvii "The majority of men . . ." Cauterucci, Christina. "The Majority of American Men Believe Sexism Is Over, According to a New Poll." *Slate,* August 18, 2016, http://www.slate.com/blogs/xx_factor/2016/08/18/the_majority_of_u_s_men_believe_sexism_is_over.html

xvii "Strike one for being . . ." Reuben, E., Paola Sapienza, and Luigi Zingales. "How stereotypes impair women's careers in science." *Proceedings of the National Academy of Sciences of the United States of America* 111 (2014): 4403–4408. doi: 10.1073/pnas.1314788111

xviii "A 2014 survey . . ." Williams, Joan C., Katherine W. Phillips, and Erika V. Hall. "Double Jeopardy?: Gender Bias Against Women of Color in Science." *Center for WorkLife Law* (2014), http://www.uchastings.edu/news/articles/2015/01/double-jeopardy-report.pdf

xviii "What's more, while . . ." The American Association of University Women. "The Simple Truth About the Gender Pay Gap." http://www.aauw.org/research/the-simple-truth

xx "Even though women . . ." Guo, Jeff. "Women Are Dominating Men at College. Blame Sexism." *Washington Post,* December 11, 2014, https://www.washingtonpost.com/news/storyline/wp/2014/12/11/women-are-dominating-men-at-college-blame-sexism/?utm_term=.a09de7905db8; "Women CEOs of the S&P 500." Catalyst. Accessed June 14, 2017, http://www.catalyst.org/knowledge/women

-ceos-sp-500; 2020 Women on Boards Gender Diversity Index, 2016, https://www.2020wob.com/sites/default/files/2020GDI-2015Report.pdf; "Quick Take: Women in Law." Catalyst. April 19, 2017, http://www.catalyst.org/knowledge/women-law-canada-and-us#footnote19_qrsu4e0

xx "1 in 4 . . ." Rockefeller Foundation and Global Strategy Group. "Women in Leadership: Tackling Corporate Culture from the Top." Accessed August 4, 2017, https://assets.rockefellerfoundation.org/app/uploads/20170728121141/Women-in-Leadership-Tackling-Corporate-Culture-from-the-Top.pdf

xx "According to a . . ." Sandberg, Sheryl. "Sheryl Sandberg: Women Are Leaning In—but They Face Pushback." *Wall Street Journal*, September 27, 2016, https://www.wsj.com/articles/sheryl-sandberg-women-are-leaning-inbut-they-face-pushback-1474963980

xx "The World Economic Forum . . ." "The Global Gender Gap Report." *World Economic Forum*, 2016, http://www3.weforum.org/docs/GGGR16/WEF_Global_Gender_Gap_Report_2016.pdf

xx "If women participated . . ." Aguirre, DeAnne, Leila Hoteit, Christine Rupp, and Karim Sabbagh. "Empowering the Third Billion. Women and the World of Work in 2012." *Booz and Company*, 2012. https://www.strategyand.pwc.com/media/file/Empowering-the-third-billion_Briefing-report.pdf

xx "At least eight . . ." Smale, Alison, and Claire Cain Miller. "Germany Sets Gender Quota in Boardrooms." *New York Times*, March 6, 2015, https://www.nytimes.com/2015/03/06/world/europe/german-law-requires-more-women-on-corporate-boards.html?mcubz=0

xviii "In the U.K. . . ." Lawrie, Eleanor. "Gender pay gaps must be declared by UK companies." BBC News, April 6, 2017, http://www.bbc.com/news/business-39502872; Allen, Katie. "Gender Pay Gap: Women Earn £300,000 Less Than Men over Working Life." *The Guardian*, March 7, 2016.

xx "Prime Minister Shinzō . . ." Ryall, Julian. "Japan Has a Problem—but It Isn't Young Women Who Don't Give Birth." *The Telegraph*, December 10, 2014. http://www.telegraph.co.uk/women/womens-life/11284634/Japanese-economy-Japan-has-a-problem-but-it-isnt-young-women-who-dont-give-birth.html; Tyson, Laura D'Andrea. "Japan's Women to the Rescue." *New York Times*, August 23, 2013, https://nyti.ms/2rw3v6D

xxi "Research has shown . . ." Kanter, Rosabeth Moss. *Men and Women of the Corporation*. New York: Basic Books, 1993; Kanter, Rosabeth Moss. "Some effects of proportions on group life: Skewed sex ratios and responses to token women." *American Journal of Sociology* 82, no. 5 (1977), http://www.journals.uchicago.edu/doi/pdfplus/10.1086/226425

xxi "Here I am . . ." Kenneth Jacobs, transcript from event, September 23, 2015.

Chapter 1: The Secret Lives of Women (a Primer for Men)

1 "Research tells me . . ." Kortt, Michael, and Andrew Leigh. "Does size matter in Australia?" *The Economic Record* 86, no. 272 (2010), http://andrewleigh.org//pdf/BodySize.pdf

1 "Linda Hudson, former . . ." Linda Hudson, personal interview, May 13, 2015.

1 "Dr. Carmen Quatman..." Carmen Quatman, email message to author, June 25, 2015.

2 "'Speak up—but...'" Streitfeld, David. "In Ellen Pao's Suit vs. Kleiner Perkins, World of Venture Capital Is Under Microscope." *New York Times,* March 5, 2015, https://nyti.ms/2uQ4Gw4

2 "That's one reason..." Cuddy, Amy. "Your Body Language May Shape Who You Are." TED, 2012, Video. https://www.ted.com/talks/amy_cuddy_your_body_language_shapes_who_you_are

2 "She's found that..." Carney, Dana R., Amy J. C. Cuddy, and Andy J. Yap. "Power Posing: Brief Nonverbal Displays Affect Neuroendocrine Levels and Risk Tolerance." *Psychological Science* 20, no. 10 (2010): 1–6. doi: 10.1177/0956797610383437

2 "The poses not..." Shontell, Alyson. "How to Become Powerful: Start By Sitting in a Powerful Pose." *Business Insider,* October 14, 2010, http://www.businessinsider.com/how-to-become-powerful-start-by-sitting-in-a-powerful-pose-2010-10

2 "Not surprisingly..." Kellaway, Lucy. "Power Posing and Flattery Beat an MBA Any Day." *Financial Times,* October 4, 2010, https://www.ft.com/content/ca32abb6-cda1-11df-9c82-00144feab49a

2 "A woman's looks..." Parker-Pope, Tara. "Beauty Discrimination During a Job Search." *New York Times,* November 30, 2010, https://well.blogs.nytimes.com/2010/11/30/beauty-discrimination-during-a-job-search/?_r=0; Ruffle, Bradley J., Ze'ev Shtudiner. "Are Good-Looking People More Employable?" *Management Science,* 61, no. 8 (2014), http://dx.doi.org/10.2139/ssrn.1705244

2 "One study found..." Johnston, David W. "Physical appearance and wages: Do blondes have more fun?" *Economics Letters,* 108, 10–12 (2010). doi: 10.1016/j.econlet.2010.03.015

2 "Women who wear..." Goudreau, Jenna. "Wear More Lipstick to Get a Promotion?" *Forbes,* October 14, 2011, https://www.forbes.com/sites/jennagoudreau/2011/10/14/wear-more-lipstick-to-get-a-promotion/#255c985e7556

2 "Thin women outearn..." Zagorsky, Jay L. "Health and wealth: The late-20th century obesity epidemic in the U.S." *Economics & Human Biology* 3, no. 2 (2005): 296–313, http://www.sciencedirect.com/science/article/pii/S1570-677X(05)00030-4

2 "Multiple studies have..." Hamermesh, Daniel S., and Jeff E. Biddle. "Beauty and the Labor Market." *The American Economic Review* 84, no. 5 (1994): 1174–1194, http://www.ux1.eiu.edu/~lsghent/hamerbiddle.pdf

2 "But there too..." Zarya, Valentina. "How a Little Lipstick Could Add Thousands to Your Paycheck." *Fortune,* May 19, 2016, http://fortune.com/2016/05/19/makeup-more-money/

3 "The average woman..." https://blog.mint.com/consumer-iq/splurge-vs-save-which-beauty-products-are-worth-the-extra-cost-0413/?display=wide

3 "Women pay more..." New York City Department of Consumer Affairs, "From Cradle to Cane: The Cost of Being a Female Consumer," December 2015, http://

www1.nyc.gov/assets/dca/downloads/pdf/partners/Study-of-Gender-Pricing-in-NYC.pdf

3 "That can add..." Senate Judiciary Committee. "Gender Tax Repeal Act of 1995," Bill No: AB 1100, amended in Senate, August 31, 1995. *The Assembly Committee on Consumer Protection, Governmental Efficiency and Economic Development,* "Gender Discrimination in the Pricing and Availability of Products and Services," 1994, http://leginfo.ca.gov/pub/95–96/bill/asm/ab_1051–1100/ab_1100_cfa_950831_152302_sen_floor.html

4 "'Over the course...'" Spar, Debora. *Wonder Women: Sex, Power, and the Quest for Perfection.* New York: Sarah Crichton Books, 2013.

4 "And that's before..." Pompa, Frank, and Sharon Jayson. "Men vs. Women: How Much Time Spent on Kids, Jobs, Chores?" *USA Today,* March 14, 2013, https://www.usatoday.com/story/news/nation/2013/03/14/men-women-work-time/1983271/

4 "One study found..." Peck, Emily. "Why an Outsized Number of Blondes Are Leading the Country." *Huffington Post,* August 24, 2016, http://www.huffingtonpost.com/entry/blonde-leaders-sexism_us_57bdd4f5e4b00c67eca12176?bprpb9

4 "Hillary Clinton, who..." "Did You Know Most of the Women in Power." *Makers,* August 29, 2016, http://www.makers.com/blog/blonde-women-in-power. Jennifer Berdahl and Natalya Alonso, who presented their research at the Academy of Management's annual meeting.

4 "Researchers theorize that..." Peck, Emily. "Why an Outsized Number of Blondes Are Leading the Country." *Huffington Post,* August 24, 2016, http://www.huffingtonpost.com/entry/blonde-leaders-sexism_us_57bdd4f5e4b00c67eca12176

4 "Onstage, either..." Matrix Archives (2001–2017), *New York Women in Communications,* http://nywici.org/matrix/matrix-archives

5 "Comedian Amy Schumer..." Gray, Emma. "Amy Schumer's 'I'm Sorry' Skewers a Culture That Makes Women Apologize Constantly." *Huffington Post,* May 5, 2015, http://www.huffingtonpost.com/2015/05/14/amy-schumer-im-sorry-not-sorry_n_7276504.html.

5 "It wasn't that far..." Wieczner, Jen. "Hillary Clinton Is the First to Say 'I'm Sorry' in a Presidential Concession Speech." *Fortune,* November 14, 2016, http://fortune.com/2016/11/14/hillary-clinton-concession-speech-sorry-hallelujah/

5 "Some female executives..." Rohman, Jessica, and Tabitha Russell. "How to Create a Great Workplace for Women." *Fortune,* September 15, 2016, http://fortune.com/2016/09/15/create-great-workplace-women/

6 "It highlights those..." Grose, Jessica. "Telling Women to Apologize Less Isn't about Empowerment. It's about Shame." *Washington Post,* January 4, 2016, https://www.washingtonpost.com/posteverything/wp/2016/01/04/sorry-language-shamers-but-women-just-dont-need-your-new-email-policing-app/?utm_term=.5151db69daa7

6 "Boys gain status..." Tannen, Deborah. *Talking from 9 to 5: Men and Women at Work.* New York: HarperCollins, 1994.

7 "She sighed . . ." Deborah Tannen, personal interview, November 17, 2014.

7 "Perhaps it shouldn't . . ." Fingerhut, Hannah. "In both parties, men and women differ over whether women still face obstacles to progress." *Pew Research Center,* August 16, 2016, http://www.pewresearch.org/fact-tank/2016/08/16/in-both-parties-men-and-women-differ-over-whether-women-still-face-obstacles-to-progress/#

7 "while the majority . . ." PerryUndem. "The State of the Union on Gender Equality, Sexism, and Women's Rights," CTNewsJunkie, January 17, 2017, http://www.ctnewsjunkie.com/upload/2017/01/336804316-PerryUndem-Gender-Equality-Report.pdf

7 "As sociologist Michael . . ." Kimmel, Michael S. "Why Men Should Support Gender Equity." *The Role of Women in World Peace & the Role of Men and Boys in Gender Equity* (2005), http://www.lehman.edu/deanhum/womenstudies-to-be-removed/pdf/Section10.pdf

7 "That explains why . . ." "Paradigm for Parity: A Call to Action and Model for Gender Equality." *Paradigm for Parity,* 2016, https://static1.squarespace.com/static/57e9765e9f7456c76dc1c1c0/t/5873a40ccd0f6899ba02d384/1483973644868/Paradigm_For_Parity-Full.1.5.17_BD.pdf

8 "Being blind to . . ." O'Reilly, Lara. "Saatchi & Saatchi Chairman Kevin Roberts Thinks the Gender Diversity in Advertising Is 'Over'." *Business Insider,* July 29, 2016, http://www.businessinsider.com/kevin-roberts-on-women-in-leadership-roles-2016-7

8 "His comments provoked . . ." Ibid; Davies, Robert and Jasper Jackson. "Saatchi & Saatchi Boss Resigns amid Sexism Row." *The Guardian,* August 3, 2016, https://www.theguardian.com/media/2016/aug/03/saatchi-saatchi-boss-kevin-roberts-resigns-amid-sexism-row

8 "That blind spot . . ." Hirtenstein, Anna, and David Hellier. "Tesco Chairman Regrets Saying White Men on Boards Are Endangered." *Bloomberg,* March 11, 2017, https://www.bloomberg.com/news/articles/2017-03-11/tesco-chairman-regrets-saying-white-men-on-boards-are-endangered

8 "He later backtracked . . ." Ibid.

8 "research has shown . . ." http://www.npr.org/templates/transcript/transcript.php?storyId=197390707; DeBaise, Colleen. "Making Hollywood Less Sexist, One Crowd Scene at a Time." *Huffington Post,* March 24, 2015, http://www.huffingtonpost.com/colleen-debaise/making-hollywood-less-sexist-one-crowd-scene-at-a-time_b_6856698.html

8 "While they perceive . . ." Cutler, Anne, and Donia R. Scott. "Speaker sex and perceived apportionment of talk." *Applied Psycholinguistics* 11, no. 3 (1990): 253–272. http://pubman.mpdl.mpg.de/pubman/item/escidoc:68785:7/component/escidoc:506904/Cutler_1990_Speaker+sex.pdf

9 "60 to 80 . . ." Mendelberg, Tali, and Christopher F. Karpowitz. "More Women, but Not Nearly Enough." *New York Times,* November 8, 2012, https://campaign-stops.blogs.nytimes.com/2012/11/08/more-women-but-not-nearly-enough/

9 "That goes for . . ." Smith, Stacy L., Marc Choueiti, and Katherine Pieper. "Inequality in 800 Popular Films: Examining Portrayals of Gender, Race/Ethnicity, LGBT, and Disability from 2007–2015." *Media, Diversity, & Social*

Change Initiative (2009), http://annenberg.usc.edu/pages/~/media/MDSCI/
Dr%20Stacy%20L%20Smith%20Inequality%20in%20800%20Films%20
FINAL.ashx

9 "Consider Glen Mazzara ..." Lev-Ram, Michal. "Why This Former 'The Walking Dead' Producer Banned 'Manterrupting.'" *Fortune*, March 8, 2016, http://fortune.com/2016/03/08/glen-mazzara-diversity-writers/

10 "They didn't believe ..." Glen Mazzara, personal interview, July 28, 2017.

10 "Indeed, less than ..." Smith, Stacy L., Marc Choueiti, and Katherine Pieper. "Inclusion or Invisibility? Comprehensive Annenberg Report on Diversity in Entertainment." USC Annenberg School for Communication and Journalism, http://annenberg.usc.edu/pages/~/media/MDSCI/CARDReport%20FINAL%2022216.ashx; Mandell, Andrea. "Study: Just 7% of Top 2016 Films Were Directed by Women." *USA Today*, January 12, 2017, https://www.usatoday.com/story/life/movies/2017/01/12/study-just-7-top-2016-films-were-directed-women/96495880/

10 "'I was complicit ...'" Lev-Ram, Michal. "Why This Former 'The Walking Dead' Producer Banned 'Manterrupting'." *Fortune*, March 8, 2016, http://fortune.com/2016/03/08/glen-mazzara-diversity-writers/

11 "And when researchers ..." Karpowitz, Christopher F., Tali Mendelberg, and Lee Shaker. "Gender Inequality in Deliberative Participation." *American Political Science Review* (2002). doi: 10.1017/S0003055412000329

11 "Christine Lagarde, head ..." Parker, Ceri. "'When the woman starts talking, the men switch off'—Christine Lagarde on why gender parity is taking so long." World Economic Forum, January 18, 2017, https://www.weforum.org/agenda/2017/01/when-the-woman-starts-talking-the-men-switch-off-davos-participants-on-why-gender-parity-is-taking-so-long/

11 "She doesn't hesitate ..." Christine Lagarde, "Davos 2017—Disrupting the Status Quo of Gender Roles." World Economic Forum, 2017. Online video. January 18, 2017, https://youtu.be/-MoaKjOTTY4?t=34m30s

11 "'You can see ...'" Linda Hudson, personal interview, December 4, 2014.

11 "They almost never ..." Snyder, Kieran. "How to Get Ahead as a Woman in Tech: Interrupt Men." *Slate*, July 23, 2014, http://www.slate.com/blogs/lexicon_valley/2014/07/23/study_men_interrupt_women_more_in_tech_workplaces_but_high_ranking_women.html

11 "A Northwestern University ..." Jacobi, Tonja, and Dylan Schweers. "Justice, Interrupted: The Effect of Gender, Ideology and Seniority at Supreme Court Oral Arguments." *Virginia Law Review* (2017), http://ssrn.com/abstract=2933016

12 "'It takes endurance ...'" Kim Metcalf-Kupres, personal interview, January 18, 2017.

14 "Topping the list ..." "Moving Women Forward into Leadership Roles." *KPMG Women's Leadership Study*, 2015, http://womensleadership.kpmg.us/content/dam/kpmg-womens-leadership-golf/womensleadershippressrelease/FINAL%20Womens%20Leadership%20v19.pdf

14 "It's so common ..." Murphy, Tim, and Tasneem Raja. "Ladies Last: 8 Inventions by Women That Dudes Got Credit For." *Mother Jones*, October 15, 2013, http://www.motherjones.com/media/2013/10/ada-lovelace-eight-inventions-women-erasure-credit/

14 "The classic example . . ." Ruiz, Rebecca. "What to Do When You're a Woman and a Man Takes Credit for Your Success." *Mashable*, February 17, 2016, http://mashable.com/2016/02/17/man-takes-credit-woman/#5wprmWjaNmqK

15 "'Then, when they . . .'" Lev-Ram, Michal. "Why This Former 'The Walking Dead' Producer Banned 'Manterrupting.'" *Fortune*, March 8, 2016, http://fortune.com/2016/03/08/glen-mazzara-diversity-writers/

15 "Mazzara has since . . ." Glen Mazzara, personal interview, July 28, 2017.

16 "Then each makes . . ." Allyn, Jennifer. "30% Club: Growth Through Diversity," event from the 30% Club, September, 23, 2015.

16 "The first bill . . ." Stolberg, Sheryl G. "Obama Signs Equal-Pay Legislation." *New York Times*, January 29, 2009, https://nyti.ms/2jL18Gw

18 "When given a mix . . ." "Saying it like it isn't: Mixed messages from men and women in the workplace." *Journal of Applied Social Psychology* 32, no. 12 (2002): 2435–2457, https://pdfs.semanticscholar.org/cdd9/cd05f70f41fea6784d a74b464d6dfe376f8c.pdf

19 "His work helped . . ." Frances, Taplett, personal email to the author, July 26, 2017.

19 "The bottom line . . ." Matt Krentz, personal interview, March 17, 2015, and email correspondence, July 2017.

Chapter 2: She'll Make You More Successful

21 "But now that . . ." "Tupperware!" *American Experience, PBS.* (2004). WGBH Educational Foundation, http://www.pbs.org/wgbh/americanexperience /features/general-article/tupperware-plastics/

21 "Then he and . . ." Doll, Jen. "How a Single Mom Created a Plastic Food-Storage Empire." *Mental Floss*, June 6, 2017, http://mentalfloss.com/article/59687/ how-single-mom-created-plastic-food-storage-empire

22 "He was sure . . ." Kealing, Bob. *Tupperware Unsealed: Brownie Wise, Earl Tupper, and the Home Party Pioneers.* Gainsesville: University Press of Florida, 2008.

22 "An astonishing 85 percent . . ." "Women Make Up 85% of All Consumer Purchases." *Bloomberg*, July 22. Online video. https://www.bloomberg.com/news/ videos/b/9e28517f-8de1–4e59-bcda-ce536aa50bd6

23 "Clothing designers struggled . . ." Desta, Yohana. "5 Fashion Brands Actually Eyeing Bigger Pockets for the iPhone 6 Plus." *Mashable*, September 30, 2014, http://mashable.com/2014/09/30/iphone-6-plus-pockets/#1FmspquzwZqy

23 "Apple remains 68 percent . . ." "Inclusion & Diversity." *Apple*, 2017, https:// www.apple.com/diversity/

23 "So this creaky . . ." Belluck, Pam. "Chilly at Work? Office Formula Was Devised for Men." *New York Times*, August 3, 2015, http://www.nytimes.com/2015/08/04/ science/chilly-at-work-a-decades-old-formula-may-be-to-blame.html?_r=0

23 "A 2011 study . . ." Bose, Dipan, Maria Segui-Gomez, and Jeff R. Crandall. "Vulnerability of Female Drivers Involved in Motor Vehicle Crashes: An Analysis of US Population at Risk." *American Journal of Public Health* 101, no. 12 (2011): 2368–2373. doi: 10.2105/AJPH.2011.300275

24 "Because medical testing . . ." Cahill, Larry. "Equal ≠ The Same: Differences in the Human Brain." *Cerebrum: The Dana Forum on Brain Science* 5 (2014), https:// www.ncbi.nlm.nih.gov/pmc/articles/PMC4087190/

24 "Even today, most..." Karp, Natasha A. "Prevalence of sexual dimorphism in mammalian phenotypic traits." *Nature Communications* 15475 (2017), https://www.nature.com/articles/ncomms15475

24 "For starters, we'd..." Morais, Betsy. "The Unfunniest Joke in Technology." *The New Yorker,* September 9, 2013, http://www.newyorker.com/tech/elements/the-unfunniest-joke-in-technology

24 "'Here's What Would...'" Moore, Tracy. "Here's What Would Happen If More Women Designed/Marketed Lady Products." *Jezebel,* July 24, 2014, http://jezebel.com/heres-what-would-happen-if-more-women-designed-marketed-1608471511

25 "Buzzfeed weighed in..." Chack, Erin. "21 Pointlessly Gendered Products." *Buzzfeed,* January 24, 2014, http://www.buzzfeed.com/erinchack/pointlessly-gendered-products#.jnoRL5X70

24 "More practically, rather..." Ehrenberg, Rachel. "Building a Better Breast Pump." *The Atlantic,* September 15, 2014, http://www.theatlantic.com/health/archive/2014/09/building-a-better-breast-pump/380734/

26 "Female executives make..." Huang, Jiekun, and Darren J. Kisgen. "Gender and corporate finance: Are male executives overconfident relative to female executives?" *Journal of Financial Economics* 108, no. 3 (2013): 822–839, https://doi.org/10.1016/j.jfineco.2012.12.005

26 "Firms with the..." "Companies with More Women Board Directors Experience Higher Financial Performance, According to Latest Catalyst Bottom Line Report." Catalyst, October 23, 2013.

26 "Companies whose top..." Dawson, Julia, Richard Kersley, and Stefano Natella. "The CS Gender 3000: The Reward for Change." Credit Suisse Research Institute, September 2016, http://publications.credit-suisse.com/tasks/render/file/index.cfm?fileid=5A7755E1-EFDD-1973-A0B5C54AFF3FB0AE

26 "One study concluded..." Goodman, Leah M. "If Women Are So Good At Managing Money, Why Are So Few of Them Doing It?" *Newsweek,* January 26, 2016, http://www.newsweek.com/2016/02/05/hedge-fund-women-419481.html

27 "There's a reason..." Goudreau, Jenna. "Warren Buffett Invests Like a Girl?" *Forbes,* June 27, 2011, https://www.forbes.com/sites/jennagoudreau/2011/06/27/warren-buffett-invests-like-a-girl/#4e49fae68450

27 "The evidence also..." Zenger, Jack, and Joseph Folkman. "Are Women Better Leaders Than Men?" *Harvard Business Review,* March 15, 2012, https://hbr.org/2012/03/a-study-in-leadership-women-do

27 "'They're afraid to...'" Ibid.

28 "Home Depot founder..." Flaherty, Joseph. "How Home Depot Copied Apple to Build an Ingenious New Bucket." *Wired,* December 31, 2013, http://www.wired.com/2013/12/home-depot-reinvents-buckets/

28 "This wasn't rocket..." Scot Herbst, personal interview, March 2, 2015.

28 "The plastic bucket..." Alfred, Randy. "July 28, 1907: Tupperware's First Burp." *Wired,* September 28, 2009, https://www.wired.com/2009/07/dayintech_0728/

29 "She was a..." "Tupperware!" *American Experience, PBS.* (2004). WGBH Educational Foundation, http://www.pbs.org/wgbh/americanexperience/features/general-article/tupperware-plastics/

29 "'There is nothing...'" Ibid.

29 "She wasn't eligible..." Kealing, Bob. *Tupperware Unsealed: Brownie Wise, Earl Tupper, and the Home Party Pioneers.* Gainsesville: University Press of Florida, 2008.

31 "An ad for Lysol..." "10 Most Sexist Print Ads from the 1950s." *Business Pundit*, December 10, 2012, http://www.businesspundit.com/10-most-sexist-print-ads-from-the-1950s/8/

32 "She gave out Cadillacs..." "Tupperware!" *American Experience, PBS.* (1996–2017). WGBH Educational Foundation, http://www.pbs.org/wgbh/americanexperience/features/general-article/tupperware-plastics/

32 "She sometimes ordered..." Ibid.

32 "Brownie had the ability..." Ibid.

32 "Researchers have found..." Tom, Pamela."Political Correctness in Diverse Workplace Fosters Creativity." *Berkeley Haas News*, November 25, 2014, http://newsroom.haas.berkeley.edu/research-news/political-correctness-diverse-workplace-fosters-creativity

32 "In one experiment..." Goncalo, Jack A., et al. "Creativity from Constraint? How the Political Correctness Norm Influences Creativity in Mixed-sex Work Groups." *Administrative Science Quarterly* 20, no. 10 (2014): 1–30. doi: 10.1177/0001839214563975

33 "In the mixed group..." Phillips, Katherine. "Diversity Helps Your Business but Not the Way You Think." *Forbes*, June 2, 2009, http://www.forbes.com/2009/06/02/diversity-collaboration-teams-leadership-managing-creativity.html

35 "Fast-forward to..." Ratliff, Kate A., and Shigehiro Oishi. "Gender Differences in Implicit Self-Esteem Following a Romantic Partner's Success or Failure." *Journal of Personality and Social Psychology* 105, no. 4 (2013): 688–702. doi: 10.1037/a0033769

35 "Women's self-esteem..." Marcotte, Amanda. "New Research Shows That Men Feel Insecure When Their Partners Succeed, but Women Don't." *Slate*, August 30, 2013, http://www.slate.com/blogs/xx_factor/2013/08/30/gender_differences_and_self_esteem_new_research_shows_that_men_feel_insecure.html

36 "When a man..." Ratliff, Kate A., and Shigehiro Oishi. "Gender Differences in Implicit Self-Esteem Following a Romantic Partner's Success or Failure." *Journal of Personality and Social Psychology* 105, no. 4 (2013): 688–702. doi: 10.1037/a0033769

36 "Even among young..." Verel, Patrick. "Being the Breadwinner Still Large Part of Male Identity, Study Finds." *Fordham University*, August 23, 2012, http://legacy.fordham.edu/campus_resources/enewsroom/archives/archive_2501.asp

36 "The hit to..." Paulhus, Delroy L., and Oliver P. John. "Egoistic and Moralistic Biases in Self-Perception: The Interplay of Self-Deceptive Styles with Basic Traits and Motives." *Journal of Personality* 66, no. 6 (1998): 1025–1060, http://onlinelibrary.wiley.com/doi/10.1111/1467-6494.00041/abstract

36 "One study found..." Furnham, Adrian, Joanna Moutafi, and Tomas Chamorro-Premuzic. "Personality and Intelligence: Gender, the Big Five, Self-Estimated and Psychometric Intelligence." *International Journal of Selection and Assessment* 13, no. 1 (2005): 11–24. doi: 10.1111/j.0965–075X.2005.00292

36 "In another experiment..." Konnikova, Maria. "The Confidence Game: Why We Fall for It... Every Time." *Columbia Business School,* November 29, 2016, http://www8.gsb.columbia.edu/leadershiplab/events/authortalks/konnikova

37 "Yet the reverse..." Munsch, Christin L. "Her Support, His Support: Money, Masculinity, and Marital Infidelity." *American Sociological Review* 80, no. 3 (2015): 469–495. doi: 10.1177/0003122415579989

37 "'Many men who...'" Grant, Adam. "Why So Many Men Don't Stand Up for Their Female Colleagues." *The Atlantic,* April 29, 2014. https://www.theatlantic.com/business/archive/2014/04/why-men-dont-stand-up-for-women-to-lead/361231/

37 "Working with women and other..." Chris Brassell, personal interview, March 12, 2015.

38 "Researchers have found..." Ratner, R. K., and Dale T. Miller. "The norm of self-interest and its effects on social action." *Journal of Personality and Social Psychology* 81, no 1 (2001) 5–16. doi: 10.1037/0022–3514.81.1.5

39 "What's more, championing..." Johnson, Stefanie K. "Women and Minorities Are Penalized for Promoting Diversity." *Harvard Business Review,* March 23, 2016, https://hbr.org/2016/03/women-and-minorities-are-penalized-for-promoting-diversity

39 "Back at his office..." Dunn, Laura. "Women in Business Q&A: Sue Sears Is Vice President of Global Diversity & Inclusion at Kimberly-Clark Corporation." *Huffington Post,"* August 9, 2014, http://www.huffingtonpost.com/laura-dunn/women-in-business-qa-sue_b_5664315.html; Bob Brand, email exchange, August 2, 2017.

39 "Falk already considered..." This note covers all subsequent Falk quotes to author. Tom Falk, personal interview, March 26, 2015.

40 "In China, where..." Bob Brand, email exchange, August 2, 2017.

40 "Some other companies..." Mundy, Liza. "Why Is Silicon Valley So Awful to Women?" *The Atlantic,* April 2017, https://www.theatlantic.com/magazine/archive/2017/04/why-is-silicon-valley-so-awful-to-women/517788/?utm_campaign=digest&utm_medium=email&utm_source=app

40 "They were 'threatened...'" Sue Dodsworth, personal interview, March 17, 2015.

40 "Other male executives..." Sue Sears, personal interview, March 17, 2015.

42 "Perhaps Earl Tupper..." "Tupperware!" *American Experience, PBS.* (1996–2017). WGBH Educational Foundation, http://www.pbs.org/wgbh/americanexperience/features/general-article/tupperware-plastics/

43 "With the help..." Minnick, Mimi. "Brownie Wise Papers." *Archives Center, National Museum of American History,* July 1995, http://amhistory.si.edu/archives/d7509.htm

43 "Brownie herself published..." "Tupperware!" *American Experience, PBS.*

(2004). WGBH Educational Foundation, http://www.pbs.org/wgbh/american-experience/features/general-article/tupperware-plastics/

43 "He instructed his . . ." Wise, Brownie. *Best Wishes, Brownie Wise: How to Put Your Wishes to Work*. Orlando: Podium Publishing, 1957.

43 "After she sued . . ." Dickinson, Joy W. "Rise and Fall of the 'Sunshine Cinderella'". *Orlando Sentinel*, June 8, 2008, http://articles.orlandosentinel.com /2008–06–08/news/brownie08_1_bob-kealing-tupperware-brownie-wise

44 "'There's a Tupperware party . . .'" This note covers subsequent references and comments quoted to author. Rick Goings, personal interview, November 10, 2015.

Chapter 3: We're All a Little Bit Sexist

46 "In their 2013 . . ." Banaji, Mahzarin R., Anthony G. Greenwald, and Eric Martin. *Blindspot: Hidden Biases of Good People*, New York: Delacorte Press, 2013.

46 "Multiple studies encompassing . . ." Rankin, Kenrya. "Study Unveils Subconscious Racial Bias in Asian, Black, White, Biracial People." *Colorlines*, August 24, 2015, http://www.colorlines.com/articles/study-unveils-subconscious-racial-bias-asian-black-white-biracial-people

47 "Not long ago . . ." Society for Industrial and Organizational Psychology. Brian Welle. http://www.siop.org/lec/2011/welle.aspx

47 "Over coffee in . . ." This note covers subsequent references and comments quoted to author. Brian Welle, personal interviews, January 27, 2015; July 8, 2015; July 22, 2017.

47 "It analyzes everything . . ." Kuang, Cliff. "6 Ways Google Hacks Its Cafeterias So Googlers Eat Healthier." *Co. Design*, March 26, 2012, http://www .fastcodesign.com/1669355/6-ways-google-hacks-its-cafeterias-so-googlers-eat-healthier; Goo, Sara Kehaulani. "Building a 'Googley' Workforce." *Washington Post*, October 21, 2006, http://www.washingtonpost.com/ wp-dyn/content/article/2006/10/20/AR2006102001461.html

47 "In designing its . . ." Holson, Laura M. "Putting a Bolder Face on Google." *New York Times*, February 28, 2009, http://www.nytimes.com/2009/03/01/ business/01marissa.html?_r=0

47 "Members of its . . ." Derose, Chris. "How Google Uses Data to Build a Better Worker." *The Atlantic*, October 7, 2013, https://www.theatlantic.com/business/ archive/2013/10/how-google-uses-data-to-build-a-better-worker/280347/

47 "According to Laszlo . . ." Bock, Laszlo. *Work Rules!: Insights from Inside Google That Will Transform How You Live and Lead*. New York: Grand Central Publishing, 2015.

49 "It boasts more . . ." Google Diversity. Accessed July 26, 2017, https://www .google.com/diversity/at-google.html

49 "The financial services . . ." Mercer, LLC. "When Women Thrive Businesses Thrive." Presented for the World Economic Forum, Davos-Klosters, Switzerland, January, 2017, https://www.mercer.com/content/dam/mercer/attachments/ global/glb-2017-davos-wwt-wef-summary.pdf

51 "In 1973, organizational . . ." Schein, Virginia E. "The relationship between sex role stereotypes and requisite management characteristics." *Journal of*

Applied Psychology 57, no. 2 (1993): 95–100, http://psycnet.apa.org/doiLanding?doi=10.1037%2Fh0037128

51 "'Acting as men . . .'" Wiley, Mary G., and Arlene Eskilson. "The Interaction of Sex and Power Base on Perceptions of Managerial Effectiveness." *Academy of Management Journal* 25, no. 3 (1982): 671–677. doi: 10.2307/256089; Wiley, Mary G., and Arlene Eskilson. "Speech style, gender stereotypes, and corporate success: What if women talk more like men." *Sex Roles* 12 (1985): 993–1007, http://link.springer.com/article/10.1007/BF00288100

51 "Studying sex differences . . ." Goodman, Walter. "TELEVISION REVIEW: Of Women and Men, and La Difference." *New York Times,* February 1st, 1995, http://www.nytimes.com/1995/02/01/movies/television-review-of-women-and-men-and-la-difference.html

54 "A study of . . ." Gorey, Colm. "High-Paying Jobs' Ads Shown Less to Women on Google, Study Finds." *Silicon Republic,* July 8, 2015, https://www.siliconrepublic.com/careers/high-paying-jobs-ads-shown-to-women-less-google; Datta, Amit. "Automated Experiments on Ad Privacy Settings." *Proceedings on Privacy Enhancing Technologies* 1, (2015). https://doi.org/10.1515/popets-2015-0007

54 "'Code is not neutral . . .'" Wiener, Anna. "Hacking Technology's Boys' Club." *New Republic,* January 31, 2016, https://newrepublic.com/article/128795/hacking-technologys-boys-club

55 "UN Women, a . . ." "UN Women ad series reveals widespread sexism." UN Women, October 21, 2013, http://www.unwomen.org/en/news/stories/2013/10/women-should-ads

55 "These unconscious biases . . ." Heilman, M. E., and Haynes M. C. "No credit where credit is due: Attributional rationalization of women's success in male-female teams." *Journal of Applied Psychology* 90, no. 5 (2005): 905–916.

55 "Similarly, even though . . ." Sheltzer, Jason M., and Joan C. Smith. "Elite male faculty in the life sciences employ fewer women." *Proceedings of the National Academy of Sciences of the United States of America* III, no. 28 (2014): 10107–10112. doi: 10.1073/pnas.1403334111

55 "These biases start . . ." Mondschein, Emily R., Karen E. Adolph, and Catherine S. Tamis-LeMonda. "Gender bias in mother's expectations about infant crawling." *Journal of Experimental Child Psychology* 77 (2000): 304–316. doi: 10.1006/jecp.2000.2597

55 "Parents of male . . ." Stephens-Davidowitz, Seth. *Everybody Lies: Big Data, New Data, and What the Internet Can Tell Us About Who We Really Are.* New York: Dey Street Books, 2017.

56 "All of the teachers . . ." Marcotte, Amanda. "Teachers Give Girls Better Grades on Math Tests When They Don't Know They Are Girls." *Slate,* Feb 10, 2015, http://www.slate.com/blogs/xx_factor/2015/02/10/teacher_bias_in_math_new_study_finds_teachers_grade_boys_more_generously.html

56 "Not only students . . ." O'Shaughnessy, Lynn. "Teen girls face leadership bias." CBS News, August 28, 2015, http://www.cbsnews.com/news/teen-girls-face-leadership-bias/

56 "Women are 33 percent . . ." Meyer, Ali. "Women now 33 percent more likely than

men to earn college degrees." CNS News, March 31, 2014, http://cnsnews.com/news/article/ali-meyer/women-now-33-more-likely-men-earn-college-degrees

56 "Yet professors are..." Sarah L. Eddy, Sara E. Brownell, and Mary Pat Wenderoth. "Gender gaps in achievement and participation in multiple introduction biology classrooms." *Life Sciences Education* 16, No. 4 (2017): http://www.lifescied.org/content/13/3/478; Hancock, Adrienne B., and Benjamin A. Rubin. "Influence of Communication Partner's Gender on Language." *Journal of Language and Social Psychology* (May 11, 2014), http://isites.harvard.edu/fs/html/icb.topic58474/krupnick.html

56 "The researchers concluded..." Yong, Ed. "XY Bias: How Male Biology Students See Their Female Peers." *The Atlantic,* February 16, 2016, https://www.theatlantic.com/science/archive/2016/02/male-biology-students-underestimate-their-female-peers/462924/

56 "New female grads..." Babcock, Linda, Sara Laschever, Michele Gelfand, and Deborah Small. "Nice Girls Don't Ask." *Harvard Business Review,* October 2003, https://hbr.org/2003/10/nice-girls-dont-ask

56 "At every level..." Waller, Nikki, and Joann S. Lublin. "What's Holding Women Back in the Workplace?" *Wall Street Journal,* September 30, 2015, https://www.wsj.com/articles/whats-holding-women-back-in-the-workplace-1443600242

57 "Social scientists have..." Nordell, Jessica. "It's Not Foot in Mouth Disease." *Medium,* December 6, 2015, https://medium.com/@jessnordell/it-s-not-foot-in-mouth-disease-6fdc3e2b08bc

57 "Adding to the burden..." Gutiérrez y Muhs, Gabriella, Yolanda Flores Niemann, Carmen G. González, and Angela P. Harris. *Presumed Incompetent: The Intersections of Race and Class for Women in Academia.* Utah State University Press, 2012.

57 "Other studies have..." Swim, Janet K., and Lawrence J. Sanna. "He's skilled, she's lucky: a meta-analysis of observers' attributions for women's and men's successes and failures." *Personality and Social Psychology Bulletin,* 22, no. 5 (1999): 507–519. doi: 10.1177/0146167296225008

57 "When women make..." Heilman, Madeline E. "Sex stereotypes and their effects in the workplace: what we know and what we don't know." *Journal of Social Behavior and Personality* 10 (1995): 3–26.

57 "They literally took..." Banaji, Mahzarin R., and Anthony G. Greenwald. *Blind Spot: Hidden Biases of Good People.* New York: Bantam Books, 2016.

58 "These tiny biases have outsize..." "Male-Female Differences: A Computer Simulation," http://www.ruf.rice.edu/~lane/papers/male_female.pdf

58 "And you can't..." Brian Nosek, personal interview, January 21, 2015.

58 "Researchers estimated that..." Kristof, Nicholas. "She Gets No Respect." *New York Times,* June 11, 2014, https://www.nytimes.com/2014/06/12/opinion/nicholas-kristof-she-gets-no-respect.html

59 "The company's roots..." Bright Futura. "20 Billionaire College Dropouts," May 26, 2012, http://www.brightfutura.com/20-billionaire-college-dropouts/

59 "The world's first..." World Wide Web Foundation. "History of the Web." Accessed July 27, 2017, http://webfoundation.org/about/vision/history-of-the-web/

59 "With the right code..." Google, Inc. "Our Story: From the Garage to the

Googleplex." Accessed July 27, 2017, https://www.google.com/intl/en/about/our-story/

60 "But he was . . ." Malseed, Mark. "The Story of Sergey Brin." *Moment,* February 2007, http://web.archive.org/web/20130121055147/http://www.oldsite.momentmag.net/moment/issues/2007/02/200702-BrinFeature.html

60 "Sergey's mother was . . ." Epstein, Nadine. "Genia Brin's Double Parkinson's Mutation." Northwest Parkinson's Foundation, https://nwpf.org/stay-informed/news/2012/07/genia-brin%E2%80%99s-double-parkinson%E2%80%99s-mutation/

60 "He spent hours . . ." McPherson, Stephanie Sammartino. *Sergey Brin and Larry Page: Founders of Google.* New York: Twenty-First Century Books, 2010.

60 "So when, in . . ." Swift, Mike. "Susan Wojcicki: The Most Important Googler You've Never Heard Of." *The Mercury News,* February 3, 2011, http://www.mercurynews.com/2011/02/03/susan-wojcicki-the-most-important-googler-youve-never-heard-of/

61 "And while it's . . ." Laszlo Bock, personal interview, July 20, 2017.

61 "Bock, who joined . . ." Brian Welle, personal interview, July 8, 2017.

62 "There's Women Who . . ." LinkedIn. "Women Who Code." Accessed July 27, 2017, https://www.linkedin.com/company-beta/3233332/; Black Girls Code. "Measuring Our Impact." Accessed July 27, 2017, http://www.blackgirlscode.com/what-we-do.html; Guynn, Jessica. "No Boys Allowed: Girls Who Code Takes on Gender Gap." *USA Today,* August 12, 2014, https://www.usatoday.com/story/tech/2014/08/12/girls-who-code-facebook-sheryl-sandberg/13784445/

63 "If it held . . ." Romei, Valentina. "Half of the Global CEOs Are in Their 50s." *Financial Times,* September 11, 2015, http://blogs.ft.com/ftdata/2015/09/11/half-of-the-global-ceos-are-in-their-50s/

63 "In the early . . ." Contorno, Steve. "Rand Paul Says More than Half of Students at Medical, Dental and Law Schools Are Females." *Politifact,* January 28, 2014, http://www.politifact.com/truth-o-meter/statements/2014/jan/28/rand-paul/rand-paul-says-more-half-students-medical-dental-a/

63 "Yet fast-forward . . ." American Bar Association—Commission on Women in the Profession. "A Current Glance at Women in the Law." *American Bar Association,* 2014, https://www.americanbar.org/dam/aba/marketing/women/current_glance_statistics_july2014.authcheckdam.pdf

63 "Researchers have found . . ." Castilla, Emilio J., and Stephen Benard. "The paradox of meritocracy in organizations." *Administrative Science Quarterly* 55, (2010): 543–576. doi: 10.2189/asqu.2010.55.4.543

63 "In one experiment, psychologists . . ." Sachdeva, S., Iliev, R., Medin, D. L. (2009). "Sinning Saints and Saintly Sinners: the Paradox of Moral Self-Regulation." *Psychological Science.* 20(4): 523–528, http://groups.psych.northwestern.edu/medin/documents/SachdevaSinningSaints.pdf

64 "They didn't feel . . ." Ibid.

64 "GitHub is such . . ." Rusli, Evelyn. "Torment Claims Make Startup Grow Up." *Wall Street Journal,* July 18, 2014, http://www.wsj.com/articles/harassment-claims-make-startup-github-grow-up-1405639553

64 "It once commissioned . . ." Orsini, Lauren. "Why GitHub's CEO Ditched Its Divisive 'Meritocracy' Rug." *Readwrite,* January 24, 2014, http://readwrite .com/2014/01/24/github-meritocracy-rug/

65 "GitHub itself is . . ." Rusli, Evelyn. "Torment Claims Make Startup Grow Up." *Wall Street Journal,* July 18, 2014, http://www.wsj.com/articles/harassment-claims-make-startup-github-grow-up-1405639553

66 "So in 2012 . . ." Brian Welle, personal interview, July 8, 2017.

66 "A 2008 *Harvard* . . ." Evans, Jon. "Women in Tech: It's Not Just a Pipeline Problem." *Tech Crunch,* August 23, 2014, https://techcrunch.com/2014/08/23/just-another-white-dude-writing-about-diversity/

66 "A survey of . . ." Vassallo, Trae, et al. "Elephant in the valley." Accessed July 27, 2017, https://www.elephantinthevalley.com/

66 "In 2017, a . . ." Louise Matsakis, Jason Koebler, and Sarah Emerson. "Here Are the Citations for the Anti-Diversity Manifest Circulating at Google." *Vice,* August 7, 2017, https://motherboard.vice.com/en_us/article/evzjww/here-are-the-citations-for-the-anti-diversity-manifesto-circulating -at-google.

66 "The company fired . . ." Rachel Sandler. "Ads Posted Outside Google Offices Slam CEO for Firing Controversial Memo's Author," *USA Today,* August 11, 2017, https://www.usatoday.com/story/tech/2017/08/11/anti-google-ads -appear-outside-google-offices-response-controversial-memo/559603001/

66 "Google has also . . ." Levin, Sam. "Accused of Underpaying Women, Google Says It's Too Expensive to Get Wage Data." *The Guardian,* May 26, 2017, https://www .theguardian.com/technology/2017/may/26/google-gender-discrimination -case-salary-records

Chapter 4: The Twelve Most Terrifying Words in the English Language

69 "Whatever quality the . . ." Uhlmann, Eric, and Geoffrey L. Cohen. "Constructed criteria: redefining merit to justify discrimination." *American Psychological Society* 16 no. 6 (2005), https://ed.stanford.edu/sites/default/files/ uhlmann_et_2005.pdf

69 "'You've had your . . .'" "The Trouble with Women at Work-1959 Educational Film-S88TV1," YouTube video, posted by Tomorrow Always Comes, April 21, 2014, https://www.youtube.com/watch?v=paIVEeyoqfE

70 "After the passage . . ." Anand, Rohini, and Mary-Frances Winters. "A retrospective view of corporate diversity training from 1964 to the present." *Academy of Management Learning & Education* 7, no. 3 (2008): 356–372, http://www .wintersgroup.com/corporate-diversity-training-1964-to-present.pdf

70 "'Women don't write . . .'" Povich, Lynn. "Women in the Workplace: How 'Good Girls' Fight Back." *LA Times,* October 7, 2012, http://articles.latimes .com/2012/oct/07/opinion/la-oe-povich-newsweek-discrimination-gender -20121007

70 "In her lively . . ." Povich, Lynn. *The Good Girls Revolt: How the Women of Newsweek Sued Their Bosses and Changed the Workplace.* New York: PublicAffairs, 2012.

70 "It took two . . ." Ibid.

70 "By the time . . ." Palmeira, Amanda. "Sung Their Way into the Newsroom: How Women at the *Detroit News* Changed Journalism." BA Thesis, University of Central Florida, 2012, http://etd.fcla.edu/CF/CFH0004306/Palmeira_Amanda _N_201212_BA.pdf

70 "Thomas wasn't terribly . . ." Covert, Bryce. "Woman Accusing Clarence Thomas Is Just One of Many Alleged Victims." *Think Progress*, October 28, 2016, https://thinkprogress.org/clarence-thomas-harassment-accusers -3608a700bf29

71 "The only exception . . ." Dobbin, Frank, Alexandra Kalev, and Erin Kelly. "Diversity management in corporate America." *American Sociological Association* 6, no. 4 (2007): 21–27. doi: 10.1525/ctx.2007.6.4.21

71 "In other words . . ." Frank Dobbin, personal interview, May 13, 2015.

71 "Unfortunately, he found, . . ." Dobbin, Frank, and Alexandra Kalev. "Why Diversity Programs Fail." *Harvard Business Review,* July–August, 2016, https:// hbr.org/2016/07/why-diversity-programs-fail

72 "Some surmised . . ." Anand, Rohini, and Mary-Frances Winters. "A retrospective view of corporate diversity training from 1964 to the present." *Academy of Management Learning & Education* 7, no. 3 (2008): 356–372, http://www .wintersgroup.com/corporate-diversity-training-1964-to-present.pdf

72 "The irony is . . ." Dobbin, Frank, Alexandra Kalev, and Erin Kelly. "Diversity management in corporate America." *American Sociological Association* 6, no. 4 (2007): 21–27, doi: 10.1525/ctx.2007.6.4.21

72 "The men who . . ." Dover, Tessa L., Brenda Major, and Cheryl R. Kaiser. "Members of high-status groups are threatened by pro-diversity organizational messages." *Journal of Experimental Social Psychology* 62 (January 2016): 58–67. doi: 10.1016/j.jesp.2015.10.006

73 "They were certain . . ." Dover, Tessa L., Brenda Major, and Cheryl R. Kaiser. "Diversity Policies Rarely Make Companies Fairer, and They Feel Threatening to White Men." *Harvard Business Review,* January 4, 2016, https://hbr .org/2016/01/diversity-policies-dont-help-women-or-minorities-and-they- make-white-men-feel-threatened

73 "The managers who . . ." Grant, Adam, and Sheryl Sandberg. "When Talking About Bias Backfires." *New York Times,* December 6, 2014, https://www .nytimes.com/2014/12/07/opinion/sunday/adam-grant-and-sheryl-sandberg -on-discrimination-at-work.html

73 "As individuals, we . . ." Thomas-Hunt, Melissa C., and Carlos Santos. "Everybody's Biased, So I Can Be Too." University of Virginia Darden School of Business, November 5, 2015, https://ideas.darden.virginia.edu/2015/11/every- bodys-biased-so-i-can-be-too/

73 "Yet companies continue . . ." Guo, Jeff. "Why We Should Give Up Trying to Make People Less Sexist." *Washington Post,* March 15, 2016, https://www .washingtonpost.com/news/wonk/wp/2016/03/15/why-we-should-give-up- trying-to-make-people-less-sexist/

73 "It's all led . . ." "Diversity Fatigue." *The Economist,* February 11, 2016, https:// www.economist.com/news/business/21692865-making-most-workplace -diversity-requires-hard-work-well-good-intentions-diversity

74 "Whatever it is . . ." Duguid, M. M., and M. C. Thomas-Hunt. "Condoning stereo-typing? How awareness of stereotyping prevalence impacts expression of stereotypes." *Journal of Applied Psychology* 100, no. 2 (2015): 343–359. doi: 10.1037/a0037908

74 "In one study . . ." Hebl, Michelle R., Jessica Bigazzi Foster, Laura M. Mannix, and John F. Dovidio. "Formal and interpersonal discrimination: a field study of bias toward homosexual applicants." *Personality and Social Psychology Bulletin*, 28, no. 6 (2002), https://pdfs.semanticscholar.org/dded/244d61d10907b1270d5caf5428fb8cc2c12b.pdf

75 "At Google, about . . ." Roya Soleimani, email interview with author, January 22, 2016; Kelly, Heather. "Google commits $150 million to diversity." CNN, May 7, 2015, http://money.cnn.com/2015/05/06/technology/google-diversity-plan/

75 "At least 20 percent . . ." Giang, Vivian. "The Growing Business of Detecting Unconscious Bias." *Fast Company,* May 5, 2015, https://www.fastcompany.com/3045899/the-growing-business-of-detecting-unconscious-bias

75 "'We do that . . .'" Dominic Barton, personal interview, November 16, 2015.

75 "By some estimates . . ." Lublin, Joann S. "Bringing Hidden Biases Into the Light." *Wall Street Journal,* January 9, 2014, https://www.wsj.com/articles/bringing-hidden-biases-into-the-light-1389311814?tesla=y; Association for Talent Development. "$164.2 Billion Spend on Training and Development by U.S. Companies." December 12, 2013, https://www.td.org/Publications/Blogs/ATD-Blog/2013/12/ASTD-Releases-2013-State-of-the-Industry-Report

77 "The company says . . ." Bertie Thompson, email interview with author, July 22, 2017.

77 "Facebook engineer that . . ." Seetharaman, Deepa. "Facebook's Female Engineers Claim Gender Bias." *Wall Street Journal,* May 2, 2017, https://www.wsj.com/articles/facebooks-female-engineers-claim-gender-bias-1493737116

79 "'I didn't get . . .'" Guynn, Jessica. "Facebook Takes Heat for Diversity 'Pipeline' Remarks." *USA Today,* July 15, 2016, https://www.usatoday.com/story/tech/news/2016/07/15/facebook-diversity-pipeline-silicon-valley/87142058/

79 "Among others, it . . ." *Collins English Dictionary,* 12th ed., s.v. "horns and halo effect." New York: HarperCollins Publishers, 2014, http://www.thefreedictionary.com/horns+and+halo+effect; Google. "Took: Use Unbiasing Checklists." re:Work. Accessed August 1, 2017, https://rework.withgoogle.com/guides/unbiasing-use-structure-and-criteria/steps/use-unbiasing-checklists/

80 "As a diagnostic . . ." Laszlo Bock, personal interview, July 20, 2017.

80 "But Google does . . ." Rudulph, Heather Wood. "Interview Insider: How to Get Hired at Google." *Cosmopolitan,* February 12, 2015, http://www.cosmopolitan.com/career/news/a36390/interview-insider-google-career-jobs/

80 "In other words . . ." Chatman, Jennifer A. "Matching people and organizations: selection and socializing in public accounting firms." *Administrative Science Quarterly* 36 (1991): 459–484, http://faculty.haas.berkeley.edu/chatman/papers/34_matchingpeopleorgs.pdf

80 "A global survey . . ." Rivera, Lauren A. "Guess Who Doesn't Fit in at Work." *New York Times,* May 30, 2015, https://www.nytimes.com/2015/05/31/opinion/sunday/guess-who-doesnt-fit-in-at-work.html?_r=0

81 "In 2017, even Facebook reported . . ." "Facebook Diversity Update: Building a More Diverse, Inclusive Workforce." https://fbnewsroomus.files.wordpress .com/2017/08/fb_diversity_2017_final.pdf

81 "At the bottom . . ." https://blog.twitter.com/en_us/topics/company/2017/ building-a-more-inclusive-twitter-in-2016.html

81 "In 2014, 21 percent . . ." "Google says 21 percent of tech hires in 2014 were women." CNBC, June 2, 2015, http://www.cnbc.com/2015/06/02/google-says-21-percent-of-tech-hires-in-2014-were-women.html

81 "Nancy Lee, a former . . ." Weise, Elizabeth and Swartz, Jonathan. "Diversity Debate Divides Silicon Valley," *USA Today,* August 6, 2017. https://www .usatoday.com/story/tech/2017/08/06/diversity-debate-divides-silicon -valley/543487001/

81 "As James Alitzer . . ." Bowles, Nellie. "Push for Gender Equality in Tech? Some Men Say it's Gone Too Far," *New York Times,* September 23, 2017, https://www.nytimes.com/2017/09/23/technology/silicon-valley-men -backlash-gender-scandals.html

82 "The few who did . . ." Sue Shellenbarger. "The XX Factor: What's Holding Women Back?" *Wall Street Journal,* May 7, 2012, https://www.wsj.com/articles /SB10001424052702304746604577381953238775784

82 "And in a . . ." Kang, Cecilia. "Google Data-mines Its Approach to Promoting Women." *Washington Post,* April 2, 2014, https://www.washingtonpost .com/news/the-switch/wp/2014/04/02/google-data-mines-its-women-problem/?utm_term=.5eeaaa9781b6

82 "'tell them for . . .'" "Women in the Google Workplace." *Wall Street Journal* video, May 1, 2012, http://www.wsj.com/video/women-in-the-google-workplace /16A9B911-E7D9-4E1D-99E1-979CB1B0F35C.html

82 "Once, when the . . ." WNYC Studios. "What Google Is Doing to Solve Its Gender Problem." Host Manoush Zomorodi, April 29, 2015, http://www.wnyc.org/ story/google-test-case-gender-bias/

82 "The firm has . . ." Google. "Took: Give Your Own Unbiasing Workshop." re:Work. Accessed August 1, 2017, https://rework.withgoogle.com/guides/unbiasing -hold-everyone-accountable/steps/give-your-own-unbiasing-workshop/

83 "The succinctly monikered . . ." Hitt, Jack. "The Amateur Future of Space Travel." *New York Times,* July 1, 2007, http://www.nytimes.com/2007/07/01/ magazine/01nasa-t.html

83 "In 2011, Google . . ." http://time.com/money/4098469/paid-parental-leave -google-amazon-apple-facebook/; https://qz.com/604723/when-google -increased-paid-maternity-leave-the-rate-at-which-new-mothers-quit-dropped-50/; http://fortune.com/best-companies/google/

83 "Attrition rates for . . ." Bock,Laszlo. *Work Rules!: Insights from Inside Google That Will Transform How You Live and Lead.* New York: Grand Central Publishing, 2015.

83 "That set off . . ." Lev-Ram, Michal. "Exclusive: Twitter to Give All New Parents 20 Weeks of Paid Leave." *Fortune,* April 5, 2016, http://fortune.com/2016/04/05/ twitter-20-weeks-parental-leave/; Tepper, Taylor. "Facebook Workers Just Got a Better Parental Leave Policy. Here's When You'll Get Yours." *Time,* Decem-

ber 3, 2015, http://time.com/money/4129990/facebook-paid-parental-leave/; Fairchild, Caroline. "Change.org Boosts Paid Parental Leave Perks for All New Parents." *Fortune*, October 20, 2014, http://fortune.com/2014/10/20/paid -parental-leave-tech-companies/

83 "Netflix and Virgin..." Taylor, Tess. "Netflix Transforms Employee Bene-fits-Year Long Parental Leave Policy." *The Balance*, September 16, 2016, https:// www.thebalance.com/netflix-parental-leave-1177969; Guilford, Gwynn. "Richard Branson Just Gave the Paternity Leave Cause a Major Boost." *Quartz*, June 10, 2015, https://qz.com/425002/richard-branson-just-gave-the-paternity -leave-cause-a-major-boost/

84 "At least ninety-six..." Kurtzleben, Danielle. "Lots of Other Countries Man-date Paid Leave. Why Not the U.S.?" NPR, July 15, 2015, http://www.npr.org/ sections/itsallpolitics/2015/07/15/422957640/lots-of-other-countries-mandate -paid-leave-why-not-the-us; Cole, Diane. "New Dads in Togo Are Guaran-teed Something That U.S. Dads Aren't." NPR, March 14, 2015, http://www.npr.org/ sections/goatsandsoda/2015/03/14/392632777/new-dads-in-togo-are-guaranteed -something-that-u-s-dads-arent

84 "Apple's sprawling new..." Murphy, Mike. "Apple's New $5 Billion Campus Has a 100,000-Square-Foot Gym and No Daycare." *Quartz*, May 16, 2017, https:// qz.com/984785/apples-new-5-billion-apple-park-campus-has-a-100000- square-foot-gym-and-no-daycare-aapl/

84 "His vision of..." Bergstein, Brian. "Google Execs Have Ideas on How to Run Your Business." *MIT Technology Review*, September 29, 2014, https://www .technologyreview.com/s/531056/google-execs-have-ideas-on-how-to-run- your-business/

86 "Notably, the decor..." Cheryan, Sapna, Victoria C. Plaut, Paul G. Davies, and Claude M. Steele. "Ambient belonging: How stereotypical cues impact gender participation in computer science." *Journal of Personality and Social Psy-chology* 97, no. 6 (2009): 1045–1060, http://dx.doi.org.ezproxy.cul.columbia .edu/10.1037/a0016239

87 "In tech, there's..." Cooke-Garza, Kennedy. "The Cool Girl Trap: Or, Why Sexism in Tech Isn't Going Away." *Medium*, October 6, 2015, https://medium .com/endless/the-cool-girl-trap-or-why-sexism-in-tech-isn-t-going-away- 825b9a7642f5

87 "'She laughs along...'" Ibid.

88 "She ultimately was..." Ibid.

88 "The audience cheered..." Yadron, Danny. "Thoughts on Gender Equality in Tech, Interrupted." *Wall Street Journal*, March 16, 2015, https://blogs.wsj.com/ digits/2015/03/16/thoughts-on-gender-equality-in-tech-interrupted/

Chapter 5: She's Pretty Sure You Don't Respect Her

90 "Even today, 40 to..." Grant, Adam, and Sheryl Sandberg, "When Talking About Bias Backfires." *New York Times*, December 6, 2014, http://www.nytimes .com/2014/12/07/opinion/sunday/adam-grant-and-sheryl-sandberg-on -discrimination-at-work.html?_r=0

90 "The old joke . . ." Merrill, Andrea. "#IlookLikeASurgeon: Breaking Stereo-types and Promoting Diversity," *Huffington Post*, September 3, 2015, http://www.huffingtonpost.com/andrea-merrill/look-like-a-surgeon-breaking-stereotypes_b_8079862.html

90 "I first spoke . . ." This note covers subsequent comments quoted to author. Andrea Merrill, personal interview, July 5, 2016.

90 "Researchers have found . . ." Neumann, Janice, "Why Are Female Doctors Introduced by First Name While Men Are Called 'Doctor'?" *Washington Post*, June 23, 2017, https://www.washingtonpost.com/national/health-science/why-are-female-doctors-introduced-by-first-name-while-men-are-called-doctor/2017/06/23/b790ddf2-4572-11e7-a196-a1bb629f64cb_story.html?utm_term=.f34ca94e348f

90 "I always feel. . . ." Andrea Merrill, personal interview, July 5, 2016.

91 "When a man . . ." Kay, Katty, and Claire Shipman. *The Confidence Code*. New York: HarperCollins Publishers, 2014.

91 "'Female doctors often. . .'" Gjerberga, Elisabeth, and Lise Kjølsrødb. "The doctor-nurse relationship: how easy is it to be a female doctor co-operating with a female nurse?" Social Science and Medicine Work Research Institute, 2001, https://www.med.upenn.edu/gastro/documents/Thedoctor-nurserelationshipHoweasyisittobeafemaledoctoreco-operatingwithafemalnurse.pdf

91 "Purdue University researcher . . ." "MTSU Professor Gauges Politeness to Male, Female Bosses." *MTSUS News*, July 17, 2013, http://www.mtsunews.com/mtsu-professor-gauges-politeness-to-male-female-bosses/

91 "To test her . . ." Ibid.

92 "Here are some . . ." Xiaowei Shi, "Did You Become More Polite When Talking to a Male Supervisor? The Impact of Supervisor's Gender on Employees' Upward Influence Behavior," final draft, part of docotoral dissertation for Purdue University, sent to me by the author on December 9, 2014.

92 "About 40 percent of . . ." "Women and Leadership." Pew Research Center, January 14, 2015, http://www.pewsocialtrends.org/2015/01/14/women-and-leadership/

93 "Women may be . . ." Vial, Andrea C., Jaime L. Napier, and Victoria L. Brescoll. "A bed of thorns: Female leaders and the self-reinforcing cycle of illegitimacy." *The Leadership Quarterly* 27, 2016, http://dx.doi.org/10.1016/j.leaqua.2015.12.004 1048–9843.

93 "One study, drawing . . ." "Men benefit more than women from having authority." Phys.org, March 26, 2013, http://phys.org/news/2013-03-men-benefit-women-authority-job.html; Koenig, Anne M., Alice H. Eagly, Abigail A. Mitchell, and Tiina Ristikari. "Are leader stereotypes masculine? A meta-analysis of three research paradigms." *Psychological Bulletin* 137 no. 4 (2011): 616–42, https://www.semanticscholar.org/paper/Are-leader-stereotypes-masculine-A-meta-analysis-o-Koenig-Eagly/b2650126e807ea06514f dc9f95b128846c87046e; Hogg, Michael A., and Deborah J. Terry. "Social iden-tity and self-categorization processes in organizational contexts." *Acad-*

emy of Management Review 25, no. 1 (2000): 121–140, https://imcesec.files
.wordpress.com/2014/01/social-identity-and-self-categorization-process
-in-organizational-contexts-2.pdf

93 "The official definition..." Tobar, Hector. "Neckbeard, Mansplain, Now in
Oxford Dictionaries Online: Amazeballs." *LA Times*, August 14, 2014, http://
www.latimes.com/books/jacketcopy/la-et-jc-neckbeard-mansplain-amazeballs
-oxford-dictionary-words-20140814-story.html

94 "Orthopedic surgery is..." Association of American Medical Colleges. *2016
Physician Specialty Data Report*, 2016, https://www.aamc.org/download/471786/
data/2016physicianspecialtydatareportexecutivesummary.pdf

95 "Dr. Barres was..." Cornelia, Dean. "Dismissing 'Sexist Opinions' About
Women's Place in Science." *New York Times*, July 18, 2006, http://www.nytimes
.com/2006/07/18/science/18conv.html?_r=0

96 "he 'told me...'" Ibid.

96 "Later, as a..." Begley, Sharon. "He, Once a She, Offers Own View on Sci-
ence Spat." *Wall Street Journal*, July 13, 2006, http://www.wsj.com/articles/
SB115274744775305134

96 "After Dr. Barres transitioned..." Michelle Higgins, personal interview, July
20, 2017.

96 "As his presentation..." Ibid.

96 "Dr. Barres later..." Barres, Ben A. "Does Gender Matter?" *Nature*, 2006,
http://www.nature.com/nature/journal/v442/n7099/full/442133a.html

96 "This is why..." Nordell, Jessica. "Why Aren't Women Advancing at Work?
Ask a Transgender Person." *New Republic*, August 28, 2014, https://newrepublic
.com/article/119239/transgender-people-can-explain-why-women-dont
-advance-work

96 "*Quartz* editor..." McBee, Thomas Page. "Until I Was a Man, I Had No Idea How
Good Men Had It at Work." *Quartz*, May 13, 2016, https://qz.com/680275/until-
i-was-a-man-i-had-no-idea-how-good-men-had-it-at-work/

97 "'Men are assumed...'" Schilt, Kristen. *Just One of the Guys?: Transgender Men
and the Persistence of Gender Inequality.* Chicago: University of Chicago Press,
2011.

97 "Caitlin, suddenly, was..." Carrol, Meredith. "Jon Stewart: Welcome to Being
a Woman in America, Caitlyn Jenner." *Babble*, June 5, 2015, https://www.babble
.com/parenting/jon-stewart-welcome-to-being-a-woman-in-america-caitlyn
-jenner/

97 "'It's really heartening...'" Oh, Inae. "The American Media Is a Sexist Shit-
show. Welcome, Caitlyn Jenner." *Mother Jones*, June 3, 2015, http://www
.motherjones.com/mixed-media/2015/06/jon-stewart-welcomes-caitlyn
-jenner-medias-sexism

98 "She transitioned in..." Neely, Tucker. "Martine Rothblatt: She Founded
SiriusXM, a Religion and a Biotech. For Starters." *Washington Post*, December 2014,
https://www.washingtonpost.com/lifestyle/magazine/martine-rothblatt-she-
founded-siriusxm-a-religion-and-a-biotech-for-starters/2014/12/11/5a8a4866–
71ab-11e4-ad12–3734c461eab6_story.html?utm_term=.b0e5a64af8c3

98 "As she told . . ." Hackett, Robert. "Highest-Paid Female Executive Seeks
 Immortality—Digitally." *Fortune*, September 12, 2014, http://fortune
 .com/2014/09/12/highest-paid-female-executive-seeks-immortality-digitally/

98 "'We need to . . .'" Goodkind, Nicole. "Highest-Paid Female CEO Used to Be
 a Man." *Yahoo Finance*, September 25, 2014, http://finance.yahoo.com/news/
 highest-paid-female-ceo-martine-rothblatt-talks-pay-gap-231516214.html

98 "There are an . . ." Flores, Andrew R., Jody L. Herman, Gary J. Gates, and Taylor
 N. T. Brown. "How Many Adults Identify as Transgender in the United States."
 The Williams Institute, 2016, https://williamsinstitute.law.ucla.edu/wp
 -content/uploads/How-Many-Adults-Identify-as-Transgender-in-the-United
 -States.pdf

98 "The NIH has . . ." Barres, Ben A. "Does Gender Matter?" *Nature*, 2006, http://
 www.nature.com/nature/journal/v442/n7099/full/442133a.html

99 "In 2016, he . . ." Polk, Sam. "How Wall Street Bro Talk Keeps Women Down."
 New York Times, July 7, 2016, https://www.nytimes.com/2016/07/10/opinion/
 sunday/how-wall-street-bro-talk-keeps-women-down.html?mtrref=www
 .google.com&gwh=E17B2B13EFD0FB9040D04D76A5A3BD4B&gwt=pay
 &assetType=opinion

99 "Women run fewer . . ." Maxey, Daisy. "Where Are the Female Fund Manag-
 ers?" *Wall Street Journal*, July 6, 2015, http://www.wsj.com/articles/SB1167062
 717502099336630458106629274274464; Financial Women's Association. "A
 Deep Dive into the Women-Run Hedge Fund Universe." Kyria Capital Man-
 agement, June 2015, http://fwa.org/pdf_2016/20150630_a_deepdive_into_
 women-run_hedge_funds.pdf

99 "There are 11 . . ." Jones, Meredith. "Wall Street has a problem with women.
 Here's why you should worry." World Economic Forum, October 20, 2015,
 https://www.weforum.org/agenda/2015/10/wall-street-has-a-problem-with-
 women-heres-why-you-should-worry/

99 "At Goldman Sachs . . ." "Goldman Sachs Lags Behind National Averages for
 Female Leadership." Reuters, May 13, 2016, http://fortune.com/2016/03/19/
 goldman-sachs-10000-women/

99 "Female-led funds . . ." Goodman, Leah McGrath. "If Women Are So Good at
 Managing Money, Why Are So Few of Them Doing It?" *Newsweek*, January 26,
 2016, http://www.newsweek.com/2016/02/05/hedge-fund-women-419481.html

99 "The same is . . ." Palvia, Ajay, Emilia Vähämaab, and Sami Vähämaa. "Are
 Female CEOs and Chairwomen More Conservative and Risk Averse? Evidence
 from the Banking Industry During the Financial Crisis." *Journal of Business
 Ethics* 131, no. 3 (2015): 577–594. doi: 10.1007/s10551-014-2288-3

99 "What's more, male . . ." Sommer, Jeff. "How Men's Overconfidence Hurts
 Them as Investors." *New York Times*, March 14, 2010, http://www.nytimes
 .com/2010/03/14/business/14mark.html

99 "A prominent hedge . . ." Tharp, Paul. "Trading Places." *New York Post*, October
 11, 2007, http://nypost.com/2007/10/11/trading-places-3/

99 "Polk got his . . ." Polk, Sam. "How Wall Street Bro Talk Keeps Women Down."
 New York Times, July 7, 2016, http://www.nytimes.com/2016/07/10/opinion/
 sunday/how-wall-street-bro-talk-keeps-women-down.html

100 "JPMorgan Chase CEO..." Oh, Inae. "Jamie Dimon Doubts Elizabeth Warren 'Fully Understands' Global Banking." *Mother Jones,* June 11, 2015, http://www .motherjones.com/politics/2015/06/jamie-dimon-elizabeth-warren/

100 "Or when former..." Swanson, Emily. "Michael Hayden Says Dianne Feinstein Too 'Emotional' to Be Objective on Intelligence Report." *Huffington Post,* April 7, 2014, http://www.huffingtonpost.com/2014/04/06/feinstein-cia-report _n_5100652.html

100 "Similarly, when Supreme..." Bianco, Marcie. "Sexist Critics Dismiss Justice Sotomayor's Impassioned Affirmative Action Dissent as 'Emotional.'" *Mic,* April 24, 2014, https://mic.com/articles/88297/sexist-critics-dismiss -justice-sotomayor-s-impassioned-affirmative-action-dissent-as-emotional #.j9Tltekps

101 "In my own..." "Said to Lady Journos." *Tumblr.* Accessed July 28, 2017, http:// saidtoladyjournos.tumblr.com

101 "Female entrepreneurs have..." Kane, Shanley, and Amelia Greenhall. "Shit Men Say to Women Founders." *Model View Culture.* April 7, 2014, https:// modelviewculture.com/pieces/shit-men-say-to-women-founders

101 "The proposal was..." Dunkley, Emma. "HSBC Wants Half of Senior UK Managers to Be Women." *Financial Times,* November 25, 2015, https://www .ft.com/content/ccc75fe6–9387–11e5-bd82-c1fb87bef7af

101 "Merrill Lynch alone..." Dobbin, Frank, and Alexandra Kalev. "Why Diversity Programs Fail." *Harvard Business Review,* July–August 2016, https://hbr .org/2016/07/why-diversity-programs-fail

101 "The proportion of..." Ibid.

101 "Ninety-four percent..." Kaufman, Aaron. "The Startling Statistics That Prove Venture Capitalists Are More Likely to Fund White Males over Minorities and Women." *Elite Daily,* March 24, 2014, http://elitedaily.com/money/ venture-capitalists-still-overwhelmingly-fund-white-male-entrepreneurs -minorities-women/; Brush, Candida G., Patricia G. Greene, Lakshmi Balachandra, and Amy E. Davis. *Diana Report Women Entrepreneurs 2014: Bridging the Gender Gap in Venture Capital,* 2014, http://www.babson.edu/news-events/ babson-news/Pages/140930-venture-capital-funding-women-entrepreneurs -study.aspx

102 "The industry's frat-house..." Lyons, Dan. "Jerks and the Start-Ups They Ruin." *New York Times,* April 1, 2017, https://www.nytimes.com/2017/04/01/ opinion/sunday/jerks-and-the-start-ups-they-ruin.html

102 "One female entrepreneur..." Mundy, Liza. "Why Is Silicon Valley So Awful to Women?" *The Atlantic,* April 2017, https://www.theatlantic.com/magazine/ archive/2017/04/why-is-silicon-valley-so-awful-to-women/517788/?utm_ campaign=digest&utm_medium=email&utm_source=app

102 "'real problem with...'" Lyons, Dan. "Jerks and the Start-Ups They Ruin." *New York Times,* April 1, 2017, https://www.nytimes.com/2017/04/01/opinion/ sunday/jerks-and-the-start-ups-they-ruin.html

102 "'Men rarely do...'" Polk, Sam. "How Wall Street Bro Talk Keeps Women Down." *New York Times,* July 7, 2016, https://www.nytimes.com/2016/07/10/ opinion/sunday/how-wall-street-bro-talk-keeps-women-down.html?

mtrref=www.google.com&gwh=E17B2B13EFD0FB9040D04D76A5A3BD
4B&gwt=pay&assetType=opinion.

103 "An analysis of . . ." Williams, Melissa J., "The Price Women Leaders Pay for Assertiveness—and How to Minimize It." *Wall Street Journal*, May 31, 2016, https://www.wsj.com/articles/the-price-women-leaders-pay-for-assertivenessand-how-to-minimize-it-1464660240

103 "It bears noting . . ." Doherty, Elissa, and Alex White. "Stay-at-Home Dads Fight for Acceptance." *Herald Sun*, July 12th 2011, http://www.heraldsun.com.au/news/stay-at-home-dads-battle-for-respect/news-story/13e65363cd0d45859d31d5fc88f0ea58

103 "It 'can backfire . . .'" Rudman, Laurie A. "Self-promotion as a risk factor for women: the costs and benefits of counterstereotypical impression management." *Journal of Personality and Social Psychology* 74, no. 3 (1998): 629–645, http://search.committee.module.rutgers.edu/pdf/Rudman_self_promoing.pdf

103 "That's a handicap . . ." Cuddy, Amy J. C., Susan T. Fiske, and Peter Glick. "When professionals become mothers, warmth doesn't cut the ice." *Journal of Social Issues* 60, no. 4 (2004): 701–718, http://www.people.hbs.edu/acuddy/2004,%20cuddy,%20fiske,%20&%20glick,%20JSI.pdf; Fiske, S T, Juan Xu, Amy C. Cuddy, and Peter Glick. "(Dis)respecting versus (dis)liking: status and interdependence predict ambivalent stereotypes of competence and warmth." *Journal of Social Issues* 55, no. 3 (1999): 473–489. doi: 10.1111/0022–4537.00128; Prentice, Deborah A., and Erica Carranza. "What women and men should be, shouldn't be, are allowed to be, and don't have to be: the contents of prescriptive gender stereotypes." *Psychology of Women Quarterly* 26, no. 4 (2002): 269–281, http://journals.sagepub.com/doi/pdf/10.1111/1471–6402.t01–1–00066; Brescoll, Victoria L., and Eric Luis Uhlmann. "Can an angry woman get ahead?" *Psychological Science* 19 (2008): 268–275. doi: 10.1111/j.1467–9280.2008.02079.x

104 "'You're sitting in . . .'" Barnes, Brooks. "Amy Pascal's Hollywood Ending, Complete with Comeback Twist." *New York Times*, July 8, 2017, https://www.nytimes.com/2017/07/08/business/media/amy-pascal-sony-pictures.html?_r=0

104 "Television producer Glen . . ." Glen Mazzara, personal interview, July 28, 2017.

104 "For women, though, . . ." Krentz, Matt, et al. "The Rewards of an Engaged Female Workforce." Boston Consulting Group, October 27, 2016, https://www.bcg.com/publications/2016/people-organization-leadership-talent-rewards-engaged-female-workforce.aspx

104 "'Yes, I'm angry . . .'" Miller, S.A., "Donald Trump Stokes Fire at Iowa Rally: 'I'm Angry at Stupidity.'" *The Washington Times*, January 15, 2016, http://www.washingtontimes.com/news/2016/jan/15/trump-stokes-fire-iowa-rally-im-angry-stupidity/

104 "'I'm angry because . . .'" Chipman, Kim. "Donald Trump to South Carolina Governor Nikki Haley: 'Yes, I'm Angry.'" *Bloomberg*, January 14, 2016, https://www.bloomberg.com/news/trackers/2016-01-15/donald-trump-to-s-c-gov-haley-yes-i-m-angry-

104 "A CNN poll . . ." Malone, Clare. "Why Donald Trump?" *FiveThirtyEight*, March 23, 2016, http://fivethirtyeight.com/features/why-donald-trump/

105 "His slogan, 'Make..." Hollander, Paul. "Donald Trump, Human Nature, and the Craving for Respect." *The American Interest,* April 27, 2016, http://www.the-american-interest.com/2016/04/27/donald-trump-human-nature-and-the-craving-for-respect/

105 "When she was..." Gehl, Robert. "Hillary Clinton Is Getting Angry: She's Entitled to the Nomination, Dammit!" *Downtrend,* April 2, 2016, http://downtrend.com/robertgehl/hillary-clinton-is-getting-angry-shes-entitled-to-the-nomination-dammit

105 "A *Politico* piece..." Thrush, Glenn. "5 Takeaways from the Democratic Debate." *Politico,* February 2, 2016, http://www.politico.com/story/2016/02/five-takeaways-from-the-democratic-debate-219187#ixzz4DUBX83oQ

105 "'I haven't quite...'" Howard, Adam. "Trump: 'I haven't quite recovered' from Clinton's 'shouting.'" MSNBC April 27, 2016, http://www.msnbc.com/msnbc/trump-i-havent-quite-recovered-clintons-shouting

105 "At another he..." Diamond, Jeremy. "Trump unleashes on Clinton after day of attacks." CNN, June 2, 2016, http://www.cnn.com/2016/06/02/politics/trump-unleashes-on-clinton/index.html

105 "Participants believe they..." Arizona State University. "Angry Men Gain Influence, Angry Women Lose Influence, Study Shows." *ScienceDaily,* October 26, 2015, www.sciencedaily.com/releases/2015/10/151026172546.htm

106 "The researchers concluded..." Salerno, Jessica M., and Liana C. Peter-Hagene. "One angry woman: Anger expression increases influence for men, but decreases influence for women, during group deliberation." *Law and Human Behavior* 39, no. 6 (2015): 581–592. doi: 10.1037/lhb0000147

106 "Yet if a..." Covert, Bryce. "The Gender Wage Gap Goes All the Way to the Top." *Think Progress,* August 26, 2015, https://thinkprogress.org/the-gender-wage-gap-goes-all-the-way-to-the-top-f492c57867fe#.qknec6qzj

106 "The media plays..." The Rockefeller Foundation & Global Strategy Group. "Does the media influence how we perceive women in leadership?" Women in Leadership: Why It Matters, 2016, https://assets.rockefellerfoundation.org/app/uploads/20161028122206/100x25_MediaLanguage_report1.pdf

107 "Women are marched..." Reingold, Jennifer. "Why Top Women Are Disappearing From Corporate America." *Fortune,* September 9, 2016, http://fortune.com/women-corporate-america/

107 "Men also appear..." Sorkin, Andrew Ross. "Do Activist Investors Target Female C.E.O.s?" *New York Times,* February 9, 2015, https://dealbook.nytimes.com/2015/02/09/the-women-of-the-s-p-500-and-investor-activism/

107 "One aggressor, Nelson Peltz..." Sellers, Patricia. "Corporate raider Nelson Peltz simply can't resist women." *Fortune,* January 12, 2015, http://fortune.com/2015/01/12/nelson-peltz-women-dupont/

107 "Women leaders are..." Favaro, Ken, Per-Ola Karlsson, and Gary L. Neilson. "The 2013 Chief Executive Study: Women CEOs of the last 10 years." *Strategy&,* April 29, 2014, https://www.strategyand.pwc.com/reports/2013-chief-executive-study

108 "The female CEO..." Bigelow, Lyda, Leif Lundmark, Judi McLean Parks, and Robert Wuebker. "Skirting the issues: experimental evidence of gender bias in

IPO prospectus evaluations." *Journal of Management* 40, no. 6 (2014): 1732–1759. doi: 10.1177/0149206312441624

108 "The women who . . ." Babcock, Linda, and Sara Laschever. *Women Don't Ask: Negotiation and the Gender Divide.* Princeton, N.J.: Princeton University Press, 2009. Kindle edition.

108 "Indeed, the magazine . . ." Snyder, Kieran. "The Abrasiveness Trap: High-Achieving Men and Women Are Described Differently in Reviews." *Fortune,* August 26, 2014, http://fortune.com/2014/08/26/performance-review-gender-bias/

108 "One unintentionally hilarious . . ." Cain, Susan. *Quiet: The Power of Introverts in a World That Can't Stop Talking.* New York: The Crown Archetype Publishing Group, 2012. Kindle edition.

108 "While that study . . ." Women's Media Center. "The Problem." Accessed August 3, 2017, http://www.womensmediacenter.com/pages/the-problem

108 "One analysis calculated . . ." Women's Media Center. "The Status of Women in the U.S. Media 2015." 2015, https://wmc.3cdn.net/7d039991d7252a5831_0hum68k6z.pdf

109 "That came across with. . ." Gardiner, Beck, Mahana Mansfied, Ian Anderson, Josh Holder, Daan Louter, and Monica Ulmanu. "The Dark Side of Guardian Comments," *The Guardian,* April 12, 2016, https://www.theguardian.com/technology/2016/apr/12/the-dark-side-of-guardian-comments

110 "In a *Vox* . . ." Taub, Amanda. "The Guardian Study's Hidden Lesson: Trolls Reinforce White Male Dominance in Journalism." *Vox,* April 13, 2016, http://www.vox.com/2016/4/13/11414942/guardian-study-harassment

110 "But women are . . ." Duggan, Maeve. "Online Harassment." Pew Research Center, October 22, 2014, http://www.pewinternet.org/2014/10/22/online-harassment/

111 "Researchers have shown . . ." Dobbin, Frank, Daniel Schrage, and Alexandra Kalev. "Resisting the Iron Cage: The Effects of Bureaucratic Reforms to Promote Equity." September 30, 2014. doi: 10.2139/ssrn.2513869

111 "Some 71 percent of . . ." Johnson, Stefanie K., Jessica Kirk, and Ksenia Keplinger. "Why We Fail to Report Sexual Harassment." *Harvard Business Review,* October 4, 2016, https://hbr.org/2016/10/why-we-fail-to-report-sexual-harassment; Vagianos, Alanna. "1 in 3 Women Has Been Sexually Harassed at Work, According to Survey." *Huffington Post,* February 19, 2015, http://www.huffingtonpost.com/2015/02/19/1-in-3-women-sexually-harassed-work-cosmopolitan_n_6713814.html; Ahn, Lauren, and Ruiz Michelle. "Survey: 1 in 3 Women Has Been Sexually Harassed at Work." *Cosmopolitan,* February 16, 2015, http://www.cosmopolitan.com/career/news/a36453/cosmopolitan-sexual-harassment-survey/?dom=fb_hp&src=social&mag=cos

111 "Until then, the . . ." Flint, Joe, and Michael Rothfield. "Scope of Federal Probe into Fox News Broadens." *Wall Street Journal,* May 4, 2017, https://www.wsj.com/articles/scope-of-federal-probe-into-fox-news-broadens-1493938947

111 "Just months later . . ." Boehlert, Eric. "A Hotbed of Sexual Harassment and Victim-Blaming, Fox News Fixates on the Clintons' Private Life." *Media*

Matters, October 4, 2016, https://mediamatters.org/blog/2016/10/04/hotbed
-sexual-harassment-and-victim-blaming-fox-news-fixates-clintons-private
-life/213511

112 "O'Reilly too was..." Steel, Emily, and Michael S. Schmidt. "Bill O'Reilly Is
Forced Out at Fox News." *New York Times,* April 19, 2017, https://www.nytimes
.com/2017/04/19/business/media/bill-oreilly-fox-news-allegations.html

112 "Sexual harassment claims..." Barnes, Brooks. "Fox Reveals Cost of Sexual
Harassment Allegations: $45 Million." *New York Times,* May 10, 2017, https://
www.nytimes.com/2017/05/10/business/media/fox-news-sexual-harassment
-21st-century-fox.html?_r=0

111 "A University of British Columbia..." Berdahl, Jennifer L. "The Sexual Ha-
rassment of Uppity Women." *Journal of Applied Psychology* 92, no. 2 (2007):
425–437. doi: 10.1037/0021–9010.92.2.425

112 "it allows a..." Lautenberger, Diana, Valerie M. Dandar, Claudia L. Raezer,
and Rae Anne Sloan. "The State of Women in Academic Medicine: The Pipeline
and Pathways to Leadership." Association of American Medical Colleges, 2014,
https://members.aamc.org/eweb/upload/The%20State%20of%20Women%20
in%20Academic%20Medicine%202013–2014%20FINAL.pdf

113 "'We are still...'" Merrill, Andrea L. "Why Are Women So Underrepresented in
Surgery Leadership?" *KevinMD,* June 1, 2015, http://www.kevinmd.com/blog
/2015/06/why-are-women-so-underrepresented-in-surgery-leadership.html

113 "'Would my female...'" Merrill, Andrea. "Calling Attention to the Disparity
in Surgery: Here's What I Learned." *KevinMD,* July 3, 2015, http://www.kevinmd
.com/blog/2015/07/calling-attention-to-the-disparity-in-surgery-heres-
what-i-learned.html

114 "The advice columnist..." Huang, Alice. "Help! My Adviser Won't Stop
Looking Down My Shirt!" *Science Careers,* June 1, 2015, http://web.archive
.org/web/20150601150626/http://sciencecareers.sciencemag.org/career_
magazine/previous_issues/articles/2015_06_01/caredit.a1500140

115 "He subsequently became..." The History Makers. Accessed July 29, 2017,
http://www.thehistorymakers.com/biography/dr-augustus-white-iii

116 "'Here was this...'" White III, Augustus. *Seeing Patients.* Cambridge, M.A.:
Harvard University Press, 1969.

116 "They're less likely..." Ibid.

116 "Dr. White defines..." Dillon Sam. "Harvard Chief Defends His Talk
on Women." *New York Times,* January 18, 2005, http://www.nytimes
.com/2005/01/18/us/harvard-chief-defends-his-talk-on-women.html

117 "Yet even as..." This note covers all of Dr. White's remarks to the author in this
chapter. Augustus White III, personal interview, April 14, 2015.

116 "When I asked..." Dominic Barton, personal interview, November 16, 2015.

117 "And Uber's..." Frances Frei, personal interview, August 21, 2015.

118 "The backlash was..." Dockterman, Eliana. "*Science* Deletes Column Advis-
ing Student to 'Put Up with' Advisor Staring Down Her Shirt." *Time,* June 3,
2015, http://time.com/3908382/science-advice-column-researcher-breasts
-advisor/

118 "'There may be . . .'" Merrill, Andrea. "Calling Attention to the Disparity in Surgery: Here's What I Learned." *KevinMD*, July 3, 2015, http://www.kevinmd.com/blog/2015/07/calling-attention-to-the-disparity-in-surgery-heres-what-i-learned.html

Chapter 6: She Deserves a Raise. But She Won't Ask for It.

120 "Researchers ultimately concluded . . ." Lipman, Joanne. "Let's Expose the Gender Pay Gap," *New York Times*, August 13, 2015, https://www.nytimes.com/2015/08/13/opinion/lets-expose-the-gender-pay-gap.html?_r=0

120 "The gap is . . ." Artz, Benjamin, Amanda H. Goodall, and Andrew J. Oswald. "Do Women Ask?" Warwick Economics Research Papers, no. 1127, July 2016, http://www2.warwick.ac.uk/fac/soc/economics/research/workingpapers/2016/twerp_1127_oswald.pdf

120 "An Australian study . . ." Cohn, Laura. "Women Ask for Raises as Much as Men Do—but Get Them Less Often." *Fortune*, September 6, 2016, http://fortune.com/2016/09/06/women-men-salary-negotiations/

121 "American women earn . . ." United States Department of Labor. "The Economics Daily," March 8, 2017, https://www.bls.gov/opub/ted/2017/womens-median-earnings-82-percent-of-mens-in-2016.htm

121 "A comprehensive study . . ." Hill, Catherine, Kevin Miller, and Kathleen Benson. "The Simple Truth About the Gender Pay Gap." American Association of University Women, 2016, http://www.aauw.org/aauw_check/pdf_download/show_pdf.php?file=The-Simple-Truth

121 "A Catalyst survey . . ." Carter, Nancy M., and Christine Silva. "The Myth of the Ideal Worker: Does Doing All the Right Things Really Get Women Ahead?" Catalyst, 2011, http://www.catalyst.org/knowledge/myth-ideal-worker-does-doing-all-right-things-really-get-women-ahead

121 "Female M.B.A.s . . ." Greenhouse, Steven. "M.B.A.'s Have Biggest 'Mommy Penalty,' Doctors the Smallest." *New York Times*, December 6, 2010, http://economix.blogs.nytimes.com/2010/12/06/m-b-a-s-have-biggest-mommy-penalty-doctors-the-smallest/?_r=0

122 "When the researchers . . ." Babock, Linda. *Women Don't Ask*. New York: Bantam Books, 2007.

123 "The syndrome continues . . ." Evans, Lisa. "Why Are Women Entrepreneurs Paying Themselves Less Than They Deserve?" *Fast Company*, March 17, 2014, http://www.fastcompany.com/3027709/why-are-women-entrepreneurs-paying-themselves-less-than-they-deserve

123 "Yet the men . . ." Babock, Linda. *Women Don't Ask*. New York: Bantam Books, 2007.

123 "Linda Babcock and . . ." Small, Deborah A., and Linda Babcock. "Who Goes to the Bargaining Table? The Influence of Gender and Framing on the Initiation of Negotiation." *Journal of Personality and Social Psychology* 93, no. 4 (2007): 600–613. doi: 10.1037/0022–3514.93.4.600

124 "Carol Frohlinger and . . ." Sheryl Sandberg. *Lean In*. New York: Knopf Doubleday Publishing Group, 2013.

124 "The first camp..." Barron, Lisa A. "Ask and you shall receive? Gender differences in negotiators' beliefs about requests for a higher salary." *Human Relations* 56, no. 6 (2003): 635–662, http://journals.sagepub.com/doi/pdf/10.1177/00187267030566001

125 "This time, while..." Bowles, Hannah Riley, Linda Babcock, and Lei Lai. "Social incentives for gender differences in the propensity to initiate negotiations: sometimes it does hurt to ask." *Organizational Behavior and Human Decision Processes* 103, 1 (2007): 84–103, http://www.sciencedirect.com/science/article/pii/S0749597806000884

126 "Yet the women..." Gerhart, Barry A., and Sara L. Rynes. "Determinants and Consequences of Salary Negotiations by Graduating Male and Female MBAs." *Center for Advanced Human Resource Studies,* 1989, http://digitalcommons.ilr.cornell.edu/cahrswp/413

126 "One study found..." Weber, Lauren. "Gender Wage Gap Widens at Age 32, Report Finds." *Wall Street Journal,* June 21, 2016, http://www.wsj.com/articles/gender-wage-gap-widens-at-age-32-report-finds-1466537493

126 "Crunching the numbers..." "Lifetime Wage Gap for Women Compared with Men." National Women's Law Center. March 28, 2017, https://nwlc.org/resources/the-lifetime-wage-gap-state-by-state/

126 "The pay gap..." Hegewisch, Ariane, and Asha DuMonthier. "The Gender Wage Gap: 2015." *Institute for Women's Policy Research,* March 2016, https://iwpr.org/wp-content/uploads/wpallimport/files/iwpr-export/publications/C437%20Gender%20Wage%20Gap%20FS%20March%202016.pdf

126 "When Glassdoor surveyed..." Glassdoor. "Global Salary Transparency Survey." Accessed July 30, 2017, https://press-content.glassdoor.com/app/uploads/sites/2/2016/04/GD_Survey_GlobalSalaryTransparency-FINAL.pdf

127 "'This study raises...'" Carter, Nancy M., and Christine Silva. "The Myth of the Ideal Worker." Catalyst, 2011, http://www.catalyst.org/system/files/The_Myth_of_the_Ideal_Worker_Does_Doing_All_the_Right_Things_Really_Get_Women_Ahead.pdf

127 "Massachusetts, New York..." Fu, Lisa. "60% of Women Want Employers to Stop Asking About Salary History." *Fortune,* July 12, 2017, http://fortune.com/2017/07/12/salary-history-employer-questions/

127 "It's too soon..." PayScale. "Is Asking for Salary History... History?" Accessed July 20, 2017, http://www.payscale.com/data/salary-history

127 "In an encouraging..." PayScale. "About Who We Are." Accessed August 3, 2017, http://www.payscale.com/about; Salary.com. "About Us." Accessed August 3, 2017, http://www.companalyst.com/company/; Glassdoor. "About Us." Accessed August 3, 2017, https://www.glassdoor.com/about/index_input.htm

128 "At the time..." "Jennifer Lawrence: 'Why Do I Make Less Than My Male Co-Stars?'" *Lenny Letter,* October 15, 2015, http://www.lennyletter.com/work/a147/jennifer-lawrence-why-do-i-make-less-than-my-male-costars/

128 "Subsequently other actresses..." Brennan, Christine. "Brennan: U.S. Women's Soccer Team Sends Powerful Message." *USA Today,* March 31, 2016,

https://www.usatoday.com/story/sports/columnist/brennan/2016/03/31/hope-solo-carli-lloyd-alex-morgan-powerful-message/82466586/

129 "Clare Klemmer, a ..." Caplin, Joan. "How I Negotiated a Nearly $20,000 Pay Increase." *Money,* July 6, 2016. http://time.com/money/4364804/negotiate-pay-increase/

129 "It ended up ..." Davis, Julie Hirschfeld. "Obama Moves to Expand Rules Aimed at Closing Gender Pay Gap." *New York Times,* January 29, 2016, http://www.nytimes.com/2016/01/29/us/politics/obama-moves-to-expand-rules-aimed-at-closing-gender-pay-gap.html?_r=0; McGirt, Ellen. "Benioff to CEOs: Pick One Thing." *Fortune,* April 4, 2017, http://fortune.com/2017/04/04/benioff-to-ceos-pick-one-thing/

130 "'Every CEO needs ...'" Zillman, Claire. "Salesforce CEO Marc Benioff: We're Erasing Our Gender Pay Gap—Again." *Fortune,* January 20, 2017, http://fortune.com/2017/01/20/salesforce-marc-benioff-gender-pay-gap-davos/

130 "Tech firms Intel ..." Masungaga, Samantha. "Gap Says Audits Show Its Workers Get Equal Pay for the Same Work." *Los Angeles Times,* November 27, 2015, http://www.latimes.com/business/la-fi-gap-fair-pay-20151127-story.html; Launey, Kristen M., and Marjorie Soto, "Pay Equity Extends to Race Ethnicity, Without Banning Salary Inquiries." Cal-Peculiarities, October 27, 2016, http://www.calpeculiarities.com/2016/10/27/pay-equity-extends-to-race-ethnicity-without-banning-salary-inquiries/

130 "President Obama ..." O'Hara, Mary Emily. "Trump Pulls Back Obama-Era Protections for Women Workers." NBC News, April 3, 2017, http://www.nbcnews.com/news/us-news/trump-pulls-back-obama-era-protections-women-workers-n741041

130 "three-quarters of ..." Ingraham, Christopher. "White House gender pay gap more than triples under Trump." *Washington Post,* June 5, 2017, https://www.washingtonpost.com/news/wonk/wp/2017/07/05/white-house-gender-pay-gap-more-than-triples-under-trump/?utm_term=.deae4c2e7495

130 "The wage-gap disclosures ..." Department for Education, Government Equalities Office. "Department for Education Reports Gender Pay Gap," June 28, 2017, https://www.gov.uk/government/news/department-for-education-reports-gender-pay-gap; Lipman, Joanne. "Let's Expose the Gender Pay Gap." *New York Times,* August 13, 2015, https://www.nytimes.com/2015/08/13/opinion/lets-expose-the-gender-pay-gap.html?_r=0

131 "Indeed, when the BBC ..." Bond, David. "Theresa May Criticises BBC as Star Salaries Reveal Gender Gap." *Financial Times,* July 19, 2017, https://www.ft.com/content/eaef2e2c-6c61-11e7-b9c7-15af748b6od0

131 "A few years earlier ..." Sarah Churchman, personal interview, August 6, 2015.

131 "A *Harvard Business Review* ..." Ashton, Deborah. "Does Race or Gender Matter More to Your Paycheck?" *Harvard Business Review,* June 10, 2014, https://hbr.org/2014/06/does-race-or-gender-matter-more-to-your-paycheck

131 "For starters, about ..." Huet, Ellen. "Rise of the Bias Busters: How Unconscious Bias Became Silicon Valley's Newest Target." *Forbes,* November 2, 2015, https://www.forbes.com/sites/ellenhuet/2015/11/02/rise-of-the-bias-busters

-how-unconscious-bias-became-silicon-valleys-newest-target/#14c5eb
of19b5

132 "As we've already . . ." Brooks, Chad. "Gender Equality in the Workplace Can Boost Profits." *Huffington Post,* October 7, 2014, http://www.huffingtonpost.com/2014/10/07/gender-diversity-business-study_n_5945312.html

132 "An analysis of . . ." Badal, Sangeeta Bharadwaj, "The Business Benefits of Gender Diversity." Gallup, January 20, 2014.

132 "Economists estimate that . . ." Reader, Ruth. "Paying Men and Women Equally Could Add \$4.3 Trillion to US Economy." *Mic,* April 12, 2016, https://mic.com/articles/140411/equal-pay-day-paying-men-and-women-equally-could-add-43-trillion-to-us-economy#.oF1Ttxtbs

132 "A full twenty-five . . ." "Still Looking at the Dow Jones Gender Gap." Independent Association of Publishers' Employees, March 8, 2016, http://iape1096.org/news/2016/08_stilllooking.php

132 "A 2016 analysis . . ." Paquette, Danielle. "Pay Doesn't Look the Same for Men and Women at Top Newspapers: New Data Show How Much More Men Make Than Women at Top Newspapers." *Washington Post,* May 10, 2016, https://www.washingtonpost.com/news/wonk/wp/2016/03/10/pay-doesnt-look-the-same-for-men-and-women-at-top-newspapers/

133 "A similar study . . ." Amanatullah, Emily T., and Michael W. Morris. "Negotiating gender roles: gender differences in assertive negotiating are mediated by women's fear of backlash and attenuated when negotiating on behalf of others." *Journal of Personality and Social Psychology* 98, no. 2 (2010): 256–267. doi: 10.1037/a0017094

133 "In one, students . . ." Callahan-Levy, C. M., and L. A. Messe. "Sex differences in the allocation of pay." *Journal of Personality and Social Psychology* 37, no. 3 (1979): 433-446.

134 "Women made lower . . ." Wade, Mary E. "Women and salary negotiation: the costs of self-advocacy." *Psychology of Women Quarterly* 25 (2001): 65–76. doi: 10.1111/1471–6402.00008; Amanatullah, Emily T., and Michael W. Morris. "Negotiating gender roles: gender differences in assertive negotiating are mediated by women's fear of backlash and attenuated when negotiating on behalf of others." *Journal of Personality and Social Psychology* 98, no. 2 (2010): 256–267. doi: 10.1037/a0017094

134 "Steve Boehm, who led . . ." Steve Boehm, personal interview, August 8, 2017, and November 2014.

134 "Virginia Rometty, IBM's . . ." Barnett, Megan. "IBM's Ginny Rometty: Growth and comfort do not coexist." *Fortune,* October 5, 2011, http://fortune.com/2011/10/05/ibms-ginni-rometty-growth-and-comfort-do-not-coexist/

135 "Yet within two . . ." Coffmarr, Julie, and Bill Neuenfeldt. "Everyday Moments of Truth: Frontline Managers Are Key to Women's Career Aspirations." Bain & Company, June 17, 2014, http://www.bain.com/publications/articles/everyday-moments-of-truth.aspx

135 "Kimberly-Clark adopted . . ." Lublin, Joann S. "How Companies Are Different When More Women Are in Power." *Wall Street Journal,* September 27, 2016,

https://www.wsj.com/articles/how-companies-are-different-when-more-women-are-in-power-1474963802

136 "The survey also..." "Women in the Workplace." McKinsey & Company, LeanIn. Accessed July 30, 2017, https://womenintheworkplace.com/

136 "One study found..." Hewlett, Sylvia Ann, Kerrie Peraino, Laura Sherbin, and Karen Sumberg. "The Sponsor Effect: Breaking Through the Last Glass Ceiling." *Harvard Business Review*, January 12, 2011, https://hbr.org/product/the-sponsor-effect-breaking-through-the-last-glass-ceiling/10428-PDF-ENG

136 "A survey of..." Miller, Claire Cain. "It's Not Just Mike Pence. Americans Are Wary of Being Alone with the Opposite Sex." *New York Times*, July 1, 2017, https://www.nytimes.com/2017/07/01/upshot/members-of-the-opposite-sex-at-work-gender-study.html

137 "Another study by..." Waldman, Katy. "Tips for Finding a Great Mentor: Be White and Be Male." *Slate*, April 23, 2014, http://www.slate.com/blogs/xx_factor/2014/04/23/mentorship_in_academia_study_finds_that_professors_prefer_to_mentor_white.html

137 "And when researchers..." Ewing Marion Kauffman Foundation. "Sources of Economic Hope: Women's Entrepreneurship." Ewing Marion Kauffman Foundation, 2014, http://www.id8nation.com/women-entrepreneurs-face-obstacles/#sthash.5ZD7xg2Z.dpbs

137 "KPMG surveyed more..." Veihmeyer, John, and Lynne Doughtie. "KPMG Women's Leadership Study." KPMG Foundation, 2015, http://womensleadership.kpmg.us/content/dam/kpmg-womens-leadership-golf/womensleadership-pressrelease/FINAL%20Womens%20Leadership%20v19.pdf

137 "Male bosses, he..." Glen Mazzara, personal interview, July 28, 2017.

137 "Even when women..." Ibarra, Herminia, Nancy M. Carter, and Christine Silva. "Why Men Still Get More Promotions Than Women." *Harvard Business Review*, September 2010, https://hbr.org/2010/09/why-men-still-get-more-promotions-than-women

137 "Frank Dobbin, the..." Dobbin, Frank, and Alexandra Kalev. "Why Diversity Programs Fail." *Harvard Business Review*, July–August 2016, https://hbr.org/2016/07/why-diversity-programs-fail

138 "A third of..." Ibarra, Herminia, Nancy M. Carter, and Christine Silva. "Why Men Still Get More Promotions Than Women." *Harvard Business Review*, September 2010, https://hbr.org/2010/09/why-men-still-get-more-promotions-than-women

138 "Over a seven-year..." Chatterjee, Soumen. "How DHL & Sun Microsystems Nailed It with Mentoring Program." LinkedIn, December 22, 2015, https://www.linkedin.com/pulse/how-dhl-sun-microsystems-nailed-mentoring-program-soumen-chatterjee

138 "Research by Catalyst..." Carter, Nancy, and Christine Silva. "Mentoring: Necessary but Insufficient for Advancement." Catalyst, 2010, http://www.catalyst.org/system/files/Mentoring_Necessary_But_Insufficient_for_Advancement_Final_120610.pdf

139 "Harvard's Dobbin has pinpointed..." Dobbin, Frank, and Alexandra Kalev.

"Why Diversity Programs Fail." *Harvard Business Review*, July–August, 2016, https://hbr. org/2016/07/why-diversity-programs-fail

139 "That year, Cathy . . ." Zarya, Valentina. "Exclusive: Deloitte Enters the Paid Leave Arms Race with 16 Weeks of Family Leave." *Fortune*, September 8, 2016, http://fortune.com/2016/09/08/deloitte-family-leave/

139 "'I didn't have . . .'" Cathy Engelbert, personal interview, January 18, 2017.

140 "It's telling that . . ." Waller, Nikki, and Joann S. Lublin. "What's Holding Women Back in the Workplace?" *Wall Street Journal*, September 30, 2015, https://www.wsj.com/articles/whats-holding-women-back-in-the-work-place-1443600242

140 "Indeed, tech executive . . ." "Steve Boehm." LinkedIn. Accessed August 2, 2017, https://www.linkedin.com/in/stboehm/

140 "Almost half . . ." della Cava, Marco. "EBay Becomes a Little More Diverse," *USA Today*, April 29, 2015, https://www.usatoday.com/story/tech/2015/04/29/ebay-diversity-numbers-up-a-point-as-company-splits/26574871/

140 "You'd think . . ." Steve Boehm, personal interviews, November 2014 and August 8, 2017.

142 "Tragically, in 2001 . . ." Vogt, Tom. "WSU Professor Dies: Doctors Fail to Save Her Baby." *The Columbian*, May 1, 2001, https://www.highbeam.com/doc/1P2–23474606.html

142 "'She was a . . .'" This note covers all of Irving's remarks to the author in this chapter. Blake Irving, personal interview, November 5, 2015.

142 "When she passed . . ." Irving, Blake. "Organizational Change." Anita Borg Institute. YouTube video, November, 30, 2015, https://www.youtube.com/watch?v=oUpQeKVVkHs&index=20&list=PLdZRvkf2LLVx8EVfAnmw7TqE7rRPooiyi

142 "There was the . . ." Shire, Emily. "The Five Most Sexist Super Bowl Ads Ever." *Daily Beast*, January 31, 2015, http://www.thedailybeast.com/articles/2015/01/31/the-5-most-sexist-ads-in-super-bowl-history.html; "GoDaddy Bar Refaeli Kiss Super Bowl Commercial." *Clever News*. YouTube video. February 1, 2013, https://www.youtube.com/watch?v=t-10ixpSShs

143 "GoDaddy created a . . ." GoDaddy. "GoDaddy Women in Technology." Accessed July 30, 2017, https://www.godaddy.com/careers/diversity

143 "'Can I be . . .'" Blake Irving, personal interview, November 5, 2015.

Chapter 7: Blind Auditions

146 "The most famous . . ." Chicago Symphony Orchestra Association. "Winners of 2017 Crain-Maling Foundation Chicago Symphony Orchestra Youth Auditions Announced." March 16, 2017, https://cso.org/globalassets/about/pr-press-releases/2016–17/crain-maling-2017-winner-announced.pdf

147 "They found that . . ." Goldin, Claudia, and Cecilia Rouse. "Orchestrating Impartiality: The Impact of 'Blind' Auditions on Female Musicians." NBER Working Paper No. 5903, issued January 1997, http://www.nber.org/papers/w5903

147 "Firms including Bloomberg . . ." Miller, Claire Cain. "Is Blind Hiring

the Best Hiring?" *New York Times,* February 25, 2016, http://www.nytimes
.com/2016/02/28/magazine/is-blind-hiring-the-best-hiring.html?_r=0

147 "The audition process . . ." Kedar Iyer, personal interview, March 17, 2016.

148 "And of those . . ." Kedar Iyer, email exchange, March 19, 2016.

148 "Other companies are . . ." Bohnet, Iris. "Interviewing Job Candidates? Try
Doing It Blind." *Wired,* May 20, 2016, http://www.wired.co.uk/article/job
-interviews-first-impressions

149 "Born and raised . . ." Bee, Samantha. *I Know I Am, But What Are You?* New York:
The Gallery Group, 2010.

149 "'I am still . . .'" Morris, Alex. "How Samantha Bee Crashed the Late-Night
Boys' Club." *Rolling Stone,* June 30, 2016, http://www.rollingstone.com/tv/fea-
tures/how-samantha-bee-crashed-the-late-night-boys-club-20160630#ixzz4DX-
SiiQDS

149 "In 2003, when . . ." Ibid.

149 "*Harvard Business Review* . . ." Mohr, Tara Sophia. "Why Women Don't Apply for
Jobs Unless They're 100% Qualified." *Harvard Business Review,* August 2014,
https://hbr.org/2014/08/why-women-dont-apply-for-jobs-unless-theyre-
100-qualified

149 "'I had to . . .'" "'Full Frontal' Showrunner: 'It's a Feminist Show Because We Are
All Feminists.'" *All Things Considered,* NPR, February 10, 2016, http://www.npr
.org/2016/02/10/466306540/full-frontal-showrunner-its-a-feminist-show-
because-we-are-all-feminists

150 "Even though *The* . . ." Steiger, Katy. "The Underside of Jon Stewart's Legacy at
'The Daily Show.'" February 11, 2015, https://thinkprogress.org/the-underside-
of-jon-stewarts-legacy-at-the-daily-show-2af7e1cc5311/

150 "Even John Oliver . . ." Levy, Nicole. "How John Oliver Tried to Shake Up the
Late-Night Writers' Room." *Politico,* August 6, 2014, http://www.capitalnewyork
.com/article/media/2014/08/8550268/how-john-oliver-tried-shake-late-night-
writers-room; IMDb, "Last Week Tonight with John Oliver: Full Cast & Crew."
Accessed August 3, 2017, http://www.imdb.com/title/tt3530232/fullcredits/

150 "She found that . . ." Rivera, Lauren A. "Hiring as Cultural Matching: The Case
of Elite Professional Service Firms." *American Sociological Review,* 2012. doi:
10.1177/0003122412463213

151 "'It's such a . . .'" Blake, Meredith. "Samantha Bee Has the Solution for Hol-
lywood's Diversity Problem: 'Just Hire People.'" *Los Angeles Times,* Febru-
ary 8, 2016, http://www.latimes.com/entertainment/tv/showtracker/la-et-st
-samantha-bee-has-the-solution-for-hollywood-diversity-how-about-you-
hire-someone-20160208-story.html

151 "'I have literally . . .'" Morris, Alex. "How Samantha Bee Crashed the Late-
Night Boys' Club." *Rolling Stone,* June 30, 2016, http://www.rollingstone.com/tv
/features/how-samantha-bee-crashed-the-late-night-boys-club-
20160630#ixzz4DXSiiQDS

152 "'It's not like . . .'" Kruger, Pamela. "Samantha Bee Talks About How She
Avoided White Dude Comedy." *Fortune,* April 20, 2016, http://fortune
.com/2016/04/20/samantha-bee-white-dude-comedy/

152 "Blendoor's founder, Stephanie . . ." O'Connor, Clare. "Black Woman Engineer

Launches 'Blind' Job Match App to Take Bias Out of Tech Hiring." *Forbes,* March 3, 2016, https://www.forbes.com/sites/clareoconnor/2016/03/03/black-woman -engineer-launches-blind-job-match-app-to-take-bias-out-of-tech-hiring /#6b40d3823949; Bohnet, Iris. "Interviewing Job Candidates? Try Doing It Blind." *Wired,* May 20, 2016, http://www.wired.co.uk/article/job-interviews -first-impressions

152 "'I knew from . . .'" McGee, Chantel. "Can This 'Blind' Hiring App Help Solve Silicon Valley's Diversity Issue?" *Daily Dot,* January 30, 2017, https://www .dailydot.com/debug/stephanie-lampkin-blendoor-diversity/

152 "A Chrome extension . . ." Google Chrome. "Unbias—LinkedIn anonymiser for recruit . . ." Accessed July 30, 2017, https://chrome.google.com/webstore/ detail/unbias-linkedin-anonymise/amikjdcghpcjpanknfdokfpknknjifon ?hl=en-GB

152 "Interviewing.io allows employers . . ." Mundy, Liza. "Why Is Silicon Valley So Awful to Women?" *The Atlantic,* April 2017, https://www.theatlantic. com/magazine/archive/2017/04/why-is-silicon-valley-so-awful-to-women /517788/?utm_campaign=digest&utm_medium=email&utm_source=app

153 "Researchers have shown . . ." Highhouse, Scott. "Stubborn Reliance on Intuition and Subjectivity in Employee Selection." *Industrial and Organizational Psychology* 1 (2008): 333–342, http://blogg.hrsverige.nu/wp-content/ uploads/2010/04/Stubborn1.pdf

153 "When Northwestern's Rivera . . ." Dobbin, Frank, and Alexandra Kalev. "Why Diversity Programs Fail." *Harvard Business Review,* July–August 2016, https:// hbr.org/2016/07/why-diversity-programs-fail

153 "A Harvard Business School . . ." Hoffman, Mitchell, Lisa B. Kahn, and Danielle Li. "Discretion in Hiring." Harvard Business School Working Paper 16–055, 2015, http://www.hbs.edu/faculty/Publication%20Files/16–055_32146994– 78d3–42f0-bb05-c30329cf4.aef.pdf

153 "Unilever and Mercer . . ." Bohnet, Iris. *What Works: Gender Equality by Design.* New York: Harvard University Press, 2016.

153 "Morgan Stanley says . . ." Antilla, Susan. "Decades After 'Boom-Boom Room' Suit, Bias Persists for Women." *New York Times,* May 22, 2016, https:// www.nytimes.com/2016/05/23/business/dealbook/decades-after-boom- boom-room-suit-bias-persists-for-women.html?mtrref=www.google .com&gwh=6C9DBE634F5D93505BEA0F2D8963A961&gwt=pay

153 "Compose, a software . . ." Joseph, Jeffrey. "What Companies Use Blind/Anonymous Resumes and What Benefits Have They Reported?" Cornell University, ILR School, http://digitalcommons.ilr.cornell.edu/cgi/viewcontent.cgi ?article=1108&context=student

153 "So-called diversity . . ." The Female Quotient. Modern Guide to Equality," 2017, http://www.catalyst.org/system/files/the_modern_guide_to_equality.pdf

153 "Employers in European . . ." Joseph, Jeffrey. "What Companies Use Blind/ Anonymous Resumes and What Benefits Have They Reported?" Cornell University, ILR School, http://digitalcommons.ilr.cornell.edu/cgi/viewcontent .cgi?article=1108&context=student

153 "In France, for . . ." Krause, Annabelle. "Anonymous job applications in

Europe." *Journal of European Labor Studies,* 2012, https://doi.org/10.1186/2193–9012–1–5

153 "Australia created a . . ." Minister for Finance. "Recruit Smarter: A Better Way to Do Business." The Premier of Victoria, May 20, 2016, http://www.premier.vic.gov.au/recruit-smarter-a-better-way-to-do-business/

153 "In the U.K. . . ." Joseph, Jeffrey. "What Companies Use Blind/Anonymous Resumes and What Benefits Have They Reported?" Cornell University, ILR School, http://digitalcommons.ilr.cornell.edu/cgi/viewcontent.cgi?article=1108&context=student

154 "Hiring managers 'are . . .'" Bohnet, Iris. "How to Take the Bias Out of Interviews." *Harvard Business Review,* April 18, 2016, https://hbr.org/2016/04/how-to-take-the-bias-out-of-interviews

154 "Consulting firm McKinsey . . ." Barton, Dominic. "Corporate IMPACT Champion." HeForShe. Accessed August 1, 2017, http://www.heforshe.org/en/impact/dominic-barton

154 "'We found . . .'" Dominic Barton, personal interview, November 16, 2015.

155 "There's a long . . ." Thormahlen, Marianne. "The Brontë Pseudonyms: A Woman's Image—The Writer and Her Public," *Victorian Web.* Accessed August 1, 2017, "http://www.victorianweb.org/authors/bronte/cbronte/thormahlen.html

155 "A modern-day equivalent . . ." Cohn, Laura. "This Female Exec Changed Her Name to a Man's to Get a Job. Should You?" *Fortune,* June 7, 2016, http://fortune.com/2016/06/08/name-bias-in-hiring/

155 "More recently, the . . ." John Paul Titlow. "These Women Entrepreneurs Created a Fake Male Cofounder to Dodge Startup Sexism." *Fast Company,* August 29, 2017, https://www.fastcompany.com/40456604/these-women-entrepreneurs-created-a-fake-male-cofounder-to-dodge-startup-sexism

155 "'Women, 'are you . . .'" Greathouse, John. "Why Women in Tech Might Consider Just Using Their Initials Online." *Wall Street Journal,* September 28, 2016, https://blogs.wsj.com/experts/2016/09/28/why-women-in-tech-might-consider-just-using-their-initials-online/

155 "The response to . . ." Greathouse, John. Twitter Post. September 29, 2016, https://twitter.com/johngreathouse/status/781584645691289600

155 "After former Uber . . ." Balakrishnan, Anita. "Here's the full 13-page report of recommendations for Uber." CNBC, June 13, 2017, https://www.cnbc.com/2017/06/13/eric-holder-uber-report-full-text.html

156 "Or where then-CEO . . ." Rapkin, Mickey. "Uber Cab Confessions." *GQ,* February 27, 2014, http://www.gq.com/story/uber-cab-confessions?currentPage=1

156 "'All the HR . . .'" Cauterucci, Christina. "All the HR Suggestions in the World Can't Change the Soul of Uber." *Slate,* June 13, 2017, http://www.slate.com/blogs/xx_factor/2017/06/13/all_the_hr_suggestions_in_the_world_can_t_change_uber_s_soul.html

156 "The company hired . . ." Swisher, Kara. "Uber Has Hired HBS's Frances Frei as a Top Leadership and Strategy Exec to Fix Its Management Mess." *Recode,* June 5, 2017, https://www.recode.net/2017/6/5/15741982/uber-hires-hbs-frances-frei-leadership-strategy-exec-fix-management-mess

156 "Shortly after she joined . . ." Frances Frei, personal interview, August 8, 2017.

156 "We've come a . . ." "The Passaic Daily News v. Blair." *Justia.* Accessed August 2, 2017, http://law.justia.com/cases/new-jersey/supreme-court/1973/63-n-j-474–0 .html

156 "Textio, a tech . . ." Miller, Claire Cain. "Is Blind Hiring the Best Hiring?" *New York Times,* February 25, 2016, https://www.nytimes.com/2016/02/28/magazine /is-blind-hiring-the-best-hiring.html?_r=0; Giang, Vivian. "The Growing Business of Detecting Unconscious Bias." *Fast Company,* May 5, 2015, https://www.fastcompany.com/3045899/the-growing-business-of-detecting -unconscious-bias; Miller, Claire Cain. "Is Blind Hiring the Best Hiring?" *New York Times,* February 25, 2016, https://www.nytimes.com/2016/02/28/ magazine/is-blind-hiring-the-best-hiring.html?_r=0

157 "Textio's software singles . . ." Mundy, Liza. "Why Is Silicon Valley So Awful to Women?" *The Atlantic,* April 2017, https://www.theatlantic.com/magazine/ar-chive/2017/04/why-is-silicon-valley-so-awful-to-women/517788/

157 "On a sliding . . ." Jones, Stacy, and Grace Donnelly. "Walmart's New Jobs Approach Could Be Undermined by Gender Bias." *Fortune,* April 4, 2017, http:// fortune.com/2017/04/04/walmart-jobs-gender-bias/

157 "Trying to democratize . . ." Gaucher, Danielle, Justin Friesen, and Aaron C. Kay. "Evidence that gendered wording in job advertisements exists and sustains gender inequality." *Journal of Personality and Social Psychology* 101, no. 1 (2011): 109—128. doi: 10.1037/a0022530

159 "Cardinal Health's Paul . . ." This note covers subsequent Gotti comments quoted to author. Paul Gotti, personal interview, November 20, 2014.

160 "According to one . . ." "10 Things Women Do That Absolutely Terrify Men." *Daily Edge,* May 23, 2015, http://www.dailyedge.ie/things-women-do-that-scare-men-2098452-May2015/

160 "A Reddit thread . . ." "Men of Reddit: Is It Scary, Annoying or Sad When a Girl Cries over You?" *Reddit.* Accessed August, 2017, "https://www.reddit.com/r/ AskMen/comments/3nwjqr/men_of_reddit_is_it_scary_annoying_or_sad_ when_a/

160 "It's ingrained in . . ." IMDb, *A League of Their Own* (1992) quotes, http://www .imdb.com/title/tt0104694/quotes, accessed November 13, 2017

160 "Barbara Annis and John . . ." Adams, Susan. "8 Blind Spots Between the Sexes at Work." *Forbes,* April 26, 2013, http://www.forbes.com/sites/susanadams /2013/04/26/8-blind-spots-between-the-sexes-at-work/#68ddb2d5195d

160 "Scientists have found . . ." Kreamer, Anne. *It's Always Personal: Navigating Emotion in the New Workplace.* New York: Random House, 2011.

161 "'Let me tell . . .'" Bilefsky, Dan. "Women Respond to Nobel Laureate's 'Trouble with Girls.'" *New York Times,* June 11, 2015, https://www.nytimes .com/2015/06/12/world/europe/tim-hunt-nobel-laureate-resigns-sexist-women -female-scientists.html

161 "They're also afraid . . ." Lipman, Joanne. "Women at Work: A Guide for Men." *Wall Street Journal,* December 12, 2014, https://www.wsj.com/articles/women -at-work-a-guide-for-men-1418418595

162 "But despite stellar . . ." Biernat, Monica, M. J. Tocci, and Joan C Williams. "The Language of Performance Evaluations." *Social Psychological and Personality Science* 3, no. 2 (2012). doi: 10.1177/1948550611415693

162 "When the manager . . ." UGM Consulting, "How Unconscious Bias Can Contaminate Performance Reviews," August 6, 2010, http://www.ugmconsulting.com/UGM%20Briefing%20Aug%206%202010%20How%20Unconscious%20Bias%20can%20contaminate%20%20Performance%20Reviews.pdf

162 "Women also . . ." Brizendine, Louann. *The Female Brain*. New York: Three Rivers Press, 2007; Traub, Leslie. "Bias in Performance Management Review Process." Cook Ross, 2013, http://www.cookross.com/docs/unconsciousbiasinperformance2013.pdf

163 "A man gets . . ." Dowd, Maureen. "The Women of Hollywood Speak Out." *New York Times*, November 20, 2015, http://www.nytimes.com/2015/11/22/magazine/the-women-of-hollywood-speak-out.html?_r=0

163 "A recent study . . ." Goudreau, Jenna. "Crying at Work, a Woman's Burden." *Forbes*, January 11, 2011, http://www.forbes.com/sites/jennagoudreau/2011/01/11/crying-at-work-a-womans-burden-study-men-sex-testosterone-tears-arousal/#2fad4a084e54

163 "Studies have associated . . ." Gelstein, Shani, et al. "Human tears contain a chemosignal." Weizmann Institute of Science, Department of Neurobiology, 2011, http://faculty.washington.edu/beecher/Gelstein_et_al_2011.pdf

163 "The scientists theorized . . ." Macrae, Fiona. "The Brain Scans Which Reveal Why Men REALLY Don't Understand Women." *Daily Mail*, April 16, 2013, http://www.dailymail.co.uk/sciencetech/article-2309812/The-brain-scans-reveal-men-REALLY-dont-understand-women.html

164 "'It was a fairly . . .'" Reuben Gur, personal interview, August 20, 2015.

165 "To me, those . . ." Ragini Verma, personal interviews, July 27, 2015, and July 2017.

165 "When these 3-D . . ." Ingalhalikar, Madhura, et al. "Sex differences in the structural connectome of the human brain." *Proceedings of the National Academy of Sciences* 111, no. 2 (2014): 823–828, http://www.pnas.org/content/111/2/823.abstract

166 "This suggests that . . ." Ibid.

166 "Her findings showed . . ." Morgan, James. "Women 'better at multitasking' than men, study finds." BBC, October 24, 2013, http://www.bbc.com/news/science-environment-24645100

167 "Its chief executive . . ." Frey, Jennifer, and Hanna Rosin. "Lifestyles of the Rich and Infamous/Enron's Elite Indulged in Cars, Homes, Art, Trips." *SF Gate*, February 27, 2002, http://www.sfgate.com/news/article/Lifestyles-of-the-rich-and-infamous-Enron-s-2870711.php; Ahrens, Frank. "Prosecution Outlines Lay's Lavish Lifestyle." *Washington Post*, May 1, 2006, https://www.washingtonpost.com/archive/business/technology/2006/05/01/prosecution-outlines-lays-lavish-lifestyle/70215dd1-e957-4f1c-a7d3-3c7061b84a5a/

167 "The company set . . ." Banerjee, Neela, with reporting from David Barboza, Audrey Warren. "Enron's Many Strands: Corporate Culture; At Enron, Lavish Excess Often Came Before Success." *New York Times*, February 26, 2002, http://

www.nytimes.com/2002/02/26/business/enron-s-many-strands-corporate-culture-enron-lavish-excess-often-came-before.html

167 "'When I read about it...'" Andrew McCallum, personal interview, February 28, 2015.

167 "Computer scientists..." Vinodkumar Prabhakaran, personal interview, July 30, 2015.

171 "Founded in 1842..." Hellsbert, Clemens. "The History of the Vienna Philharmonic." Accessed August 3, 2017, https://www.wienerphilharmoniker.at/orchestra/history

171 "Among the more..." Service, Tom. "Vienna Philharmonic's conservatism has exposed it to unsettling truths." *Guardian*, March 11, 2013, https://www.theguardian.com/music/2013/mar/11/vienna-philharmonic-history

171 "The first woman..." Perlez, Jane. "Vienna Philharmonic Lets Women Join in Harmony." *New York Times*, February 28, 1997. http://www.nytimes.com/1997/02/28/world/vienna-philharmonic-lets-women-join-in-harmony.html

171 "Almost as if..." Service, Tom. "Vienna Philharmonic's Conservatism Has Exposed It to Unsettling Truths." *The Guardian*, March 11, 2013, https://www.theguardian.com/music/2013/mar/11/vienna-philharmonic-history

172 "half a world..." "Vienna Philharmonic Orchestra's New Year's Day Concert to Air on Great Performances." *Broadway World*, December 29, 2016, http://www.broadwayworld.com/bwwtv/article/Vienna-Philharmonic-Orchestras-New-Years-Day-Concert-to-Air-on-Great-Performances-20161229

172 "Onlookers could spot..." Lebrecht, Norman. "How Few Women in Today's Vienna Phil?" *Slippedisk*, January 1, 2015, http://slippedisc.com/2015/01/how-few-women-in-todays-vienna-phil/

Chapter 8: Invisible Women

175 "If more women..." Adamy, Janet. "How to Boost U.S. GDP by $2.1 Trillion: More Women in the Workforce." *Wall Street Journal*, April 7, 2016, https://blogs.wsj.com/economics/2016/04/07/how-to-boost-u-s-gdp-by-2-1-trillion-more-women-in-the-workforce/

175 "The same is..." Abe, Shinzō. "Unleashing the Power of 'Womanomics.'" *Wall Street Journal*, September 25, 2013, https://www.wsj.com/articles/shinzo-abe-unleashing-the-power-of-8216womenomics8217-1380149475?tesla=y

176 "Around the globe..." Woetzel, Jonathan, et al. "How advancing women's equality can add $12 trillion to global growth." McKinsey Global Institute, September 20, 2015, http://www.mckinsey.com/global-themes/employment-and-growth/how-advancing-womens-equality-can-add-12-trillion-to-global-growth

178 "There's a reason..." United States Department of Labor. "Latest Annual Data: Women of Working Age." Accessed August 1, 2017, https://www.dol.gov/wb/stats/mother_families.htm

178 "A Pew Research..." Pew Research Center. "Fewer Mothers Prefer Full-time Work." July 12, 2007, http://www.pewsocialtrends.org/2007/07/12/fewer-mothers-prefer-full-time-work/

178 "In fact, daughters..." Bhattacharya, Ananya. "Kids of working moms are better off." *CNN Money,* June 15, 2015, http://money.cnn.com/2015/06/15/news/economy/working-moms-kids-better-off-harvard-study/

178 "And men who..." Miller, Claire Cain. "How to Raise a Feminist Son." *New York Times,* June 1, 2017, https://www.nytimes.com/2017/06/02/upshot/how-to-raise-a-feminist-son.html?_r=1

178 "It's an astonishing..." Groden, Claire. "An Overwhelming Majority of Americans Support Paid Parental Leave." *Fortune,* April 15, 2016, http://fortune.com/2016/04/15/an-overwhelming-majority-of-americans-support-paid-parental-leave/

178 "Even more mind-boggling..." Addati, Laura, Naomi Cassirer, and Katherine Gilchrist. "Maternity and paternity at work: law and practices across the world." International Labour Organization, 2014.

178 "Companies and politicians..." Dixon, Laura. "3 Reasons Why Paid Leave Is Worth the Cost." *Talent Economy,* December 5, 2016, http://www.talenteconomy.io/2016/12/05/3-reasons-paid-leave-worth-cost/; *Deloitte,* June 15, 2016, https://www2.deloitte.com/us/en/pages/about-deloitte/articles/press-releases/deloitte-survey-parental-leave.html

179 "And there are..." Shulevitz, Judith. "How to Fix Feminism." *New York Times,* June 10, 2016, https://www.nytimes.com/2016/06/12/opinion/sunday/how-to-fix-feminism.html?action=click&pgtype=Homepage®ion=CColumn&module=MostEmailed&version=Full&src=me&WT.nav=MostEmailed&mtrref=undefined&assetType=opinion

179 "The burden is..." Ibid.

179 "Child care is unaffordable..." Zillman, Claire. "Child Care Is Unaffordable in Every U.S. State Except This One." *Fortune,* December 9, 2016, http://fortune.com/2016/12/09/child-care-cost-us/

179 "In more than..." Shulte, Brigid. "The U.S. Ranks Last in Every Measure When It Comes to Family Policy, in 10 Charts." *Washington Post,* June 23, 2014, https://www.washingtonpost.com/blogs/she-the-people/wp/2014/06/23/global-view-how-u-s-policies-to-help-working-families-rank-in-the-world/?utm_term=.6cd92336c03e

179 "That helps explain..." Waxman, Sandra, and Simone Ispa-Landa. "Academia's 'Baby Penalty.'" *US News,* February 11, 2016, https://www.usnews.com/opinion/knowledge-bank/articles/2016-02-11/academia-must-correct-systemic-discrimination-and-bias-against-mothers

179 "In the U.S...." Budig, Michelle J., and Paula England. "The wage penalty for motherhood." *American Sociological Review* 66, no. 2 (2001): 204–225, http://courses.washington.edu/pbafadv/examples/TheWagePenaltyforMotherhood.pdf

180 "The gap exists..." Evans, Dayna. "Mothers Are Paid Less Than Fathers in Every State and at Every Education Level." *The Cut,* May 22, 2017, https://www.thecut.com/2017/05/the-gender-pay-gap-mothers.html

180 "The paradox is..." "What's holding women back?" *The Economist,* January 23, 2015, https://www.economist.com/blogs/democracyinamerica/2015/01/women-and-work

180 "'Virtually everyone—women . . .'" Peck, Emily. "Focusing on Women's Advancement Blinds Companies to Their Real Problem: Overworking Everyone." *Huffington Post,* June 11, 2015, http://www.huffingtonpost.com/2015/06/11/ harvard-overwork-study_n_7553654.html?

180 "When a man . . ." Ibid.

180 "Why not? they . . ." Eydal, Guðný Björk, and Ingólfur V. Gíslason. "Equal rights to paid parental leave and caring fathers—the case of Iceland." *Icelandic Review of Politics and Administration* 9, no. 2 (December 19, 2013): 323–344. doi: http://dx.doi.org/10.13177/irpa.a.2013.9.2.4

181 "In one survey . . ." Bellstrom, Kristen. "This Is How Much Stay-at-Home Moms Say They Should Be Paid." *Fortune,* June 6, 2016, http://fortune .com/2016/06/06/stay-at-home-moms-pay/

181 "It's no wonder . . ." Adams, Rebecca. "A Quarter of Working Moms Cry Once a Week, but There Are Solutions." *Huffington Post,* October 24, 2014, http://www .huffingtonpost.com/2014/10/24/working-moms-cry_n_6041728.html

182 "That's even truer . . ." Student Loan Hero. "A Look at the Shocking Student Loan Debt Statistics for 2017," https://studentloanhero.com/student-loan-debt-statistics/

183 "'I found that . . .'" Vanderkam, Laura. "The Problem with Part-Time Work Is That It's Rarely Part-Time." *Harvard Business Review,* May 26, 2015, https://hbr. org/2015/05/the-problem-with-part-time-work-is-that-its-rarely-part-time

184 "On the other . . ." Zarya, Valentina. "What Women Want from Their Employers, in 5 Simple Charts." *Fortune,* January 19, 2016, http://fortune.com/2016/01/20/ what-women-want-charts/

186 "Like men . . ." Julie Coffman, personal interview, November 21, 2014.

187 "In a poignant . . ." Lee, Seonaid. "Re-Recruit from the Leaky Pipeline." *Model View Culture Magazine,* July 21, 2015, https://modelviewculture.com/pieces/ re-recruit-from-the-leaky-pipeline

188 "'Now, here's the . . .'" Krawcheck, Sallie. "Sallie Krawcheck Explains Why Women's Careers Heat Up Just as Men's Slow Down." *Fortune,* May 4, 2016, http://fortune.com/2016/05/04/sallie-krawcheck-third-act/

188 "Indeed, a 2005 . . ." Hewlett, Sylvia Ann, and Carolyn Buck Luce. "Off-Ramps and On-Ramps: Keeping Talented Women on the Road to Success." *Harvard Business Review,* March 2005, https://hbr.org/2005/03/off-ramps-and-on-ramps-keeping-talented-women-on-the-road-to-success

188 "What's more, a . . ." Cohen, Patricia. "Over 50, Female and Jobless Even as Others Return to Work." *New York Times,* January 1, 2016, https://www.nytimes .com/2016/01/02/business/economy/over-50-female-and-jobless-even-as-others-return-to-work.html?_r=1&mtrref=undefined

189 "Structured somewhat like . . ." "Start Your Journey Back to Work with the Goldman Sachs Returnship Program." Goldman Sachs. Accessed July 26, 2017, http://www.goldmansachs.com/careers/experienced-professionals/return ship/flyer.pdf

190 "Other financial firms . . ." Butcher, Sarah. "How to Get into Goldman Sachs, JPM and Credit Suisse if You Haven't Worked for 5 years." eFinancialCareers,

March 25, 2015, http://news.efinancialcareers.com/us-en/203227/how-to-get-into-goldman-sachs-jpm-and-credit-suisse-if-you-havent-worked-for-5-years/

190 "A mini-industry..." Elejalde-Ruiz, Alexia. "Resume Gap? Corporate 'Returnships' for Career Breakers Could Help." *Chicago Tribune,* February 27, 2016, http://www.chicagotribune.com/business/ct-relaunch-careers-0228-biz-20160226-story.html

190 "A nonprofit..." Zillman, Claire. "These 6 Tech Companies Are Recruiting Moms Who Left the Workplace." *Fortune,* August 23, 2016, http://fortune.com/2016/08/23/tech-jobs-mom-women-return-workplace/

190 "The concept is..." Hoyle, Antonia. "Move over Millienials: The Rise of the 'Returnship' for Middle-Aged Mums." *The Telegraph,* January 23, 2017, http://www.telegraph.co.uk/women/work/move-millienials-rise-returnship-middle-aged-mums/

190 "Meanwhile, organizations like..." "What Is Reboot Accel?" ReBoot Accel. Accessed July 26, 2017, https://rebootaccel.com/what-is-reboot/

190 "'Proceed with caution...'" Koba, Mark. "Returnships for older workers: Proceed with caution." CNBC, October 14, 2013, http://www.cnbc.com/2013/10/14/returnships-for-older-workers-proceed-with-caution.html

190 "The Goldman Sachs..." Ibid.

190 "When the University..." Jones, Sandra M. "In Tough Times Jobless Turning to Alma Maters." *Chicago Tribune,* March 4, 2009, http://www.chicagotribune.com/business/chi-biz-colleges-help-alumni-jobs-march04-story.html

190 "Schools including the..." Alumni Eligibility and Services, University of Michigan University Career Center. Accessed July 26, 2017, https://careercenter.umich.edu/topic/alumni

191 "'Leaving the workforce...'" Light, Paula. "Why 43% of Women with Children Leave Their Jobs, and How to Get Them Back." *The Atlantic,* April 19, 2013, https://www.theatlantic.com/sexes/archive/2013/04/why-43-of-women-with-children-leave-their-jobs-and-how-to-get-them-back/275134/

192 "Krawcheck herself, after..." Roberts, Jeff John. "I Was Fired for Being a Woman, Sallie Krawcheck Tells Crowd." *Fortune,* October 8, 2016, http://fortune.com/2016/10/08/sallie-krewcheck-fired/

192 "'Invest like a...'" "A New Financial Era." Ellevest. Accessed July 26, 2017, https://www.ellevest.com/

192 "Other women turn..." Kathy Soll, personal interview, June 12, 2016.

192 "Teens for Food..." "The TFFJ Mission." Teens for Food Justice. Accessed July 26, 2017, http://www.teensforfoodjustice.org/about-us/about-tffj/

Chapter 9: The Next Generation

196 "It introduced a..." Kantor, Jodi. "Harvard Business School Case Study: Gender Equity." *New York Times,* September 7, 2013, http://www.nytimes.com/2013/09/08/education/harvard-case-study-gender-equity.html?pagewanted=all&_r=0

197 "Millennial men..." Pedulla, David S., and Thebaud, Sarah. "Can we finish the revolution? gender, work-family ideals, and institutional constraint." *American Sociological Review* 80, no. 1 (February 2015), http://journals.sagepub.com/doi/

abs/10.1177/0003122414564008; The General Social Survey. *2016 General Social Survey data set.* Available as of March, 29, 2017, http://gss.norc.org/getthedata/Pages/Home.aspx

197 "What's more, when . . ." Deloitte. "The 2016 Deloitte Millennial Survey." Accessed July 30, 2017, https://www2.deloitte.com/content/dam/Deloitte/global/Documents/About-Deloitte/gx-millenial-survey-2016-exec-summary.pdf

198 "They overwhelmingly disagree . . ." VanderMey, Anne. "Relax, Millennial Men Don't Actually Want to Keep Women in the Kitchen." *Fortune, April 1, 2017,* http://fortune.com/2017/04/01/millennial-men-gender-roles/

198 "As the group's . . ." Hagan, Tara. "HBS WSA Manbassadors 2013." YouTube video, October 9, 2013, https://www.youtube.com/watch?v=NSjrYrV_oZY

198 "Professors, and the . . ." Harvard Business School. *Community Values.* Accessed July 30, 2017, http://www.hbs.edu/mba/student-life/Pages/community-values.aspx

198 "'Our mission is . . .'" Frances Frei, personal interview, August 6, 2015.

199 "The group's origin . . ." Tara Hagan, personal interview, June 11, 2015.

199 "Women are still . . ." Byrne, John A., "Harvard B-School Dean Offers Unusual Apology." *Fortune,* January 29, 2014, http://fortune.com/2014/01/29/harvard-b-school-dean-offers-unusual-apology/

199 "By the time . . ." Tara Hagan, personal interview, June 11, 2015.

199 "In the last . . ." McGregor, Jena. "A Gender-Equality Club, Run by Men." *Washington Post,* August 10, 2015, https://www.washingtonpost.com/news/on-leadership/wp/2015/08/10/a-gender-equality-club-run-by-men/; Forté Foundation. Accessed July 30, 2017, http://www.fortefoundation.org/site/PageServer?pagename=allies

200 "Inside the . . ." Sam Travers, personal interview, November 18, 2015.

201 "Sitting beside . . ." Matt Simpson, personal interview, November 18, 2015.

201 "The latter reflects . . ." Harvard Business School. "From Dean Nohria: Jan 2015." Accessed July 30, 2017, http://www.hbs.edu/about/Documents/priorities_2015.pdf

202 "That trend holds . . ." Bellstrom, Kristen. "Just 1 in 10 Top Business School Case Studies Feature a Female Protagonist." March 10, 2016, http://fortune.com/2016/03/10/women-business-school-case-studies/

202 "So taking leave . . ." Harvard Business School, "Faculty & Research: Robin J. Ely." Accessed August 3, 2017, http://www.hbs.edu/faculty/Pages/profile.aspx?facId=7287

202 "The initiative, created . . ." Harvard Business School, "About: The Gender Initiative." Accessed August 3, 2017, http://www.hbs.edu/gender/about/Pages/default.aspx

202 "A petite . . ." Robin Ely, personal interview, November 18, 2015.

203 "The proportion of . . ." Harvard Business School. "Student Profile at Matriculation." Accessed August 2, 2017, http://www.hbs.edu/recruiting/data/Pages/at-a-glance.aspx

203 "Women make up . . ." Harvard Business School. Statistics Faculty & Staff. Accessed July 30, 2017, http://www.hbs.edu/about/facts-and-figures/Pages/faculty-statistics.aspx

203 "A 2012 faculty . . ." deLuzuriaga, Tania. "Survey finds faculty satisfaction rate at 81 percent." *Harvard Gazette,* May 21, 2014, http://news.harvard.edu/gazette/story/2014/05/survey-finds-faculty-satisfaction-rate-at-81-percent/

203 "Women have been . . ." "Harvard Business School Dean Apologizes to All Women." *Huffington Post,* January 31, 2014, http://www.huffingtonpost.com/2014/01/31/harvard-business-school-women_n_4697113.html

204 "What's more, it . . ." Frances Frei, personal interview, August 6, 2015.

205 "A study of . . ." Krupnick, Catherine G. "Women and Men in the Classroom: Inequality and Its Remedies." Derek Bok Center for Teaching and Learning, Harvard University. *On Teaching and Learning,* vol. 1, 1985, https://projects.vrac.iastate.edu/REU2016/wp-content/uploads/2016/05/Krupnick_1985_Diversity_Gender.pdf

205 "The tactic has . . ." Ingraham, Christopher. "New Study Finds That Men Are Often Their Own Favorite Experts on Any Given Subject." *Washington Post,* August 1, 2016, https://www.washingtonpost.com/news/wonk/wp/2016/08/01/new-study-finds-that-men-are-often-their-own-favorite-experts-on-any-given-subject/?utm_term=.db3of31db44f

205 "And as journalists . . ." Kay, Katty, and Claire Shipman. *Confidence Code.* New York: HarperCollins Publishers, 2014.

207 "That too is . . ." Heilman, M. E. "Sex stereotypes and their effects in the workplace: what we know and what we don't know." *Journal of Social Behavior and Personality* 10, no. 4 (1995): 3, ISSN 0886–1641

208 "I soon found . . ." Jennifer Braus, personal interview, July 23, 2015.

209 "As a student, he . . ." Modi, Kunal. "Man Up on Family and Workplace Issues: A Response to Anne-Marie Slaughter." *Huffington Post,* July 12, 2012, https://www.huffingtonpost.com/kunal-modi/man-up-on-family-and-work_b_1667878.html

209 "After graduation . . ." Kunal Modi, personal interview, August 19, 2015.

210 "Frei was sure . . ." Frances Frei, personal interview, August 21, 2015.

210 "'Oh yes,' she said . . ." Frances Frei, personal interview, August 21, 2015.

211 "A study by . . ." Sakai, Kelly. "Times Are Changing: Gender and Generation at Work and at Home." *Families and Work,* February 3, 2014, http://www.familiesandwork.org/times-are-changing-gender-and-generation-at-work-and-at-home/

211 "And a study published . . ." Pedulla, David S., and Thebaud, Sarah. "Can we finish the revolution? gender, work-family ideals, and institutional constraint." American Sociological Review 80.1, February 2015, http://journals.sagepub.com/doi/abs/10.1177/0003122414564008

211 "What's more, two-thirds . . ." Ely, Robin J. "Rethink what you 'know' about high achieving women." *Harvard Business Review* 92, no. 12 (December 2014): 100–109, https://hbr.org/2014/12/rethink-what-you-know-about-high-achieving-women

212 "The HBS class . . ." Brooke Boyarsky, personal interview, June 29, 2015.

212 "After her 2014 graduation . . ." Tara Hagan, personal interview, June 11, 2015.

213 "Two years after . . ." Tara Hagan, email exchange, October 2, 2017.

Chapter 10: The Best Place in the World to Be a Woman?

217 "For eight consecutive..." *The Global Gender Gap Report 2016*. World Economic Forum, 2016, http://www3.weforum.org/docs/GGGR16/WEF_GGGR16_Full_Report.pdf

217 "One in 20..." Fontaine, Paul. "Foreign Minister Writes for Guardian About Iceland's Gender Equality." *Grapevine*, June 2, 2015, https://grapevine.is/news/2015/06/02/foreign-minister-writes-for-guardian-about-icelands-gender-equality/

218 "'They were all heroes...'" Jón Steinar Gunnlaugsson, personal interview, October 20, 2015.

218 "'Icelanders are risk...'" Bowers, Simon. "Iceland's Business Vikings Facing an Extended Winter." *Taipei Times*, February 13, 2009, http://www.taipeitimes.com/News/editorials/archives/2009/02/13/2003435963

218 "They are daring..." Bowers, Simon. "Iceland's Vikings Face a Long Winter." *The Guardian*, February 8, 2009, https://www.theguardian.com/world/2009/feb/09/iceland-economy-credit-crisis

219 "We owe pretty..." Palmer, Katie M. "Why Iceland Is the World's Greatest Genetic Laboratory. *Wired*, March 25, 20015, http://www.wired.com/2015/03/iceland-worlds-greatest-genetic-laboratory/

221 "In Iceland it..." Rosenberg, Jerry M. *The Concise Encyclopedia of the Great Recession 2007–2012*. Maryland: Scarecrow Press, 2012.

221 "A retail magnate..." Martinez, Jose. "Posh Icelandic Couple Sued for Putting IKEA Kitchen in Swank Gramercy Park Hotel Pad." *NY Daily News*, February 24, 2010, http://www.nydailynews.com/new-york/posh-icelandic-couple-sued-putting-ikea-kitchen-swank-gramercy-park-hotel-pad-article-1.194927

222 "'I thought everything...'" Sigurdsson, Gunnar. *Maybe I Should Have*. Documentary by Gunnar Sigurdsson, Iceland, 2010.

223 "off their hands..." Parker, Ian. "Lost." *The New Yorker*, March 9, 2009, http://www.newyorker.com/magazine/2009/03/09/lost-19

223 "Hers was the..." Sigurdsson, Gunnar. *Maybe I Should Have*. Documentary by Gunnar Sigurdsson, Herbert Sveinbjornsson, Iceland, 2010, https://www.icelandiccinema.com/film/Maybe-I-Should-Have

223 "'I just want some women...'" Lewis, Michael. *Boomerang: Travels in the New Third World*. New York: W.W. Norton & Co., 2011.

224 "The head of Iceland's Chamber..." Ertel, Manfred. "Cleaning Up the Men's Mess: Iceland's Women Reach for Power." *Spiegel Online*, April 22, 2009, http://www.spiegel.de/international/europe/cleaning-up-the-men-s-mess-iceland-s-women-reach-for-power-a-620544.html

224 "'After the Crash...'" Ibid.

224 "The *Financial Times*..." Sunderland, Ruth. "After the Crash, Iceland's Women Lead the Rescue." *The Guardian*, February 21, 2009, https://www.theguardian.com/world/2009/feb/22/iceland-women

224 "In New Zealand..." O'Connor, Sarah. "Iceland Calls in Women Bankers to Clean Up 'Young Men's Mess.'" *Financial Times*, October 14, 2008, http://www.ft.com/cms/s/0/6107e59c-9988-11dd-9d48-000077b07658.html?ft_site=-

falcon&desktop=true#axzz4odIgxb1K; Sunderland, Ruth. "After the crash, Iceland's women lead the rescue." *The Guardian,* February 21, 2009, https://www.theguardian.com/world/2009/feb/22/iceland-women

225 "While the men . . ." "Viking Women Aim to End the Age of Testosterone," PBS *Wide Angle,* April 24, 2009, http://www.pbs.org/wnet/wideangle/blog/viking-women-aim-to-end-to-the-age-of-testosterone/4655/

227 "A *Vice* article labeled . . ." Mead, Derek. "Why Does Iceland's Proposed Porn Ban Matter?" *Motherboard,* February 20, 2017, https://motherboard.vice.com/en_us/article/ezz9z4/why-does-icelands-proposed-porn-ban-matter

229 "The night she won . . ." Tómasdóttir, Halla. "A feminine response to Iceland's financial crash." TED talk, December 2010, https://www.ted.com/talks/halla_tomasdottir

229 "Day care is heavily . . ." Eydal, Guðný Björk, and Ingólfur V. Gíslason. "Iceland." *International Review of Leave Policies and Research,* 2013, http://www.leavenetwork.org/fileadmin/Leavenetwork/Country_notes/2013/Iceland.FINALcitation.pdf

229 "Not long after . . ." England, Charlotte. "Icelandic MP Breastfeeds Baby During a Debate in Parliament." *Independent,* October 13, 2016, http://www.independent.co.uk/news/people/icelandic-mp-breastfeeds-baby-debate-parliament-al-ingi-a7358681.html

230 "'Iceland is not a female . . .'" Katrín Anna Guðmundsdóttir, personal interview, June 2, 2015.

230 "Inside, up a flight of stairs . . ."Guðmundur Gunnarsson, personal interview, October 21, 2015.

231 "Not so in Iceland . . ." "Ten Years of Vagina Victories." Accessed November 12, 2017, https://www.vday.org/timeline-targetNode=105.html

Conclusion

233 "Teresa Shook . . ." Kearney, Laila. "Hawaii Grandma's Plea Launches Women's March in Washington." Reuters, December 5, 2016, http://www.reuters.com/article/us-usa-trump-women-idUSKBN13U0GW

233 "As many as . . ." Women's March Network. "Sister Marches." Accessed August 1, 2017, https://www.womensmarch.com/sisters; Frostenson, Sarah. "The Women's March May Have Been the Largest Demonstration in US History." *Vox,* January 31, 2017, https://www.vox.com/2017/1/22/14350808/womens-marches-largest-demonstration-us-history-map

233 "'I'm a typical . . .'" Mahdawi, Arwa. "9 Men on Why They're Joining the Women's March on Washington." *The Cut,* January 12, 2017, https://www.thecut.com/2017/01/9-men-on-why-theyre-joining-the-womens-march-on-washington.html

234 "In a letter . . ." Mauldin, Jared. "Letter to the Editor: STEM." *The Easterner,* October 5, 2015, http://easterneronline.com/36007/letters-to-the-editor/letter-to-the-editor-stem/; Holohan, Megan. "We're unequal: Engineering student's humble letter praises female peers' feats." *Today,* October 7, 2015, http://

www.today.com/parents/we-re-unequal-engineering-student-s-humble
-letter-praises-female-t48856

234 "One interesting indication . . ." Feintzeig, Rachel. "Male CEOs Tell Us Their Work-Life Rules." *Wall Street Journal*, June 14, 2016, https://www.wsj.com/articles /male-ceos-tell-us-their-work-life-rules-1465896602

235 "Younger male executives . . ." Bloomberg. "People." Accessed August 1, 2017, https://www.bloomberg.com/research/stocks/private/person.asp?person Id=1477272&privcapId=37181322

235 "His reasoning is . . ." Feintzeig, Rachel, and Parker Eshelman. "How 25 Male CEOs Manage Work and Life." *Wall Street Journal*, June 16, 2016, http:// graphics.wsj.com/image-grid/ceo-work-life/%20637%20http://fortune .com/2016/04/13/ey-parental-leave-policy/

236 "The practice started . . ." Bellstrom, Kristen. "EY Comes Out Swinging at Other Consulting Firms with New Parental Leave Policy." *Fortune*, April 13, 2016, http://fortune.com/2016/04/13/ey-parental-leave-policy/; Bologna, Caroline. "Johnson & Johnson Now Offering Employees up to 17 Weeks of Parental Leave." *Huffington Post*, May 1, 2015, http://www.huffingtonpost .com/2015/05/01/johnson—johnson-parental-leave_n_7188708.html

236 "Meanwhile at last . . ." National Partnership for Women & Families. "State Paid Leave Insurance Laws: July 2017." Accessed August 1, 2017, http://www .nationalpartnership.org/research-library/work-family/paid-leave/state-paid-family-leave-laws.pdf

236 "Paradigm for Parity . . ." Paradigm for Parity. "A Call to Action and Model for Gender Equality, 2015–2016. Accessed August 1, 2017, https://static1 .squarespace.com/static/57e9765e9f7456c76dc1c1c0/t/5873a40ccdof 6899ba02d384/1483973644868/Paradigm_For_Parity-Full.1.5.17_BD.pdf

236 "Among them: unconscious-bias . . ." Cohn, Laura. "27 CEOs Pledge to Bring Gender Parity to Corporate America's Top Ranks by 2030." *Fortune*, December 7, 2016, http://fortune.com/2016/12/07/ceos-women-in-corporate-america/

236 "Chief executives of . . ." Ibid.

237 "It created a . . ." Forté Foundation. "Forté Men as Allies Initiative." Accessed August 1, 2017, http://www.fortefoundation.org/site/PageServer ?pagename=allies

237 "In Australia, the . . ." Paradigm For Parity. "A Call to Action and Model for Gender Equality." Accessed August 1, 2017, https://static1.squarespace.com/ static/57e9765e9f7456c76dc1c1c0/t/5873a40ccdof6899ba02d384/1483973644868/ Paradigm_For_Parity-Full.1.5.17_BD.pdf

237 "Kenya, for its . . ." Reiman, Joshua. "The Women's Movement Needs Men." *International Affairs Review*, November 1, 2019, http://www.iar-gwu.org/ node/216

237 "'Gender equality is . . .'" Watson, Emma. "Gender Equality Is Your Issue Too." UN Women, September 20, 2014, http://www.unwomen.org/en/news/ stories/2014/9/emma-watson-gender-equality-is-your-issue-too

237 "Internationally, these men's . . ." Jong, Hans Nicholas. "Violence Against

Women Rising: Komnas Perempuan." *The Jakarta Post*, February 8, 2017, http://www.thejakartapost.com/news/2017/02/08/violence-against-women-rising-komnas-perempuan.html; Gayle, Damien. "Hidden Rise in Violent Crime Driven by Growth in Violence Against Women." *The Guardian*, January 12, 2016, https://www.theguardian.com/society/2016/jan/13/hidden-rise-violent-crime-growth-violence-against-women

237 "Men in Argentina . . ." "Wonder women and macho men." *The Economist*, August 22, 2015, https://www.economist.com/news/americas/21661800-latin-american-women-are-making-great-strides-culture-not-keeping-up-wonder-women-and

237 "A Burundi men's . . ." Reiman, Joshua. "The Women's Movement Needs Men." *International Affairs Review*, November 1, 2010, http://www.iar-gwu.org/node/216

237 "Hundreds of men . . ." Anderson, Lisa. "Men Leave U.N. 'Barbershop' after Vow to Push for Gender Equality." Reuters, January 15, 2015, http://uk.reuters.com/article/un-barbershop-men-idUKKBN0KP0CN20150116

238 "In more extreme . . ." Adam Grant, personal interview, July 4, 2017.

238 "Venture capitalist Roger McNamee . . ." Roger McNamee, personal interview, September 23, 2017.

239 "The thing I . . ." Sam Polk, personal interview, July 28, 2017.

239 "Consulting firm McKinsey . . ." Zarya, Valentina. "These 10 Male Executives Are Committing to Reach Gender Parity in 5 Years." *Fortune*, January 21, 2016, http://fortune.com/2016/01/22/heforshe-impact-champions/; Manville, Brook. "How Dominic Barton Cultivated Community Change at McKinsey." *Forbes*, February 24, 2016, https://www.forbes.com/sites/brookmanville/2016/02/24/how-dominic-barton-cultivated-community-change-at-mckinsey/#177bc8fe3057

239 "The firm requires all . . ." Dominic Barton, personal interview, November 16, 2015.

239 "'It's been going in . . .'" Ibid.

239 "The response was . . ." Bronznick, Shifra, and Anne Weisberg. "Women in the Spotlight: If Google and SXSW Can Do It, So Can You." *Forbes*, June 3, 2014, https://www.forbes.com/sites/forbeswomanfiles/2014/06/03/women-in-the-spotlight-if-google-and-sxsw-can-do-it-so-can-you/#133a64c421a8; Rosen, Rebecca J. "A Simple Suggestion to Help Phase Out All-Male Panels at Tech Conferences." *The Atlantic*, January 4, 2013, https://www.theatlantic.com/technology/archive/2013/01/a-simple-suggestion-to-help-phase-out-all-male-panels-at-tech-conferences/266837/

240 "'The women's movement . . .'" Reiman, Joshua. "The Women's Movement Needs Men." *International Affairs Review*, November 1, 2010, http://www.iar-gwu.org/node/216

240 "As Gloria Steinem . . ." Miller, Claire Cain. "How to Raise a Feminist Son," *New York Times*, June 1, 2017, https://www.nytimes.com/2017/06/02/upshot/how-to-raise-a-feminist-son.html?_r=0

Afterword

242 "The 2018 midterm . . ." Rosenkrantz, Holly. "Record Number of Women to Serve in Congress Following 2018 Midterm Elections." CBS News, November 7, 2018, https://www.cbsnews.com/news/record-number-of-women-to-serve-in-house-congress-2018-midterm-elections/

242 "In California, new . . ." Carpenter, Julia, and Jackie Wattles. "California Has a New Law: No More All-Male Boards." CNN Business, October 3, 2018, https://money.cnn.com/2018/09/30/news/california-requires-women-board-of-directors/index.html

242 "Several states over . . ." Beitsch, Rebecca. "#MeToo Has Changed Our Culture. Now It's Changing Our Laws." *Stateline*, July 31, 2018, https://www.pewtrusts.org/en/research-and-analysis/blogs/stateline/2018/07/31/metoo-has-changed-our-culture-now-its-changing-our-laws

242 "Companies including NBCUniversal . . ." Compton, Julie. "'Returnships' Help Stay-at-Home Moms Get Back to Work." *NBC News*, April 26, 2017, https://www.nbcnews.com/better/careers/returnships-help-stay-home-moms-get-back-work-n750651

242 "After female Nike . . ." Barry, Erin. "Some Companies Are Bridging the Gender Pay Gap, But It Still Pays to Do Your Homework." CNBC, August 19, 2018, https://www.cnbc.com/2018/08/19/some-companies-are-bridging-the-gender-pay-gap.html

243 "Google's top executives . . ." Scheiber, Noam. "Google Workers Reject Silicon Valley Individualism in Walkout." *New York Times*, November 6, 2018, https://www.nytimes.com/2018/11/06/business/google-employee-walkout-labor.html

243 "At least one . . ." Weinberger, Matt. "Amazon Spins a Giant Roulette Wheel Every Week, and Whoever's Group It Lands on Needs to Do a Presentation." *Business Insider*, December 19, 2017, https://www.businessinsider.com/amazon-web-services-uses-the-wheel-to-run-big-meetings-2017-12

243 "One of the . . ." Lipman, Joanne. "Want Equality? Make New Dads Stay Home." *Wall Street Journal*, September 28, 2018, https://www.wsj.com/articles/want-equality-make-new-dads-stay-home-1538151219

244 "The percentage of . . ." Green, Jeff, Jordyn Holman, and Janet Paskin. "America's C-Suites Keep Getting Whiter (and More Male, Too)." *Bloomberg*, September 21, 2018, https://www.bloomberg.com/news/articles/2018-09-21/america-s-c-suites-keep-getting-whiter-and-more-male-too

244 "Gender inequality has . . ." Curry, Colleen. "Gender Equality Actually Got Worse in 2017, World Economic Forum Says." Global Citizen, November 2, 2017, https://www.globalcitizen.org/en/content/gender-equality-actually-got-worse-in-2018-world-e/

244 "In a recent . . ." "In Era of #MeToo, Majority of Employees Say Their Employers Fail to Take New Steps Addressing Sexual Harassment." American Psychological Association, May 15, 2018, https://www.nytimes

.com/2015/03/07/world/europe/german-law-requires-more-women-on
-corporate-boards.html?mcubz=0

244 "A HuffPost/YouGov poll . . ." "HuffPost: Sexual Harassment." Huffington Post,
April 15, 2018, https://www.nytimes.com/2015/03/07/world/europe/german-
law-requires-more-women-on-corporate-boards.htm

244 "The divide was . . ." Pramuk, Jacob. "Sen. Lindsey Graham explodes in
defense of Kavanaugh: This Is an 'Unethical Sham.'" CNBC, September 27,
2018, https://www.cnbc.com/2018/09/27/lindsey-graham-defends-brett-ka-
vanaugh-amid-christine-blase-ford-accusation.html

245 "The Twitter hashtag . . ." North, Anna. "#HimToo, The Online Movement
Spreading Myths About False Rape Allegations, Explained." Vox, October 10,
2015, https://www.vox.com/policy-and-politics/2018/10/10/17957126/himtoo-
movement-pieter-hanson-tweet-me-too

245 "False accusations are . . ." Yon, Holly. "Trump Says It's a 'Scary Time' for
Men. Here Are the Stats on False Sexual Assault Claims." CNN, October 3,
2018, https://www.cnn.com/2018/10/03/health/sexual-assault-false-reports/
index.html

245 "But an alarming . . ." Sparks, Grace. "Most People Don't Report Sexual Harass-
ment and A Majority Think That's a Real Problem." CNN, September 21, 2018,
https://www.cnn.com/2018/09/21/politics/sexual-assault-harassment-polling/
index.html

245 "When these individuals . . ." Kim, Jennifer. "Intersectionality 101: Why 'We're
Focusing on Women' Doesn't Work for Diversity & Inclusion." Medium, April
10, 2018, https://medium.com/awaken-blog/intersectionality-101-why-were-
focusing-on-women-doesn-t-work-for-diversity-inclusion-8f591d196789

246 As I noted . . ." Dastagir, Alia E. "What Do Men Get That Women Don't? Here
Are a Few Things." USA Today, March 1, 2017, https://www.usatoday.com/story/
news/2017/03/01/2017-womens-history-month/98247518/

About the author

About the book

Insights,
Interviews
& More . . .

Meet Joanne Lipman

Gannet

JOANNE LIPMAN is the editor-in-chief of the *USA Today* Network. She began her career at the *Wall Street Journal*, where she was the first woman to become deputy managing editor and supervised coverage that won three Pulitzer Prizes. She was also the founding editor-in-chief of *Condé Nast Portfolio* magazine and Portfolio.com. She lives in New York City. ⌦

Reader's Guide:
Questions for Book
Clubs and Organizations

1. What behaviors described in *That's What She Said* have you witnessed or experienced?

2. How do the everyday issues women face—being marginalized, interrupted, overlooked, underpaid, not given the same level of respect as men—relate to the #MeToo movement?

3. What are action-oriented steps that individuals or organizations can take to close the gender gap?

4. As a man, how can I navigate the new world of gender relations?

5. As a woman, how can I convince men to be part of this conversation?

6. As a young professional, how do I call out bad behavior I see among supervisors and senior executives, or older relatives?

7. How can I start a conversation about gender equality? ▶

8. What are the biggest challenges to achieving equality in our community or organization? What steps should leaders take to address those challenges?

9. Are there policy or legislative changes that you think are needed in order to achieve gender parity in the workplace?

10. *That's What She Said* includes two cheat sheets, one for individuals and one for organizations, with steps to close the gender gap. What tactics would you add?

Cheat Sheet 1: Tips and Takeaways for Men—and Women

The scores of men and women I interviewed have come up with multiple strategies to level the gender playing field. Here are a few that any one of us, male or female, can adopt:

Interrupt the interrupters. Even female Supreme Court justices are interrupted three times more frequently than male justices. As powerful as these women are, they "are just like other women," Northwestern University researchers wrote, "talked over by their male colleagues." **Solution**: Institute a "no interruptions" rule for everyone, as *The Walking Dead* producer Glen Mazzara does. Alternatively, if a woman is cut off in conversation, cut off the interrupter: "Olivia was speaking. Let's let her finish her thought first."

Use amplification and brag buddies. Women's ideas often aren't heard—until they are repeated by a man, who gets the credit. **Solution**: Take a cue from the women of the Obama administration and "amplify" the original speaker, by repeating her idea and ensuring that she is recognized for it. What's more, since women are penalized if they talk about their accomplishments, they (along with simpatico men) can become each others' "brag buddies." They can share each others' accomplishments with one another, and then each tout the other's achievements.

She's not "sorry," she's not "lucky," and she's not asking you a question. Researchers have found that women often use qualifiers ("Sorry to bother you, but . . .") to make themselves less threatening to others. If they do act assertively, they are penalized for it, considered bossy, bitchy, or difficult to work with. **Solution**: Women are highly aware of these verbal ticks and try to control them themselves. But if they don't, just ▶

Cheat Sheet 1: Tips and Takeaways for Men—and Women *(continued)*

remember the next time a woman ends a sentence in a question-mark "upspeak," imagine she is instead stating it as a fact and banging on the table.

Yeah, that's not a compliment. Women are often subjected to compliments that, intentionally or not, belittle them—like when I spent hours preparing for a television news interview, only to be told by a senior executive that I looked "cute." **Solution**: Would you say that to a man? If not, you probably should not say it to a woman, either.

She's pretty sure you don't respect her. Researchers have found that men get more respect than women—*even if they hold the exact same position*. **Solution**: Be on the lookout for slights large and small, and adjust your own behavior. When you meet a couple, do you ask the man about his work but ignore the woman? Do you listen to a man in a meeting, but look at your email when a woman speaks? That vigilance goes for all of us, myself included. In an early draft of this book, I unwittingly referred to a female doctor by her first name, but a male physician by the honorific "doctor." Turns out that this is a common slight, researchers have found. Not a mistake I'll make again.

Invite a man to a women's meeting. Women's groups, including those for female company employees, can be powerful forums. But men don't hear about the issues that are discussed. **Solution**: Invite men! At A. T. Kearney, a consulting firm, senior female executives decided to each bring a male colleague to a meeting for female employees. Those invitations became "a badge of honor," so coveted that men were begging to be included, says Beth Bovis, global head of leadership and organization. Both men and women came away with a better understanding of—and an increased comfort level with—one another.

Don't decide for her. When a new opportunity comes up, I've often heard senior executives say that Mia would be ideal, but she has a new baby at home and wouldn't want to travel . . . or she has young kids and wouldn't want to relocate . . . or she wouldn't want to take on the extra hours. **Solution**: Don't assume. Ask her. Even if she declines, present the next opportunity, and the one after that. My own bosses did that for me when my children were young— and as result, when I was ready to rev up my career they were there, still offering me opportunities.

Don't be afraid of tears. Barbara Annis and John Gray, coauthors of the book *Work with Me: The 8 Blind Spots Between Men and Women in Business*, identify emotion as one of the major pitfalls men face. Fear of tears can lead male managers to hold back from giving women the honest feedback they need to progress. **Solution**: If you're a manager, check your employee reviews to ensure you evaluate men and women equally. And by the way, if a woman does tear up, understand why: She isn't crying because she's sad. She's crying because she is frustrated—or because she's mad as hell. When men are angry, they yell; for women, crying is pretty much the same thing.

She's ready for a raise, but she won't ask for it. Men are four times more likely to ask for a raise than women—and when women do ask we typically request 30 percent less than men do, says Carnegie Mellon University economics professor Linda Babcock. **Solution**: If you're a manager, take a look at whether you are rewarding the squeaky wheel—whether men are demanding raises more often and outearning women with comparable experience on your team. And if you're an employee, arm yourself with salary data, available from companies like PayScale, Salary.com, and Glassdoor. ▶

"Hire women your mom's age."* That catchy headline on a *New York Times* op-ed by Sally Koslow, a former editor-in-chief of McCall's, perfectly captures the conundrum of older women. Many either quit or took lesser "mommy track" roles when their children were young. But as the kids fly the nest, women have as much ambition as ever, and are eager to rev up their careers. **Solution**: Hire them. Better yet, help structure work so that we don't lose them in the first place. For women who want to step back when kids are young, offer projects that don't require facetime but allow them to continue to contribute and grow—for example, by writing legal briefs or building financial models.

She deserves a promotion. She just doesn't know it yet. Men are far more likely than women to raise their hands for a bigger job, whether they're ready for it or not. Companies including Google, meanwhile, have found that qualified women often don't nominate themselves. **Solution**: Make sure qualified women are in the mix, whether they have put up their hands or not. Be prepared to twist a few arms. Several executives I spoke with told me they identify women who have the right criteria, and ask them to apply. It doesn't mean a woman will get the job—but she certainly won't get it if her name isn't in the pool to begin with. ∽

* Koslow, Sally. "Hire Women Your Mom's Age." *New York Times,* August 5, 2017, https://www.nytimes .com/2017/08/05/opinion/sunday/older-women-employment-jobs.html?smid=tw-share&_r=1&mtrref=undefined&asset Type=opinion

Cheat Sheet 2:
Tips and Takeaways for Organizations

Organizations I've encountered in reporting this book, as well as in discussions and visits since its publication, have rolled out powerful ways to bust biases. Here are a few of their strategies:

Conduct a gender wage-gap analysis. The wage gap in the U.S. has barely budged in decades, and is equally problematic abroad. **Solution**: In the U.K., new legislation requires large companies to report their gender wage gaps. Some American companies are adopting this practice voluntarily. Mark Benioff, chief executive of Salesforce, thought he already was paying women equally—until women in his organization approached him to tell him otherwise. The firm has since begun conducting annual wage gap analyses, and has paid close to $9 million over three years to close the gap.

Create financial incentives for diversity. We all respond to incentives, yet few companies build financial incentives into their diversity goals. **Solution**: Make diversity a part of compensation packages. Kimberly-Clark's executives earn bonuses based on four different "buckets" of performance. One of those buckets now includes not just hiring, but training, promoting, and retaining people from diverse backgrounds. Some other companies are starting to adopt similar policies, including Intel, which now links bonuses in part to diversity goals.

Require paternity leave. More companies are offering family leave to new dads as well as new moms. But men often don't take it, for fear of derailing their careers. That message—that having a baby will kill your career—isn't lost on women who do take leave. **Solution**: *Require* men to take leave. Boston-based Humanyze did just that, giving both men and women twelve-week paid leaves and insisting the men take it. Cofounder Ben Waber says he did so to ensure that ▶

women are on equal footing with men. "It's the right thing to do," he says. "If (companies) can make it work for women, they can make it work for men."

Introduce formal mentorship programs. Women's mentors typically give them advice—but men's champions get them promotions and jobs. One study of mid-level executives found that over a two-year period, the men received 15 percent more promotions than the women, even though more of the women had mentors. **Solution:** Formal mentorship programs. Harvard professor Frank Dobbin found that such formal programs, along with diversity managers and task forces, are more effective for women's advancement than diversity training. And a Catalyst study concluded that women who find mentors through formal programs receive about 50 percent more promotions than those who find mentors on their own.

She'll help your bottom line. Women are often boxed out of jobs or promotions because they aren't "a good fit," or they are dismissed as "diversity hires" who are a sign of lowered standards. **Solution:** Marshal the facts. Adding women makes work groups more creative. Companies with female chief financial officers make fewer, better acquisitions than those with male chief financial officers. Firms with the most female board members outperform those with the least by almost every financial measure. Mixed groups can even solve a murder more accurately than single-sex groups. Want a recipe for success? Simply add women.

Create returnships. When women (or men) step back from careers to tend to family obligations, it can be impossible for them to get back in the door just a few years later. They are virtually invisible. **Solution:** Dozens of companies, recognizing the potential of this lost generation, now offer "returnships," for both men and women who have taken time off. Structured somewhat like internships, they offer training and ease participants back into the working world. Goldman Sachs,

Morgan Stanley, and Credit Suisse have all offered returnships, while a firm called iRelaunch has worked to create similar programs with General Motors, IBM, Johnson Controls, Caterpillar, Ford, and Johnson & Johnson.

Diversify the interviewers, not just the applicants. More companies are adopting a Rooney Rule for the office, requiring a diverse slate of applicants for job openings. But bringing in female applicants is only a first step. If the interviewers aren't diverse—if, say, all the interviewers are white men— they are less likely to see her as a "cultural fit," while she may feel so uncomfortable that she rejects the job even if offered. **Solution**: Mix things up. Expand that Rooney rule to the interviewers too: ensure that not only the slate of candidates, but the interviewers are diverse.

Implement blind auditions. In the hiring and promotion processes, managers gravitate toward those with similar backgrounds, while finding reasons to reject those who are different, whether in terms of gender, race, ethnicity or sexuality. **Solution**: A growing number of companies are adopting a practice first popularized by symphony orchestras, of "blind auditions." That means stripping identifying characteristics such as name, age, and schooling from resumes, and sometimes using a real-world test to evaluate an applicant instead of just an interview. Unilever, Mercer, and Morgan Stanley are among those that have implemented blind hiring for some roles. So is comedian Samantha Bee, who used a blind application process to hire comedy writers for her show *Full Frontal*.

Set quantifiable goals. Organizations set targets for revenue, profit, earnings per share, sales, and multiple other metrics. But too often they prioritize "diversity and inclusion" without quantifying what that means. **Solution**: Define what success looks like for your organization. Is it a specific gender percentage mix of employees? A specific goal for sales to female or other underserved customers? What gets counted, gets fixed. ▶

Cheat Sheet 2: Tips and Takeaways for Organizations *(continued)*

Leadership must *own* diversity. Too many organizations offload diversity to the HR department. Yet no matter how excellent those diversity and inclusion professionals are, they can't change a company's culture. **Solution**: Diversity must belong to top leadership. That means both the chief executive officer and the chief financial officer. The most successful executives understand that diversity isn't a "nice to have" option, separate from core financial responsibilities. They understand it is, instead, a business imperative. Not only is it the right thing to do; it will make their companies more successful by virtually every measure. ∾